Tim Clarkson worked in academic librarianship before setting up a business with his wife. He gained an MPhil in archaeology (1995) and a PhD in medieval history (2003) from the University of Manchester. He is author of *The Men of the North: the Britons of Southern Scotland*, *The Picts: A History* and *Columba* (all published by Birlinn).

The
Makers of Scotland

PICTS, ROMANS, GAELS AND VIKINGS

Tim Clarkson

BIRLINN

This edition published in Great Britain in 2013 by

Birlinn Ltd
West Newington House
10 Newington Road
Edinburgh
EH9 1QS

www.birlinn.co.uk

Reprinted 2016, 2017, 2018, 2019

First published in 2011 by John Donald, and imprint of Birlinn Ltd

ISBN: 978 1 78027 173 6

British Library Cataloguing-in-Publication Data
A catalogue record for this book is available on request
from the British Library

Typeset and designed by Mark Blackadder

Printed and bound by Clays Ltd, Elcograf, S.p.A.

Contents

List of Maps		vii
Introduction		ix
1	BC to AD	1
2	The Later Roman Period	32
3	Britons, Picts and Scots	53
4	Christian Beginnings	68
5	Celt and Saxon	86
6	The Struggle for Power	117
7	The Northern Churches	138
8	The Vikings	166
9	Alba	183
10	Kings and Bishops	202
11	Overview: The Birth of Medieval Scotland	219
	Appendix A: Genealogies	231
	Appendix B: Timeline	235
	Further Reading	237
	Index	246

List of Maps

1 Scotland: mountain, river and sea   p.viii
2 Roman Scotland: peoples and frontiers   p.2
3 Scotland: old and new territorial divisions   p.54
4 Kingdoms and kindreds, sixth to
   eighth centuries AD   p.118
5 Major centres of Christianity   p.139
6 Centres of power, sixth to eighth centuries AD   p.167
7 Scotland in the Viking Age   p.184

Scotland: mountain, river and sea

Introduction

Objectives

This book aims to provide a narrative history of Scotland from the eve of the Roman invasion to the final phase of the Viking Age. It encompasses one thousand years of social, political and religious development in which various groups and individuals each played their part. The book's subtitle names four of these groups – Picts, Romans, Gaels and Vikings – all of whom contributed to the shaping of Scotland's medieval identity. Two others – the English and the Britons – are intentionally absent from the subtitle. Their omission does not diminish their role in the narrative. Indeed, both peoples were major players in early Scottish history and are accorded due prominence in the following chapters. Omitting them from the subtitle is rather an acknowledgement that their names convey no specific sense of time and place to the reader. By contrast, the mention of 'Romans' and 'Vikings' indicates the broad chronological context, while the naming of 'Picts' and 'Gaels' emphasises that this is a book about Scotland's ancient inhabitants. The narrative begins at the end of the first century BC, in the years when Rome began to take a keen interest in the British Isles. It then follows a chronological path, tracing Scotland's origins through the ensuing centuries to the battle of Carham-on-Tweed in 1018.

This is not a study of topics or themes. Broad subjects such as warfare and economics are incorporated within the narrative, but the main purpose of the book is to present a linear history. The sole exception to this rule is Christianity, a topic forming the main focus of three chapters which together chart the decline of paganism, the establishment of churches and the increasing role of the clergy in political affairs. Chapter narratives are not punctuated by citations of primary and secondary sources, or by footnotes and endnotes, but the closing pages of the book include suggestions for 'further reading' on particular topics. Throughout the book a number of maps indicate the locations of kingdoms, settlements, religious sites and other significant places. Genealogical tables in Appendix A show the kinship between important individuals, while Appendix B provides a chronological summary or 'timeline'.

Sources

The period covered by this book includes the three and a half centuries of Roman rule in Britain, from AD 43 to c.400, plus a further six hundred years which eventually saw the northern part of the island evolve into the Gaelic-speaking kingdom of Alba. Only a segment of what is now Scotland was brought within the Roman Empire, but the unconquered portion remained a source of trouble for the imperial authorities despite many attempts to subdue it. Military campaigns launched against the northern peoples were documented by Roman writers whose accounts represent a rich vein of data on early Scottish history. After the Empire abandoned Britain in the early fifth century, Roman texts effectively ceased to mention Scotland, their disappearance depriving modern historians of a contemporary record of events. Sparse information relating to the fifth and sixth centuries does exist, but much of it was created retrospectively by writers of a much later era who were less interested in historical accuracy than in reconfiguring the past in ways appropriate to their own purposes. This means that today's historian must sift each textual source very carefully, in the hope of unearthing fragments of genuine early information among passages written in the twelfth or thirteenth century or even later.

Reliable sources from the first millennium AD are scarce and are usually biased in favour of political or religious interests. A typical example is Bede, a northern English monk whose lifetime spanned the seventh and eighth centuries. Not long before his death in 735 he completed his greatest work, *The Ecclesiastical History Of The English People*, in which he frequently made reference to the peoples of early Scotland. His book is a valuable contemporary source and a repository of fascinating detail, but, notwithstanding his reputation as a meticulous scholar, the *Ecclesiastical History* needs to be treated with caution. Bede was not a historian in the modern sense, but a monastic writer who regarded history as the unfolding revelation of events predetermined by God. This meant that he constructed his narrative in ways that allowed him to demonstrate how the English – whom he believed to be a chosen people like the Israelites of the Old Testament – enacted God's will among themselves and their neighbours. In so far as the peoples of early Scotland were concerned, Bede saw some – such as the Picts – as playing a positive role in the Divine plan, while others – such as the Britons, whom he regarded with contempt – were earmarked by God to suffer well-deserved woes at the hands of English enemies. The *Ecclesiastical History* is therefore coloured by its author's biases and preferences and is not the sober textbook it might seem at first glance.

Contemporary sources written in Scotland are few in number. There is no Scottish equivalent of Bede and only a handful of eyewitness or near-contemporary accounts relating to this period have survived from northern Britain. This does not mean that reliable information cannot be found, but the task of identifying it is made more difficult. Our most detailed source is a group of texts known collectively as the Irish annals. Originating as year-by-year entries in records maintained by monasteries, these texts refer not only to ecclesiastical matters but also to events in the secular world. Although the various manuscripts in which the annals survive were written no earlier than the twelfth century, their information was copied from older documents and can be traced back to lost texts compiled many centuries earlier. One of the lost compilations was a set of annals maintained at the Hebridean monastery of Iona, a religious settlement established by the Irish priest Columba in the sixth century. The annals were destroyed when Iona fell prey to Viking raids, but a number of entries were incorporated into the two main Irish compilations – the Annals of Ulster and the Annals of Tigernach – to preserve a valuable account of Scotland's early medieval history. Iona's annalists had a keen interest in political affairs and noted important events such as battles, alliances and the deaths of kings. Like Bede, however, they were not immune from bias and crafted their words carefully, selecting events they wished to write about and ignoring others. After the middle of the eighth century, the Iona entries in the Irish annals cease, but Scottish information continued to be recorded in Ireland throughout the Viking period and beyond. Some of this data was spurious or inaccurate, or was added to the annals retrospectively, or was amended much later by scribes when manuscripts were being copied. Rigorous modern analysis of the surviving texts has revealed numerous problems and pitfalls but has enabled the older, more reliable entries to be identified, thereby allowing the Irish annals to be used as a valid source for early Scottish history.

Other types of literature are generally held in less high regard, mainly because of the lateness of their manuscripts, even if they seem to contain material of older origin. Into this category fall the Pictish and Scottish regnal lists – schedules of the reigns of kings – together with a plethora of poems and stories. All of these texts tend to be incomplete, or ambiguous, or found in different versions which contradict one another. Some include fictional characters drawn from legend. Genuine historical information or 'real' history is frequently present, awaiting identification and extraction, but it is all too often embedded in impenetrable layers of later, less reliable material. The king-lists of the Picts, for example, are a rich source of information and are often widely used as chronological guides despite posing many questions of their own. Many of the figures named in the early or upper portions of the lists are clearly fictitious. Some historical kings are listed in one or more groups of manuscripts, but are then ignored, perhaps deliberately, in others.

Equally controversial are the *vitae* or 'lives' of saints generated by writers attached to major Christian cult-centres. This type of literature is called hagiography and is encountered in several chapters of this book. Here it will be sufficient to mention that the genre has little in common with modern biography. Even the renowned Abbot Adomnán of Iona, who wrote a *vita* or 'Life' of Saint Columba at the end of the seventh century, cannot be called a biographer, regardless of the fact that he was born only thirty years after Columba's death. Adomnán was an author of great eloquence and knowledge, but his motives in writing the Life were not those of a modern historian. Like Bede, he viewed past events through the lens of his own biases and prejudices. As Bede's contemporary he nevertheless provides a useful Gaelic perspective to balance the strongly Anglocentric focus of the *Ecclesiastical History*.

Scotland's early history is full of gaps: it is not a complete or accurate record. Basic detail is lacking for many important points, such as the ethnic and geographical origins of certain kings or the locations of 'lost' kingdoms. To compound these problems, the information given by the various sources is often contradictory, allowing different interpretations to be drawn. When uncertainty arises, it is not always confined to obscure events or to little-known individuals, as the case of Cináed mac Ailpín ('Kenneth MacAlpin') illustrates all too clearly. This enigmatic ninth-century king is examined more closely in Chapter 8, but here, in this brief survey of the sources, he becomes a useful example of just how incomplete the picture can become. Cináed is one of the most famous figures in Scottish history, the king traditionally credited with unifying the Picts and Scots to form a single nation, but he is also one of the most controversial. The problem lies with the sources, which seem to be so unclear about his origins that they fail to answer the most basic questions about him: Who was he? Where did he come from? Was he a Scot or a Pict? Faced with such ambiguity we feel tempted to seek answers in places we might normally avoid, even turning to the bogus 'histories' written by John of Fordoun and Walter Bower in, respectively, the fourteenth and fifteenth century. Today, the temptation to consult such works is less compelling than it appeared one hundred years ago, chiefly because Fordoun and Bower are better understood today. Their status as custodians of supposedly genuine 'tradition' is now being vigorously challenged.

'Tradition' is itself a rather vague term, but it appears from time to time in this book, usually in relation to information of dubious reliability. Folklore and legends, often of localised origin, fall into this category. Most historians are rightly sceptical about the use of such data, even if it appears to be old, but some acknowledge its value as a starting-point for discussion where reliable information is otherwise lacking. A few traditions relating to early Scotland are of great antiquity and seem to preserve nuggets of history concealed among works of poetry or saga. The enigmatic *Berchan's Prophecy*, for example, appears to contain many such nuggets and is therefore regarded by historians as a potentially useful source. Although preserved only in a manuscript of 1722, it appears to have been originally composed in the twelfth century from older 'traditions' circulating at that time. It is a difficult and controversial source, but among its cryptic verses is a group dealing with Scottish kings of the ninth to eleventh centuries. With careful handling these verses can sometimes be used to add flesh to a sparse entry in the Irish annals, or to an allusion in a twelfth-century chronicle.

Terminology

This book deals with a period before the country now called Scotland came into being. Thus, although the narrative is chiefly concerned with Britain north of the River Tweed and Solway Firth, only a portion of this area was regarded as ethnically or politically 'Scottish' during the period studied here. In chronological terms the book traces the history of northern Britain from the end of the Iron Age to the birth of medieval Scotland. This was an era when indigenous peoples such as Picts, Scots and Britons became more or less distinct from one another in the eyes of contemporary writers. Only in the final chapters of the book, during the time of

Cináed mac Ailpín and his heirs, does an embryonic 'Scottish' identity begin to appear across a broad swathe of northern Britain. Whenever the term 'Scotland' is used in the following narrative, the meaning is usually geographical, relating to the physical landscape, rather than political or territorial. The adjective 'Scottish' is also used, either in the specific sense of 'pertaining to the early Scots' or in reference to abstract concepts such as 'Scottish history' or 'Scottish landscape'. Another adjective is 'British' which, like 'Scottish', can be used in a specific as well as a general way in early medieval contexts. Historians sometimes use it to describe a particular ethnic group, the Britons, in studies of the period before c.1100. It is used here as a broad geographical term in phrases such as 'the British Isles' or in the narrower sense of 'pertaining to the Britons'. The latter were regarded as an identifiable ethnic group by Roman writers in the first century AD and continued to play a separate political role throughout the period covered by this book.

Most personal names appear here in native, non-Anglicised forms. *Domnall* and *Dyfnwal* are therefore preferred to 'Donald', while *Cináed* is preferred to 'Kenneth'. The exception is the Pictish name *Constantin* or *Causantin* which appears in this book in its more familiar form 'Constantine'. Other Pictish names are Gaelicised, with Óengus, Nechtan and Brude representing the likely Pictish forms *Unuist*, *Naiton* and *Bridei* respectively. This choice of nomenclature might seem obstinately old-fashioned to supporters of the current trend for presenting personal names in the original languages of their bearers. In fact, the choice reflects nothing more than the present author's own preference. The same can also be said of names borne by Britons, a people whose native language was similar to the ancestor of modern Welsh. Nowadays, these names are increasingly appearing in published works in archaic forms rather than in those found in medieval Welsh literature. Here, the later forms are retained, with names such as *Dyfnwal* and *Owain* being preferred to archaic equivalents such as *Dumngual* and *Eugein*.

Structure

The following chapters form a continuous chronological narrative spanning the first millennium AD. Each chapter deals with a segment of this chronology. Viewing Scotland's early history in this way will not be to everyone's taste, but might suit those who prefer to read history as an unfolding 'tale of years'. The alternative is the looser chronology offered by chapters devoted to broad themes. As previously stated, this book's only real concessions to a thematic approach are the three chapters dealing with Christianity, the first of which includes a study of pre-Christian pagan beliefs which the new religion supplanted in the post-Roman period. The book's final chapter provides an overview of the ten centuries to AD 1000 and looks at how particular aspects of the millennium were perceived in later times. It also considers other issues, such as modern attitudes to Scotland's archaeological heritage.

CHAPTER 2
BC to AD

At the dawn of the Christian era the British Isles were inhabited by people whose society was essentially barbaric and prehistoric. Neither of these labels implies primitiveness or backwardness, despite attempts by Roman writers to portray tribes living outside the Empire as untamed, unsophisticated and – in contrast to Roman decadence – admirably uncorrupted. In describing the ancient inhabitants of Britain and Ireland as 'barbarians' we are simply distinguishing them from native communities in mainland Western Europe who had already fallen under the heel of Rome. Barbarian societies were typically those in which large urban settlements and a coin-based economy were absent.

The first millennium AD began with much of Western Europe already in Roman hands. Within the Empire's borders native cultures were being steadily eroded by a deliberate process of Romanisation. This meant that in areas such as Gaul (roughly coextensive with modern France) the distinctively Celtic character of indigenous society was giving way to the Latin culture of the conquerors. One major casualty was the ancient Gaulish language – a branch of the same linguistic group to which the tongue of the Britons belonged – which faced extinction after being replaced by Latin in all important forms of communication. Thus, at the beginning of the first millennium, the still-unconquered British Isles represented the last bastion of Celtic language and culture.

In those days the northern part of Britain was not yet called Scotland, nor was the southern part called England. The whole island was regarded by Roman travellers and other contemporary

Roman Scotland: peoples and frontiers

observers as a single geographical entity called *Britannia*. All of its inhabitants, regardless of whether they lived on the southern coast or in the far northern isles, were known collectively as 'Britons'. Their language – usually referred to by modern scholars as Brittonic or Brythonic – was the ancestor of Welsh, Cornish and Breton. Like Gaulish, it formed part of the 'P-Celtic' linguistic group which had already started to diverge from the Goidelic or 'Q-Celtic' group when the first millennium commenced. Q-Celtic includes the Gaelic languages of Ireland, Scotland and the Isle of Man, all of which derive from a single ancestral tongue once spoken in many shorelands around the northern waters of the Irish Sea.

Giving any group of ancient peoples the label 'Celtic' is not an exercise in precision but rather a convenient way to identify them as non-Roman, non-Germanic inhabitants of north-western Europe. The Celts were not in fact a homogeneous 'race', but a myriad collection of communities linked by similarities in culture and language. Most of the ancient people now described as 'Celts' would have been puzzled to find themselves lumped together in modern history books as if they were all members of a single ethnic group. The idea of a common Celtic identity is actually a fairly modern concept promoted by nineteenth-century historians searching for an umbrella term to encompass large areas of Europe – including the British Isles – which appeared to share features of a common material culture in the first millennium BC. The name 'Celts' was borrowed from the *Celtae* or *Keltoi*, a people inhabiting parts of south-western Europe when the region was conquered by Rome in the first century BC. These folk were neither the creators of Celtic culture nor, in ethnological terms, the ancestors of other Celtic nations. Their name was merely chosen as a convenient label for a prehistoric North European culture first identified in the nineteenth century at archaeological sites in Switzerland and Austria. A more accurate use of the label 'Celtic' restricts its application to a distinct sub-group of the Indo-European family of languages. It is less appropriate to give it a cultural or ethnic dimension. In this book, it is therefore used as an all-embracing term for speakers of a Celtic language, regardless of whether they lived in Gaul, the Iberian Peninsula or the British Isles. In the narrower context of early Scottish history, 'Celtic' is often used by historians to distinguish the natives of northern Britain from the Germanic immigrants with whom they came into contact during the first millennium AD.

Settlements

Celtic language and culture were well established in the British Isles and in parts of mainland Europe long before Rome grew powerful enough to build her empire. Historians and archaeologists formerly believed that a Europe-wide process of Celticisation occurred during the middle of the first millennium BC as part of the transition between the Bronze and Iron Ages. Iron was certainly replacing bronze as the main material for tools after 600 BC and its use in everyday life is rightly seen as an indicator of Celtic influence, primarily because the 'Celts' were the first ironworkers in north-western Europe. Changes in the design and location of dwellings in Britain also occurred around this time and have often been attributed to the spread of Celtic fashions from Gaul. In particular, the fortification of isolated hilltops is strongly associated with the Celts and many examples are found on the European continent. The presence of similar hillforts in Britain and Ireland is thus seen as further evidence of Celticisation crossing from Gaul to permeate Insular (i.e. British and Irish) society. Conventional wisdom rooted in past scholarship has tended to explain these social and cultural changes in terms of a mass migration by Celtic groups from mainland Europe into the British Isles after 700 BC. This has recently been challenged by an alternative explanation which, rather than imagining waves of seaborne immigrants, suggests instead that the Celtic languages and cultures of Britain and Ireland were largely home-grown. In this scenario the idea of new linguistic and cultural influences arriving from outside gives way to a simpler theory which sees the peoples of the British Isles and Continental Europe developing a shared 'Celticness' as a natural evolution of their common Indo-European origins. Any migration from the European mainland in the first millennium BC would probably have involved small numbers of people – such as groups of ambitious Gaulish warriors – seizing power in certain areas of Britain and Ireland, from where they perhaps disseminated 'foreign' influences among the natives. This would mean that the ancient Celtic peoples of the British Isles were not newcomers from elsewhere but the descendants of an indigenous population whose ancestry lay in the pre-Celtic past and whose ultimate origins reached back into the Stone Age.

If Britain and Ireland became 'Celtic' without the need for a mass immigration of European Celts in the first millennium BC, then other factors must account for the changes that make their societies recognisably 'Celtic' to modern historians and archaeologists. The practice of constructing compact, defensible hilltop fortresses can thus be explained not as a fashion imported from Gaul, but as a Europe-wide phenomenon arising from a need felt by some communities to make their homes defensible against attack. The likeliest cause of such insecurity was a perception that society was becoming more dangerous or, to put it another way, that some communities were behaving more aggressively towards their neighbours. The first hillforts in Scotland were constructed in the Bronze Age, around the beginning of the first millennium BC, and were usually larger in area and fewer in number than their later Iron Age counterparts. Ramparts at some of the smaller forts nevertheless enclosed substantial surface areas containing many houses, giving these sites the character of 'protected villages'. Other sites were even smaller, with only a few dwellings inside, but would have seemed more imposing to onlookers when located in positions of natural strength. The people who commissioned the construction of hillforts and other enclosed settlements were clearly capable of mobilising large labour forces. They were either powerful kin-groups wielding authority at local level, or entire communities undertaking co-operative projects. Earth, stone and timber provided the raw materials for rampart construction, but the actual designs varied considerably. The basic shape could be curvilinear or recti-linear, while the enclosing rampart might be a simple wooden palisade or a massive earthen bank. In some cases a palisade replaced an earlier earthwork, the former perhaps seeming – to modern eyes, at least – a less substantial, less effective type of defensive feature. A more elaborate technique involved adding timber to unmortared (drystone) walls, either by bracing with long wooden beams or by making a box-like framework. In Scotland, the distribution of these 'timber-laced' forts covers a wide geographical area, from Broxmouth in Lothian to Cullykhan, Craig Phadrig and Burghead in the north-east. Some were destroyed by fire, presumably at enemy hands, with temperatures rising high enough to fuse stone and timber together. The resulting process, known as vitrification, left the affected parts of the ramparts with a glassy appearance which so reduced their strength that a burned fort became unsuitable for reuse by its former occupants. Aside from such cases, many hillforts fell out of use within a few centuries of their construction, either through destruction or abandonment. Others continued to be occupied, with or without occasional breaks in habitation, into the first millennium AD. In a few cases the period of occupation was remarkably long and, as subsequent chapters of this book will show, a small number of northern hillforts were still being used as late as the Viking Age.

The larger hillforts constructed around 1000 BC were essentially substantial villages enclosed by ramparts. Their usefulness in military terms was minimal, mainly because they were too large for their inhabitants to defend. There were never many of them and most were abandoned when a trend for smaller forts began to gather pace in the final centuries BC. Some large sites nevertheless continued in use, serving Iron Age communities as major centres and perhaps assuming the role of local 'capitals'. Their size added prestige to their occupants, even at those sites where an exposed or elevated position made habitation seasonal rather than permanent. When the Romans encountered such places in Gaul they frequently described them as *oppida*, a term found in Julius Caesar's account of his Gallic campaigns. One of Caesar's most celebrated victories came after a prolonged siege of an *oppidum* at Alesia, a site defended by strong earthworks similar in appearance to those at the major power centres of Celtic Britain. The impressive remains of British *oppida* can still be seen today, most notably in southern England at places like Maiden Castle and Cadbury Castle. Hillforts in Scotland were generally smaller, with even the largest barely matching the southern examples in size. This has not deterred archaeologists from applying the label *oppidum* to sites such as Eildon Hill North and Traprain Law, both of which are situated in the Lowlands. Indeed, it is possible that these two settlements served the kind of proto-urban function commonly associated with their Gallic and southern British counterparts. Whether this involved permanent habitation rather than seasonal or occasional ceremonial use is hard to discern from the archaeological evidence. Both were probably first inhabited in the Bronze Age, around 1000 BC. In each case, the earthworks enclosed a large area containing the houses of a substantial population. Settlement seems to have been continuous throughout much of the Iron Age, with a marked decline in activity in the first century BC followed by a period of recovery. Eildon was finally abandoned during Roman times but Traprain had a rather longer existence, its defences perhaps being refurbished as late as the fifth century AD.

Why were hillforts built? To this question there are no simple answers. Reasons for enclosing elevated settlements with ramparts and ditches were probably as varied as the number of sites. Some hillforts were surely constructed as protection from enemies, presumably at times of local insecurity when communities within particular districts faced real perils. The plethora of forts in the Scottish Lowlands might therefore suggest that this region was especially dangerous in the Iron Age, although the proximity of many enclosed sites to their nearest neighbours casts doubt on this explanation. Factors other than warfare and raiding could have been at work. A hillfort in a prominent location was an imposing feature in the landscape and may have served its occupants as a symbol of their group identity, or as a forceful marker of their territory. It is worthy of note that few hillforts in Scotland were still inhabited in the first century AD when the Romans invaded Britain. Perhaps, after fulfilling a range of purposes for many hundreds of years, their usefulness dwindled?

Hillforts appeared all over Celtic Britain and Ireland during the first millennium BC, but they were not the only defensible settlements constructed at this time. One type of dwelling found exclusively in Scotland is the 'Atlantic roundhouse', a class of stone-built structure which includes the distinctive brochs and duns. The type as a whole is most distinctively represented by the broch, a huge stone tower with walls so thick that chambers and stairways could be accommodated within them. A low door, invariably less than the height of an average person, provided the sole point of entry. The tower's interior apparently supported one or more upper storeys, the topmost of which might be roofed with timber or open to the sky. Ruined brochs, some little more than traces on the ground, can be seen today in places as far afield as Shetland and Lothian. Their main concentration, however, is in the far northern Highlands and Western Isles. They were constructed during a period spanning, very approximately, the years 500 BC to AD 100. Why they were built is not known, but their enormous strength suggests that they were intended to present an impression of power. Whether they served as houses for high-status families, or as temporary refuges for entire communities in times of peril, is likewise an unanswered question. At some point in the early centuries AD their original or primary functions – whatever these were – evidently became redundant. Many brochs were subsequently abandoned or partly demolished, presumably because they no longer had relevance for the descendants of their builders. One of the most northerly examples, a coastal site at Jarlshof in Shetland, ceased to be inhabited around AD 200, at which point three round stone dwellings known as 'wheelhouses' were erected inside it and around it. The surrounding walls of the courtyard continued to offer protection long after the broch tower ceased to be a dwelling. Similar continuity occurred at other sites where, in some cases, a derelict broch became the central feature or landmark of a later village. The broch at Old Scatness on Shetland, built in the mid-first millennium BC, later become the focus of a surrounding settlement which was still occupied in Viking times.

Smaller than the broch was the dun, another type of stone-built 'roundhouse'. Duns are found especially in Argyll and the Inner Hebrides and, in most cases, are of comparatively simple design. A typical dun consisted of a round stone wall enclosing a small area which was either roofed or open. Outside this very broad generalisation a great variety in shape, size and setting makes duns difficult for archaeologists to classify as a single settlement type. For instance, the distinction between a dun and a circular stone-walled house is frequently a matter of interpretation. The main period of dun construction straddles the later centuries BC and the early centuries AD. Occupants may have been single extended families belonging to a fairly prosperous tier of society, but their reasons for building and occupying stone-walled roundhouses probably varied widely. To what extent they regarded duns as defensive structures rather than as physical statements of land ownership or social rank is therefore impossible to ascertain. Factors influencing the dun-dwellers' choice of habitation might, however, have been broadly similar to those that prompted other folk to build artificial islands on stretches of inland water. Just as hilltops appealed to many of the dun-builders, so lochs, rivers and estuaries attracted the attentions of others. Homesteads founded on man-made islands are found all over Scotland and are not confined to narrow periods of construction or habitation. Archaeologists call them 'crannogs', treating them as a single category of settlement regardless of their settings on rivers, sea firths or inland lochs. The oldest examples date from Neolithic times; the latest were occupied in the first millennium AD. Within such a wide chronological span it is inevitable that there are many different types but, like the duns, the generally compact size of crannogs suggests that each accommodated a single family. The most common type was a small island connected to the shore of a loch by a wooden causeway. A fine reconstruction of such a crannog can be seen and visited today, on the southern side of Loch Tay, close to the remains of actual examples from the Iron Age. It is clear from the reconstruction that these sites, despite their inaccessibility to land-based enemies, would have been easy prey to a sustained assault.

A simple deduction might be that the lower classes of Iron Age Britain lived in humbler abodes than their social superiors. This need not necessarily have been true in all areas, especially if imposing structures such as brochs were built and occupied by entire communities rather than by high-status families. Identifying houses of less prosperous character is, in any case, a difficult archaeological exercise, particularly when we consider that the excavated remains of both a simple cottage and a stone-walled barn might look identical. It seems clear, nonetheless, that the ubiquitous type of dwelling was the family homestead, usually circular or curvilinear in form, with walls constructed from timber or stone or a combination of the two. Some were scattered across the countryside as isolated farms, while others clustered together in small villages. Towards the end of the first millennium BC and in the early centuries AD some communities in the British Isles began to build underground structures, perhaps as storage for surplus agricultural produce. In archaeological terminology they are called *souterrains*, a French word describing their subterranean character. They were dug into the ground next to established homesteads and carefully lined with stone to create rooms and passages. Most were roofed with slabs or timbers, while some of the larger examples had additional sub-structures attached. Souterrains are found not only in what is now Scotland but also in Ireland, Cornwall and Brittany, their wide geographical distribution yielding a commensurate variety of designs. In Scotland they ceased to be used after the second century AD, for reasons that remain unclear. Their associated settlements frequently continued in use, so redundancy was not due to population decline or movement. Perhaps the descendants of the souterrain-builders ceased to produce enough agricultural surplus to justify the cost of maintenance?

Society and Culture

Barbarian society in Europe at the end of the first millennium BC was already shifting away from the egalitarian, co-operative systems of earlier times to a more hierarchical structure. This was not, however, a uniform process. Different groups tend to develop in different ways when separated from one another by geography, so some regions were quicker than others in moving towards social stratification. This was true of Celtic and Germanic peoples alike, with communities in some parts of Europe amalgamating into 'tribes', while others retained separate identities within a more localised network of allegiances. The resulting diversity in development means that the barbarian peoples of Gaul, Germany and the British Isles on the eve of their respective encounters with Rome presented a variety of political structures. In southern parts of Britain, where large hillforts almost certainly functioned as *oppida* or tribal capitals, society was more likely to have exhibited a well-defined hierarchy based on wealth and status. Northern Britain – including Scotland – was a region where forts and other enclosed settlements were generally smaller and less obviously 'aristocratic'. Thus, it is impossible to distinguish in terms of social class the occupants of a small, fortified hilltop in Lothian from those of a Shetland broch. Nor can we be sure that the inhabitants of either of these sites possessed more wealth or greater status than the owners of a large drystone farmstead with associated souterrains. In those areas of northern Britain where social stratification and political centralisation had perhaps become manifest in the late Iron Age, power within a 'tribe' may have been wielded by one or more dominant kindreds whose claims to authority derived from ownership of land. Similar claims by rival kindreds undoubtedly sparked aggressive competition for territory, and this would have led to inter-tribal warfare. Roman sources seem to hint that hostility on this scale was not uncommon in southern Britain but it can barely be surmised for the North. Indeed, it is difficult to imagine the numerous small hillforts in the Scottish Lowlands being used as strongholds by what would have been a veritable plethora of Iron Age warlords. Perhaps there were occasional violent contests between communities in this region in pre-Roman times, but the scatter of forts suggests minimal political development and a resistance to centralisation. It therefore seems highly unlikely that any northern part of Britain had attained a level of development in which the topmost social tier was not merely a class of major landowners but a single individual, a paramount chieftain or king. Rome acknowledged the presence of kings among the large tribal amalgams of southern Britain, but there is no evidence that any persons of this rank existed in Iron Age Scotland. Archaeological evidence north of a line drawn between Tyne and Solway seems rather to argue against, rather than in favour of, a rigid social hierarchy and a shift towards political centralisation. This is not to wholly deny the existence of a wealthy, landowning, warrior-nobility in the North at the end of the first millennium BC. Nor should we presume that powerful leaders did not arise among the hillfort inhabitants and broch-dwellers around the time of Rome's invasion of Britain in AD 43. The defiant northern warriors whom Roman forces subsequently encountered probably looked and behaved, outwardly at least, in a similar manner to the Gauls who had stood against Julius Caesar in the previous century. What we are unable to discern is their level of organisation, their social class, their group identities and their patterns of allegiance. Some of their leaders may have aspired to kingship, like their southern peers, but of this we cannot be certain.

At the lowest level of barbarian society stood those who lacked not only land but liberty as well. These were the unfree – primarily slaves – whose freedom had been forfeit from birth or through later misfortune. Above this tier was the freeman or 'free farmer', an individual whose social rank derived from land ownership. It may be that the more prosperous freemen in North Britain – those who owned more land than their neighbours – represented the class most closely associated with brochs, duns and crannogs. They presumably had opportunities for social advancement in districts where a hierarchy was already well established, or where upward mobility to positions of power was becoming an increasingly important aspiration. A poorer freeman owned less land and would have been at risk of losing his liberty altogether, especially if his smallholding was unable to sustain his family during hard times.

In such circumstances, he might be forced to give up his freedom by becoming the 'semi-free' tenant of a wealthier neighbour. If large numbers of semi-free farmers were indeed present in the Iron Age, it is possible that they were the antecedents of the servile 'bondsmen' who seem to have constituted an agricultural peasantry in many Celtic regions of the British Isles in early medieval times.

The economy of pre-Roman Britain was based on agriculture, supplemented by hunting, fishing and specialised crafts such as pottery and metalworking. This was true of all regions, including even the North with its hilly terrain and poorer soils. It was also broadly true of all periods from the Bronze Age, through the Iron Age and Roman era, to the end of the Middle Ages and the dawn of industrialisation. Much of the Scottish landscape in prehistoric times was therefore a picture of fairly stable agriculture. An alternative image of rugged mountains and densely forested glens inhabited by scattered groups of untamed tribesmen persists today, but can be traced back to the prejudices of Roman writers. To Roman eyes it was easy to regard the remote northern parts of Britain as an archetypal wilderness beyond the reach of Classical civilisation. The region north of the Forth–Clyde isthmus was duly presented in Roman literature as a barbarous, chaotic and dangerous place. Such propaganda served a useful literary purpose by drawing a stark contrast with the civilised, Romanised, Latin-speaking provinces around the Mediterranean. The reality, of course, was quite different. Northern Britain on the eve of the Roman invasion was a country of tamed farmlands, the soils of which had been intensively cultivated for more than a thousand years. Highland areas were mostly wild and bare, but so were other mountainous regions of Europe where poor drainage and unproductive soils presented challenges to agriculture. In the lowlands and river valleys the ancient peoples of Scotland had long inhabited a cultivated landscape as populous as any in the British Isles. They grew barley, wheat and oats in small fields; they tended herds of cattle and pigs and, to a lesser extent, flocks of sheep; they levelled tracts of forest in the uplands to create additional land for grazing. So intensively cultivated were the valleys and other low-lying areas of the ancient Scottish landscape that, in the three centuries before the Roman invasion, space for new farms became scarce. Settlements began to appear on the higher land as people established homes on the hillsides to exploit treeless slopes for crop-growing.

Beyond the local agricultural base a web of trading networks linked all parts of the British Isles with one another and with Continental Europe. Most of these links were established in the Bronze Age or even earlier and provided the main channels of cultural interaction between the various Celtic peoples. It was via these same trade-routes that the distinctive artistic and metal-working techniques of the 'La Tène' style eventually spread to Gaul, Spain and the British Isles. La Tène is a Swiss village where, in the mid-nineteenth century, an impressive assemblage of ornate items was discovered. These displayed a distinctive style of decoration, characterised by spirals and curving shapes, which archaeologists now regard as the first flowering of Celtic art. By the end of the first century BC many regions further afield shared elements of this common 'Celtic' culture. In northern Britain the wealthiest members of society at this time advertised their high status through weapons, armour and domestic objects adorned with circular patterns and animal designs characteristic of the La Tène style. Some of these items arrived from Gaul, Ireland or southern Britain via seaways, rivers and ancient land-routes. Others were manufactured locally by talented artisans using skills first developed in Central Europe and transmitted to all corners of the Celtic world. By the beginning of the first century AD, the upper classes of northern Britain were actively participating in a sophisticated system of long-distance trade in exotic goods with other Celtic elites, and with the Roman Empire too. Prosperous landowners in Orkney, Perthshire, Moray and the Hebrides exploited trading networks to import high-status items such as jewellery for their own personal use. To pay for these expensive treasures they exported the home-produced commodities for which Celtic Britain was renowned: furs, skins, hunting dogs and slaves.

Like their neighbours in Ireland and Gaul, the people of Iron

Age Scotland generated no documents of their own. They were not illiterate but rather pre-literate: their society functioned well enough without the need for written communication. Knowledge was preserved and transmitted orally, passing by word of mouth from generation to generation. The customs, traditions and history of each community were disseminated informally as folktales via the medium of storytelling. In addition to this informal transmission of lore, a measure of knowledge control may have been exercised by tribal elites seeking to present particular views of the past. For example, the oral declaration of a headman's genealogy at public gatherings could have been one way of reinforcing his status within the community, especially if the alleged ancestors included local gods, otherworld figures and ancient heroes. Large public events probably incorporated religious rituals presided over by high-priests who were themselves members of an elite class and whose presence bestowed a sacred aura on the authority of a headman or chief. The venues chosen for such ceremonies would have included stone circles, monoliths and other monuments of antiquity, all of which – in the eyes of a superstitious populace – endowed the proceedings with the approval of revered forebears. In Chapter 4 the role of the pagan priesthood and the religious beliefs that sustained it will be examined more fully.

Conquest

In 56 BC, a Roman fleet commanded by Julius Caesar defeated the Veneti people of northern Gaul in a decisive naval encounter at Morbihan Bay, off the Atlantic coast of what is now north-western France. This battle finally brought to an end Caesar's Gallic wars, a series of hard-fought campaigns which he later described in a detailed account. His victory at Morbihan had an additional significance: it brought the Roman military closer to Britain, a land whose people shared the Celtic culture of the newly conquered Gauls. To Caesar and his henchmen the British Isles were not a wild, windswept archipelago lurking on the edge of the known world, but an offshore corner of the European continent and a potentially profitable addition to the Roman economy. The coast of Britain was separated from mainland Europe by nothing more than a narrow channel of water, across which Caesar's Gaulish foes had frequently received moral and material support from British sympathisers. Rome could no longer allow the Britons to lurk on the edge of the civilised world as a threat to the stability of newly conquered Gaul. It was only a matter of time before her military commanders devised a plan for invasion.

In 55 BC, and again in the following year, Caesar himself led minor expeditions across the Channel. His troops clashed with Britons on both occasions, but these encounters were not intended as a prelude to conquest. It was not until AD 43, during the reign of the emperor Claudius, that a full-scale invasion was launched. Four experienced legions – the Second, Ninth, Fourteenth and Twentieth – were selected to spearhead a strike force of 40,000 men. Crossing the Channel from Gaul, the invaders quickly assimilated the south-eastern tribes, among whom some surrendered without putting up much of a fight. Other tribes entered into treaties by which they became client states of the Empire under pro-Roman rulers. Resistance elsewhere was mercilessly swept aside: communities who tried to make a brave stand against the legions were subjugated by force and earmarked for Romanisation. In some areas, however, the Britons refused to give up their independence so easily. One defiant figure from this period was Caratacus, a chieftain of the Catuvellauni. The heartland of his people lay north of the Thames and had fallen to Rome within a few years of the invasion. Fleeing westward to Wales, Caratacus continued the fight by leading the Silures and Ordovices of Wales until his defeat by Roman forces in 51. Ten years later, in what is now Norfolk, the conquered Iceni rose in revolt under their warrior-queen Boudica. After Boudica and her immense army were vanquished by the Roman governor Suetonius Paulinus in 61, the southern Britons fell into line and never again rebelled against their conquerors. The Brigantes, whose territory encompassed much of northern England east of the Pennines, initially showed friendship to Rome before turning hostile after 69. Their name means 'High Ones', perhaps in the broad sense of 'Highlanders'. It seems to be descriptive of their geographical situation rather than of their political unity, so we can probably envisage several 'Brigantian' tribal groups, each with its own identity and its own independent leadership. A faction among one of these groups rejected the pro-Roman sympathies of a queen called Cartimandua and rose in revolt around her former consort. The ensuing civil war gave Rome an opportunity to intervene on Cartimandua's behalf and led ultimately to the conquest of the entire Brigantian zone. The emperor Vespasian, an ex-soldier himself, entrusted the campaign to Petillius Cerialis, the Roman governor of Britain and an experienced tamer of insurgents. By 73, Cerialis had crushed the resistance and brought all or most of the Brigantes to heel. Pushing northward and westward as far as eastern Dumfriesshire, he imposed Rome's authority as far as the Solway Firth and placed a unit of troops at a new fort in Carlisle. This extension of Roman power northward to the Tyne and Solway brought the Empire face to face with the peoples of ancient Scotland for the first time.

In 77, when the governorship of Britain passed to Gnaeus Julius Agricola, only a handful of Britons remained in revolt in isolated pockets of conquered territory. Almost the entire area of what is now England, as well as large parts of Wales, lay under Roman rule. The next set of imperial objectives was clear: consolidation of recent territorial gains, destruction of lingering troublemakers, and a further northward drive. In the person of Agricola the military authorities had no better candidate to complete these tasks. His achievements in Britain were recorded by his son-in-law, Cornelius Tacitus, in a book bearing the simple title *Agricola*. Through the eyes of Tacitus, present-day historians are able to gain a valuable insight into how the Roman conquest of northern Britain was achieved. For Scottish historians in particular his narrative provides a unique window on their country's ancient past. Care and caution should nevertheless be applied when reading *Agricola*, despite its author's proximity to the events he describes. As a contemporary of the events and as a member of the Roman elite, Tacitus is obviously an important source, but he was rather too close to his subject to give a balanced account. Being married to Agricola's daughter undoubtedly gave him a unique perspective, but an intense admiration of his father-in-law turned his narrative into a gushing eulogy. It is therefore through a rose-tinted lens that the modern reader must view this unique and valuable source of early Scottish history.

Agricola had prior experience of the Britons from his time as a junior officer during Boudica's revolt in 61. He had also served as commander of the Twentieth Legion in the Brigantian civil war ten years later. Campaigns against rebellious tribes had taught him much about strategy and leadership as well as giving him an insight into native military organisation. When he became governor of Britain, he lost little time in drawing on the skills acquired during his youth by launching his first campaign in the same year. His targets were the troublesome Ordovices of North Wales. They were swiftly brought to heel and absorbed. In the following year he marched north to consolidate the Empire's grip on the Brigantes, subduing them by constructing forts and roads across their territory. The farthest limit of 'Brigantia' lay between the Solway Firth in the east and the Cheviot Hills in the west. Beyond these frontier districts lay uncharted lands inhabited by other peoples whom Rome was soon to meet.

Agricola's Northern Campaigns

Tacitus does not identify the tribes who dwelt north of the Brigantes. In the following century the Britons of the region between the Tyne–Solway and Forth–Clyde isthmuses were perceived by Roman geographers as being grouped into four large amalgamations: the Damnonii, Votadini, Selgovae and Novantae. Whether these four already existed in Agricola's time, or whether they were formed in response to his campaigns, Tacitus does not say. All that can be deduced is that the people of this region were first subdued by Rome in 78 – when Brigantian territory was finally conquered – or in 79 when Agricola marched north to the River Tay. The latter campaign gave Roman troops their first sight of the untamed highlands of northern Britain, but Agricola halted his advance at the Tay estuary. In the next season of summer campaigning he consolidated earlier gains in the lowlands south of the Forth and Clyde, using the narrow isthmus between the firths as a natural frontier and guarding it with a chain of forts. All territory south of this line was regarded as part of the Empire. It represented the most northerly portion of the new province of *Britannia*. The south-western corner of this region, corresponding roughly to Dumfriesshire and Galloway, still remained unconquered in 80, but absorption by Rome was merely postponed. The countdown to conquest began in the following summer when Agricola led an army across the River Annan to harass peoples whom Tacitus described as 'nations hitherto unknown'. A series of rapid campaigns brought the Romans to the far western coast of Galloway where Agricola and his officers gazed out on the Irish Sea. Here they discussed the possibility of invading Ireland, a task which Agricola believed could be handled by a single legion and a small force of auxiliaries. In the end he resolved instead to continue pursuing his ambitions in northern Britain. In the following year, 82, he again led an army beyond the Firth of Forth. A precise figure for the number of troops at his disposal for this campaign is difficult to glean from his son-in-law's narrative, but a realistic estimate is around 20,000 men or perhaps slightly more. Agricola's main aim was the pacification of tribes who seemed to be massing for an attack on the newly built Roman outposts in districts beyond the Forth. During his long northward march he dealt with various peoples along the way, quelling their most troublesome elements by direct military action. The rest were subjected to 'shock and awe' tactics. Coastal villages were raided by units of marines despatched from the large Roman fleet which shadowed the army's march into the North. This naval force not only provided tactical support, but also had a role in reconnaissance and intelligence-gathering. Agricola eventually reached the Firth of Tay and came to lands familiar to his troops from his campaign of three years earlier. This time, however, he did not halt on the southern shore, but marched up the Tay valley, following the river northward into lands previously uncharted. Here he met strong resistance from a people called *Caledones* or *Caledonii* who disrupted his march with swift ambushes and guerrilla warfare. Utilising the hills, glens and forests of their homeland, the fierce Caledonian warriors constantly harassed the invaders and caused much dismay in the ranks. They even sent raiding parties south across the Tay to attack Roman forts behind Agricola's advance. Eventually the situation became so dire that a group of senior commanders recommended withdrawal to the relative safety of the Forth–Clyde isthmus. Agricola, however, remained undaunted and resolute. Learning that the Caledonii were mustering their forces for a full-scale assault, he split his army into three divisions to prevent its being encircled and overwhelmed. With their original plan thus thwarted, the natives chose instead to attack one of Agricola's best units – the Ninth Legion – under cover of darkness. Breaking into the Ninth's camp, they swarmed among the tents, taking the sleeping soldiers by surprise. Things looked grim for the legionaries until, in the first glow of dawn, Agricola came to the rescue with the rest of the army marching up behind. Caught between defenders and reinforcements the Caledonii were driven out of the camp to retreat in disarray to nearby forests and swamps. This successful repulse of a major onslaught restored the wavering Roman morale and convinced the doubters in the officer corps that Agricola was right to continue the campaign. The native warriors returned to their homes, defeated but unbowed. They began to gather in great numbers for a last-ditch effort to expel the invader. Warriors assembled from every tribe and sept of the Caledonian confederacy, massing around a hill called Mons Graupius where they vowed to defeat the Romans or perish in the attempt. Tacitus provides an exciting account of the build-up to the battle, employing dramatic prose to draw his readers towards the decisive endgame of Agricola's campaign. The report is so laden with rhetoric that it cannot be accepted too trustingly. It is, nevertheless, a vivid portrayal of an ancient battle. To add to the drama, Tacitus offered a non-Roman viewpoint of the preparations by quoting a heroic eve-of-battle speech given by the Caledonian leader Calgacus. The latter was undoubtedly a fictional character devised by Tacitus to fit the stereotypical image of a 'noble savage' bravely defying the inexorable advance of Roman civilisation. To draw a contrast with the barbarian hero's proud words, Tacitus followed them with a stirring call-to-arms delivered by Agricola. We see the Roman general casually dismissing his opponent's words by assuring his troops that the Caledonii are 'just so many spiritless cowards'. This fired the soldiers with such enthusiasm for war that they would have gleefully charged the enemy there and then if Agricola had not held them back. Although we have no reason to believe that Calgacus – whose Celtic name means 'Swordsman' – ever existed outside the pages of *Agricola*, the battle of Mons Graupius certainly took place. According to Tacitus, it began with a headlong rush by Caledonian chariots towards the Roman line, a chaotic charge swiftly neutralised by Agricola's well-trained cavalry. This was followed by spear-throwing from both sides before six cohorts of war-hardened Dutch and Belgian auxiliaries led the Roman advance up the hill. Fierce hand-to-hand combat ensued on the lower slopes, but the superior weapons and training of the auxiliaries cut a deep swath through the Caledonian ranks. In desperation the native leaders watching from the hilltop ordered the main body of their warriors to march down the slopes in a bid to get behind the Romans, but Agricola blocked this manoeuvre with four squadrons of cavalry. Groups of disheartened natives then began to flee the battlefield, with Roman horsemen chasing after them. Some fugitives escaped into woodland where they were hunted down and slain; others scattered wildly into the trees and managed to evade the pursuit. And so the great battle ended with a decisive Roman victory. Tacitus calculated the Caledonian losses at 10,000, a hugely exaggerated figure which nevertheless conveys the important message that Mons Graupius was a major triumph for Agricola. Unfortunately, despite giving a detailed narrative of the battle, Tacitus is imprecise as to its location. Modern historians are therefore left to wonder where it took place and, in the hope of pinpointing the battlefield, a number of more or less likely sites have been suggested. One popular theory proposes Bennachie, a group of hills in Aberdeenshire, the most prominent of which is the Mither Tap whose peak might be the *mons* described by Tacitus. Archaeologists have identified a line of first-century Roman camps running north-east from the Tay estuary in a curving arc to the Aberdeenshire coast and the Moray Firth. These have been seen by supporters of the Bennachie hypothesis as marking the route taken by Agricola's army to and from the battle. An alternative theory locates the battle further south, in Strathearn in Perthshire, where the small hill of Duncrub bears a name that might be a Gaelic form of *Mons Graupius*. Not far away stood a Roman fort, the Latin name for which was *Victoria*, meaning 'Victory', a name suggestive of special significance in Roman military lore. The main argument against Duncrub is that it lies south of the Tay in a region previously consolidated by Agricola and situated a considerable distance from the Caledonian heartlands. The latter lay further north and seem to be remembered in Gaelic place-names such as *Dun Chaillean* ('Fort of the Caledonians'), now Anglicised as Dunkeld, and Schiehallion ('The Fairy Hill of the Caledonians'). Against the candidature of Bennachie is the argument that it might actually be *too* far north of the presumed limit of Agricola's advance. Both theories have merits and pitfalls, but in neither case can the matter be proved one way or another. The most realistic assessment of the puzzle is that the location of Mons Graupius will remain forever lost. Interestingly, the name of the battle was borrowed as a broad geographical term for the upland massif of the Highlands – the Grampian Mountains. The word 'Grampian' derives from a misspelling of *Graupius* in a fifteenth-century Italian edition of *Agricola*.

After the battle, Agricola dealt with a tribe called the Boresti, perhaps a belligerent sept of the Caledonian group, and secured their obedience by taking some of their nobles as hostages. He then returned to his headquarters in southern Britain, leaving garrisoned forts to watch over the Caledonii and other defeated tribes. He left behind what was effectively a militarised zone between the Forth–Clyde isthmus and the heartlands of Caledonia. Strategic concerns were vital to his planning and, to this end, he identified the main glen-routes and blocked them with forts. His strategy is still visible today in the landscape of Stirlingshire and Perthshire, where the grass-grown remains of old ramparts guard key positions along a diagonal line drawn between Loch Lomond and the Firth of Tay. At the south-western extremity of this line a small fort was built at Drumquhassle near Drymen; at the north-eastern end lay the fort of Inverquharity in Strathmore. Other sites formed an arc guarding the southern and eastern fringes of Caledonian territory, all connected by a military road leading north from Camelon on the Forth estuary. This road linked important forts such as Doune at the crossing of the River Teith, Ardoch in Strathallan, and Bertha where the rivers Tay and Almond meet on the outskirts of modern Perth. Beyond Bertha the highway turned north and east through the fertile vale of Strathmore to a terminus at Stracathro. South of Bertha it was guarded by a line of wooden watchtowers as far as the fort at Ardoch. These were placed at half-mile intervals and seem to have functioned as observation posts giving wide views across the Caledonian borderlands. Their main concentration lay on either side of the highway where it ran west to east along the Gask Ridge overlooking the River Earn. Historians and archaeologists usually interpret the 'Gask System', as it is commonly known, as a frontier defined by Agricola to demarcate the southern limit of Caledonia and to monitor the movements of its people. One possible inference is that the Earn marked an ancient boundary between the Caledonii and neighbouring tribes in Stirlingshire from whom they were in certain ways distinct. Central to Agricola's vision for the control and, perhaps, for the eventual conquest of the lands beyond the Tay was a huge new fortress capable of housing an entire legion. This was sited at Inchtuthil on the north bank of the river between the present-day villages of Caputh and Meikleour.

As a final flourish to his campaign Agricola ordered the fleet to continue its reconnaissance of the east coast, instructing an admiral to map the geography of the furthest regions. The fleet duly passed through the Pentland Firth separating the far northern tip of Britain from the Orkney Isles, thus confirming the long-held Roman belief that Britannia was indeed an island. On the far horizon the sailors believed that they had caught a glimpse of the fabled *Thule*, the most northerly of all lands. What they had most probably seen was Fair Isle between Orkney and Shetland. Leaving the waters around Orkney, a few ships continued the journey by steering south to explore the western seaways, where their crews mapped several Hebridean isles, including one inhabited by priests or druids. The rest of the fleet turned around and sailed back to harbour, bringing new geographical data which was used by Roman cartographers to update their maps and gazetteers of the Empire. Later, in the middle of the second century, a geographer called Ptolemy compiled a detailed atlas of the known world, peppering it with names of tribes and rivers and prominent landmarks. The parts of the atlas relating to the British Isles are a rich source of information on peoples and places, not only for the Romanised regions, but also for unconquered areas such as northern Scotland.

Gazing out over the Perthshire landscape today, at the dawn of the third millennium, it might seem hard for modern eyes to imagine the visual effect of Agricola's army on the march. The great valley of the Tay still provides the main route into Caledonia, as it did in the first century, but today the ancient trail trodden by Roman boots lies buried beneath the busy A9 highway. Watching the endless blur of cars and trucks speeding north or south makes it difficult to envisage not only the impressive sight of Roman regiments marching to war, but also the logistical problems that Agricola and his officers had to face. An army of 20,000 men, marching as a column in ranks of six, inevitably made a huge impact on the landscape. Tramping north from the outflow of the Tay, near to where the city of Perth now stands, the Roman invasion force would have stretched ten miles. Thus, when the scouts at the front of the column halted at a suitable place for a night-encampment, it would have taken a further three hours for the rearguard to reach the same spot. At the campsite a huge perimeter was laid out by surveyors attached to the legions and, under the supervision of specialist engineers, the soldiers dug an enclosing ditch, three feet in depth, as an emergency protection in the event of enemy assault.

The excavated earth was then piled up to form a rampart, behind which each platoon of eight men erected a tent on a designated pitch already marked out by surveyors. Training and unit cohesion were at such a high level that the entire operation, although potentially an organisational nightmare, could be completed fairly quickly. To the Caledonian warriors lurking in the nearby woods and hills the efficiency and sophistication exhibited by the Romans must have seemed daunting. Each camp, although constructed as a temporary refuge on the march, was essentially an earth-walled fortress. Many can still be seen in the Scottish landscape, sometimes as traces on the ground, but more often as outlined shapes concealed beneath modern farmland and revealed only by aerial photography. Fields that at first seem featureless to the walker offer a different picture to the airborne photographer, who sees instead the ghostly shapes of ancient ramparts, ditches and gateways revealed by subtle changes in soil depth. From these images the archaeologist gains key insights into Roman military engineering, while the historian is able to see physical evidence of the events described by Tacitus. The distribution of temporary camps indicates the route followed by the Agricolan army on its northward march from the Tay estuary.

Supplying an army with food during a campaign in hostile territory presents a challenge to any general. Large numbers of soldiers require large amounts of food each day and can neither march nor fight if they become hungry. This is a fundamental truth of military logistics and was acknowledged by all the great commanders of the ancient world: Alexander, Hannibal, Caesar, and many others. In Agricola's time the Roman army was essentially an international organisation operating on a global scale with long experience of transportation and supply. Sustaining his soldiers on their hard trek through the Caledonian hills was therefore a challenging task for Agricola, but not an especially daunting one. The Highland landscape was probably no more an untamed wilderness in the first century than it is today. It sustained a large, settled population of native farmers. From these folk the Romans were able to acquire grain, vegetables and livestock by pillaging or threats, thereby achieving the parallel gain of denying those same resources to the enemy.

The Walls

The optimism brought about by the success of Agricola's campaigns did not last. Rome's determination to extend her Empire to the furthest limits of Britain gradually dwindled after military planners assessed the long-term costs of the project. By the beginning of the second century any realistic hope of permanently conquering Caledonia had been abandoned in favour of other, more urgent priorities in the east of the Empire. The first indications that the Agricolan gains would not be consolidated came within a few years of the great battle at Mons Graupius. According to Tacitus, Agricola himself was recalled to Rome soon after his victory because his military prowess roused the emperor's jealousy. He was summoned back to the imperial court before his popularity among the troops became a political threat. The men who held the governorship of Britain after him made no attempt to build on his gains in the Highlands and instead concentrated on drawing a frontier in the Lowlands south of the Forth–Clyde isthmus. Agricolan forts in this region saw their garrisons strengthened and their defences improved. At Newstead, where the large fort of *Trimontium* nestled in the shadow of the triple-peaked Eildon Hills, the archaeological record indicates the construction of a huge new perimeter ditch and a height increase for the ramparts. South-west of Newstead a further five forts were similarly refurbished or reoccupied at this time to constitute what appears to have been a new boundary bisecting the Lowlands in a diagonal line running from the Cheviots to Galloway. Three of the five lay in Dumfriesshire – at Milton, Dalswinton and Glenlochar – and were large sites manned by substantial garrisons. The line was almost certainly the new imperial frontier in the post-Agricolan period. North of it, beyond the Forth–Clyde isthmus in the vulnerable borderland separating the Empire from its Caledonian foes, the signal-towers constructed during the campaigns of the early 80s were abandoned. Slight archaeological evidence suggests a continuing presence on the isthmus itself – at the small fort of Castlecary, for example – but the effective limit of Roman authority withdrew south of Clydesdale and the Tweed valley. The reason for the abandonment and retreat is suggested by contemporary chroniclers who describe serious trouble far away on the Danube frontier. Successive Roman defeats at the hands of Dacian tribes in what is now Romania led to an urgent need for reinforcements and made a reduction in the British garrison inevitable. An entire legion – the Second – was transferred to the East together with an unknown number of auxiliary units, the latter presumably including veterans of Agricola's campaigns uprooted from forts in Scotland. Indications of the scale of these troop withdrawals have been identified in the archaeological record at Roman sites in Perthshire. At Inchtuthil, in 87 or 88, the new legionary fortress was in the early stages of construction when the work-gangs were ordered to pack up their tools and leave the place unfinished. Inevitably, this erratic policy of abandonment and withdrawal was destined to reap a bitter harvest in the following decades.

The second century had barely begun when the emperor Trajan undertook a major war against the Dacians. A requirement for extra troops drained more units from the British garrison and coincided with attacks by volatile elements among the Britons. The insurgents were perhaps the conquered Brigantes or their semi-independent neighbours further north. This combination of internal and external troubles prompted a further retreat of the imperial frontier and the abandonment of Newstead and other forts along the Cheviot–Galloway line. Evidence of large-scale destruction at some forts might indicate aggressive action by Britons or deliberate vandalism by retreating Romans to prevent native reuse of the buildings. The crisis highlighted the logistical difficulties faced by forces of occupation intent on holding down conquered peoples while trying to maintain a viable frontier. It ushered in a less ambitious, more cautious policy with regard to northern Britain. This entailed a concentration of military resources behind a line drawn between the Solway and the mouth of the Tyne, an option considerably more manageable than trying to maintain a screen of exposed military outposts in the wild countryside beyond. Eventually, this new policy was given physical form in the shape of a massive wall of stone running from east to west to demarcate the northern limit of the imperial province of Britannia.

Construction of this wall, which we now know by its eponymous name Hadrian's Wall, was the brainchild of Hadrian who ruled as emperor from 117 to 138. Its construction commenced after 122, the year of Hadrian's visit to Britain. He ordered that the stone rampart should follow the route followed by an earlier Roman road known today as the Stanegate. The great project was undertaken by legionary detachments and gangs of native labourers working under the supervision of military engineers. Upon completion the Wall formed a continuous barrier running for eighty miles between Carlisle in the west and Wallsend in the east. Forts garrisoned by units of auxiliaries were built along the entire length, each separated from its nearest neighbour by a distance of six to nine miles. Between these forts lay smaller defensive works, the milecastles, placed at intervals of one Roman mile. The dimensions of the Wall itself were impressive: its eastern sections rose to a height of twenty feet with a breadth of ten feet. Although its primary role was to mark the northern border of the Empire, its huge scale served an additional purpose by glorifying the emperor who had devised it. Visually it must have presented a striking display of imperial power to Roman and native alike. Britons dwelling in the lands beyond the Wall were obliged to pass through designated crossing-points if they wished to trade with compatriots in the 'civilised' South. Those living immediately north of the new barrier may have been part of some larger Pennine group, but, if so, they were now cut off from the rest and had to seek Roman approval if they wished to travel southward. They are likely to have been overawed by the towering ramparts of stone and by the soldiers peering down from the battlements. Nonetheless, as events would soon demonstrate, the most rebellious native elements on both sides of the Wall remained undaunted by its presence. To them it was not so much a physical boundary as a hindrance to communication between anti-Roman factions living on either side of it.

Twenty years after completion, Hadrian's Wall lost its frontier status to another rampart located a hundred miles north. This second barrier, known today as the Antonine Wall, was a less imposing though no less ambitious attempt to divide Roman Britain from the hostile peoples of the North. It was begun in 142 or 143 on the orders of Antoninus Pius who succeeded Hadrian as emperor. Like Agricola before him, Antoninus realised that the forty-mile neck of land between the firths of Forth and Clyde provided a narrow tract of fairly easy terrain. He perceived that a barrier built across this isthmus would provide a shorter, cheaper and more easily defensible boundary than the sprawling eighty-mile span of Hadrian's Wall. Forts had already been placed south of the isthmus by Agricola sixty years earlier, but these were not well-suited as anchors for the Antonine rampart. Instead, a new line was chosen overlooking the trough created by the rivers Kelvin and Carron, with new forts built on the hills and ridges on the southern side. Of the old Agricolan bases near the isthmus only Camelon was close enough to be considered part of the new frontier, although it lay slightly north of the line. Antoninus delegated responsibility for construction to Lollius Urbicus, the governor of Britain, who came north to personally supervise the project. Before the work commenced, the governor undertook military campaigns in the region beyond Hadrian's Wall, his objective being to subdue and pacify volatile elements among the natives – perhaps the northernmost portion of the Brigantes. Having reduced these rebels to subservience, he turned his mind back to the great task, enlisting the help of the three legions who now comprised the core of Britain's garrison. Detachments of legionaries marched up from their fortresses at York, Chester and Caerleon to lend expertise and muscle to the project. No attempt was made to imitate Hadrian's imposing but enormously expensive wall of stone. Instead, the Antonine Wall was essentially an earthwork, a turf rampart, approximately twelve feet high and fourteen feet wide, with a massive ditch in front. Forts were placed at intervals of only a couple of miles, thereby giving the new frontier a somewhat huddled appearance on our modern maps of Roman Britain. The 6,000 soldiers of the Antonine garrison comprised a strike force whose main role in the event of a Caledonian assault was to advance in swift counter-attack. In peacetime they functioned as policemen and customs officials by monitoring trade and other communication across the frontier and in the hinterland behind. Crossing-points allowed the Britons to travel to and fro between the lands on either side, but all movement was closely watched. Platforms of turf on stone foundations were erected along the Wall's southern or inner side at half a dozen locations. The precise purpose of these additional structures – often described by archaeologists as 'expansions' – is unclear, but they may have formed part of a wider signalling network which used fire-beacons to warn of danger. This would have provided an effective method of alerting garrisons along the Wall if a surprise attack came down from the North.

The new defensive line made Hadrian's frontier redundant and led to some outpost forts in Stirlingshire and Perthshire being regarrisoned. New forts were built in the intervallate region – the land between the two walls – while older forts were brought back into use. Legionary detachments, including men from the renowned Twentieth Legion at Chester, came north to support the work-gangs with engineering expertise. A portion of the Twentieth was temporarily billeted in the old Agricolan fort at Newstead whose turf ramparts were now rebuilt in stone. When completed, the new system of defences in the intervallate region left the native Britons with a large Roman presence in their midst and assured them in the starkest terms that they were being closely watched. Through this region two major roads ran north towards the Antonine Wall. One road traced the western edge of the Cheviot Hills, its course running roughly parallel to the east coast, while the other turned north-west from Carlisle to meet the upper courses of the River Clyde. Today, the eastern route is known as Dere Street and can still be seen traversing the landscape of the Anglo-Scottish borderlands. It began at Corbridge, a fort somewhat south of Hadrian's Wall, and provided a continuation of the main highway linking the Wall's eastern garrisons to the military headquarters at York. The origins of Dere Street lay in the Agricolan period, but, after the construction of the Antonine Wall, its importance greatly increased. Beyond Corbridge it ran in a north-westerly direction via High Rochester in Redesdale to Newstead. From there it continued north via Inveresk near Edinburgh to Cramond on the Firth of Forth and so onward to the Antonine Wall. Along the latter the garrisons were served by a military road similar in alignment to the Stanegate running behind Hadrian's Wall. North of the Antonine line some old Agricolan forts, such as Ardoch and Bertha, having been abandoned decades earlier, were now reoccupied. A military road, essentially an extension of Dere Street, connected these outposts from a starting-point at Camelon on the north side of the turf wall. This highway ran below the steep western slopes of Stirling's Castle Rock to cross the River Forth before turning north-east towards the valleys of Earn and Tay. It was the most northerly Roman road in the Empire, but also, as we shall see in the next chapter, one of the shortest lived.

CHAPTER 2
The Later Roman Period

Consolidation of the Frontier

If the imperial authorities hoped that the Antonine Wall would bring a period of stability to Roman Britain, their optimism was dashed when trouble broke out among the northern tribes in 154 or 155. Which tribes were involved is a matter of debate, as is the question of how much disruption was caused. It is possible, for instance, that the unrest was confined to communities living north of Hadrian's Wall, or that these were joined by neighbours in Dumfriesshire, or even that the main troublemakers lay further north in Caledonia. Whatever the location of the uprising it was put down by Julius Verus, governor of Britain, and special coins were minted to celebrate the restoration of order. In the next few years, however, a decision was taken to abandon the Antonine frontier and withdraw to Hadrian's Wall. The presence of troublesome natives in the region between the two walls may have influenced the decision, but other factors, such as the strain on military resources, could have played a bigger role. When the withdrawal commenced in 158, it evacuated the Antonine line but stopped short of abandoning the region between the two walls. Some of the intervallate forts were even refurbished at this time. Buildings destroyed by fire at Birrens, known as *Blatobulgium* ('The Flour Sack') because of the distinctive shape of the nearby Burnswark Hill, were once thought to have succumbed to the native uprising of AD 154/5, but were more likely to have been demolished by the fort garrison during a makeover.

Before 160 the Antonine Wall was recommissioned and its soldiers came back to the forts, if only for a brief time. Their return to the Forth–Clyde isthmus was temporary and did not outlast the end of the decade. Trouble flared again in the early 160s, soon after the accession of Marcus Aurelius as emperor. A Roman general with the portentous name Calpurnius Agricola was ordered to quell it. The contemporary sources do not identify the culprits, who were either rebellious Britons on the northern frontier or Caledonian raiders from the lands beyond. Whoever these troublemakers were they were defeated and a semblance of stability returned. Roman sources describe another outbreak of hostilities in 169 when unidentified Britons caused trouble somewhere in the North. A war was seemingly averted by nipping the unrest in the bud, but, by 170, the Antonine Wall was again evacuated when Marcus Aurelius needed reinforcements for a campaign on the Danube. This time the troop withdrawals were intended to be permanent and many forts sustained deliberate demolition of buildings and defences. The turf frontier was abandoned, the Stirlingshire forts were left empty and the imperial boundary shrank back to Hadrian's Wall. Some forts in the intervallate region remained in use, but these were engulfed in 181, during the reign of the emperor Commodus, when the Caledonii swept down from their Highland fastnesses to plunder the wealth of the Roman province. A high-ranking general marched out to meet the marauders, but he and his troops were slain. The ensuing wave of destruction left several forts along Hadrian's Wall in ruins and spelled disaster for vulnerable outposts such as Newstead. Commodus, son and successor of Marcus Aurelius, dismissed the hapless governor of Britain and appointed a more effective replacement. The new governor, Ulpius Marcellus, defeated the Caledonii and restored control before following up his victory by making changes to troop dispositions in the intervallate region. Some forts were rebuilt and regarrisoned, but others, including Newstead, were condemned to dereliction. By the end of the second century, only a handful of outposts north of Hadrian's Wall remained in use, their soldiers providing a token military presence in a region now regarded as a buffer-zone between the imperial province of Britannia and the badlands of Caledonia. The outposts lay in the south of the intervallate region, in lands nominally given over to native rule but under the watchful eye of Rome. Beyond them, in a broad band of territory encompassing Clydesdale and Lothian, the North Britons retained a measure of independence under the authority of their own leaders. It is likely that this arrangement was monitored by the Roman army during ceremonial events and tribal assemblies at specific sites called *loci*. The Latin word *locus* simply means 'place', but in the context of barbarian tribes bound in clientship to Rome these 'places' may have held administrative and diplomatic significance. Each of the four major groupings of North Britons had one or more *loci* within its territory, some being centred on sacred stones of immense antiquity which had long been used for ceremonial purposes. A public gathering at a *locus* would have given Rome an opportunity to remind the natives of their obligations to her Empire. How much autonomy was actually delegated to the intervallate Britons is unclear, but the surviving outpost forts were doubtless a constant reminder of imperial authority. At Birrens the Roman garrison used a native hillfort at nearby Burnswark for target practice by bombarding its decaying ramparts with catapults, an exercise which may have served the dual purpose of providing in-house artillery training as well as discouraging dissent among the North Britons. The latter thus approached the third century sandwiched between two implacably hostile forces: the Empire to the south and Caledonia to the north. Treaties forged in the aftermath of troop withdrawals from the Antonine Wall created an uneasy peace between the protagonists, but neither side, still less the Britons caught in the middle, expected it to last. It was little more than a temporary respite, a breathing-space, before a new round of raiding and retribution began.

Rome and the North Britons

Native communities in the land between the two Roman walls

dwelt in the shadow of a conquering power. Their fellow-Britons living south of Hadrian's Wall in what is now northern England were subjects of the Empire and, by the third century, had grudgingly or willingly accepted the situation. Earlier revolts by the Brigantes had been brutally crushed and were never to be repeated. Acceptance of subjugation was an easier option, even if it meant a loss of pride and a tax obligation to the imperial treasury. North of the Hadrianic frontier the Britons of the intervallate region remained nominally independent while acknowledging some measure of Roman authority. Unlike their Brigantian neighbours they continued to be ruled by their own leaders but these had presumably forged long-term treaties with Rome.

South of Hadrian's Wall, the Brigantes and other conquered Britons experienced the full impact of the Roman occupation. The native upper classes, comprising the major landowning families, had watched their privileged status slip away after the conquest. Their lifestyles had collapsed as soon as Rome dismantled the old economic networks. Tithes of agricultural produce formerly rendered to local headmen were now collected by imperial taxgatherers, while a strict prohibition of civilian military activity brought an end to tit-for-tat raids by predatory bands of Britons upon their neighbours. The resulting net loss of plunder severed the native upper class from its traditional methods of amassing surplus wealth through the acquisition of cattle and slaves. In such circumstances the neutered elites of Brigantia had little choice but to accept new roles delegated to them by the imperial administration. Some were probably allowed to retain a measure of authority in local contexts, as leaders nominated by Rome to oversee districts where their ancestors had once held substantial power. Such folk would have become more or less Romanised, maintaining their elevated status by exploiting opportunities for social advancement in the northern military zone. Some, no doubt, were allowed to remain on their ancestral estates and would have continued to receive tithes from tenant farmers.

A wholly new type of civilian settlement, the *vicus*, appeared in the wake of conquest. The typical *vicus* was a small village established outside the main gate of a Roman fort and along the primary access road. It tended to attract entrepreneurs seeking business opportunities at places where large numbers of military folk had disposable incomes. By definition, the *vicus* owed its existence to the presence of the fort and was wholly dependent on the patronage of soldiers. Its inhabitants, known as *vicani*, were generally a mixed bag of individuals drawn from local native communities and from places further afield. Some manufactured clothes, shoes or craft goods in small workshops, while others established taverns and hotels. Female *vicani* included wives and girlfriends of the garrison, their residence outside the fort initially being a requirement of the Army's prohibition on married soldiers until Septimius Severus changed the law. In reality, even before the Severan reform, the authorities routinely turned a blind eye to liaisons between soldiers and native women, many of whom bore sons who eventually succeeded their fathers in the garrison.

North of Hadrian's Wall, the much briefer occupation of Roman forts made the *vici* a fleeting addition to the landscape. Even when the Antonine Wall provided a temporary screen against Caledonian incursions, the intervallate region was not a place where civilians could put down roots outside a fort. Thus, while some *vici* south of Hadrian's Wall thrived for two hundred years or more, in the lands further north a long period of habitation for *vicani* was out of the question. No fort north of today's Anglo-Scottish border was permanently garrisoned after the end of the second century, a statistic which helps to explain why archaeologists have identified so few *vici* in Scotland. One of the few examples unearthed by excavation is a large village clustering outside the east gate of the fort at Inveresk near Musselburgh in East Lothian. Another has been discovered at Carriden, known to the Romans as *Veluniate*, a fort perched on the eastern extremity of the Antonine Wall overlooking the Forth estuary. The *vicani* at Carriden were a community of sufficient stability and cohesion to be granted a measure of self-government by the military authorities. However, neither of these settlements endured for long. They were wholly dependent on their forts and disappeared when these were abandoned.

Caledonii and Maeatae

Beyond the Antonine Wall lay the enemies of Rome: the Caledonii and their neighbours. During the northern campaigns of the second century, the Empire's relationship with these barbarians was characterised by raid and counter-raid across the borderlands around the Firth of Forth. This region became a volatile conflict zone while Roman troops still garrisoned the Antonine forts, and likewise in the years following its final abandonment in the 160s. Hostilities continued until Rome forged treaties with the main barbarian groups at the end of the century, probably by paying them to stop raiding. At that time the Caledonii were still the main threat, but another people, the Maeatae, were recognised as an equally belligerent foe. Roman writers located the Maeatae immediately north of the Antonine Wall in what are now Stirlingshire and Clackmannanshire. They may have been a fusion of smaller groups on the model of the Caledonian 'confederacy' further north. Some historians wonder if these political fusions may have occurred because an aggressive foreign power held sway south of the Forth–Clyde isthmus. They see Rome's occupation of the southern part of Britain as a catalyst for political developments in the North. In this scenario the creation of large tribal confederacies is viewed as a logical progression arising from the proximity of large numbers of Roman troops. An alternative theory sees amalgamation as an outcome of conflict between neighbouring communities, rather than as a voluntary or co-operative response to the threat of Roman invasion. Indeed, Rome might even have been responsible for creating tensions by favouring some native groups while neglecting others. Thus, it is possible that the pro-Roman queen Cartimandua might not have been a 'pan-Brigantian' sovereign after all, but merely a local ruler who exploited imperial patronage to impose her will on other Pennine peoples. By applying this model further north, we might envisage the Caledonii not so much joining with their neighbours as subjugating them by force. Such a process may have placed the Caledonian leadership at the head of a large, powerful amalgamation of tribes in a region centred on the valley of the River Tay. If this is what happened, then the Maeatae may have similarly seized the initiative among their own weaker neighbours.

High on a shoulder of the Ochil Hills, commanding a wide vista across Stirlingshire and the Firth of Forth, stood the great *oppidum* or tribal centre of the ancestors of the Maeatae. This stronghold may already have been abandoned when the Maeatae themselves first came to Rome's attention, but it remained an imposing feature in the landscape. Its ancient name is unrecorded, but the hill on which it stands is known today as Dumyat, a name deriving from Gaelic *Dun Myat* ('The Fort of the Maeatae'). Five miles south-east, and a little to the south of the modern town of Clackmannan, stood an unshaped boulder venerated in pre-Christian times as a sacred stone. In the medieval period this monument became known as King Robert's Stone after its role in a folktale about Robert the Bruce, but its original name was *Clach Manonn* ('The Stone of Manau'). The stone's proximity to the heartlands of the Maeatae suggests its adoption by their forefathers as a venue for sacred rites and public ceremonies. It now sits on top of a pillar beside the old tolbooth in Clackmannan and has given its name to the town.

The Maeatae make their first appearance in the historical record around the year 200. At that time, according to the Roman writer Cassius Dio, they overturned a treaty with Rome and mustered their forces for war. They chose the right moment, for substantial numbers of Roman troops had recently been withdrawn from Britain by Clodius Albinus, an ambitious governor who hoped to set himself up as emperor. Seeking to exploit the situation, the Maeatae crossed the abandoned Antonine Wall to rampage southward, wreaking havoc wherever they went. To make matters worse, the Caledonii were preparing to break their own treaty with the Empire by joining the assault. In a desperate bid to avert a major crisis the newly appointed governor of Roman Britain, Virius Lupus, tried to placate the Maeatae with a substantial payment. The offer was accepted: the raiders went home and released a small number of Roman prisoners. But peace did not last and a new spate of raiding began. This time, no bribe was forth-coming from the imperial treasury. What the barbarians received instead was a full-scale assault. In 208, the warlike emperor Septimius Severus arrived in Britain to deal personally with the situation on the northern frontier. With him came his sons, Geta and Caracalla, two young men rescued from the sleaze of Rome by a father who regarded the Forth borderlands as a somewhat more wholesome environment. Assembling a large army, Severus marched north to hammer the Maeatae into submission and to discourage the Caledonii from joining them. His strategy seemed to work: he received pledges of peace from the barbarians and returned to his base at York. In 210, however, the Maeatae again reverted to their old ways. They may have heard a rumour that Severus was sick and unable to leave his bed. He was indeed too ill to command a new campaign, but, despite his infirmity, he had no intention of letting the enemy run amok. Leadership of the counter-attack was delegated to Caracalla who unleashed upon the Maeatae a harsh retribution. He arrived in Stirlingshire with a clear instruc-tion from his father to slaughter the natives and to leave none alive. Until this point, the Caledonii had merely observed from the sidelines, but new tales of Roman savagery towards their neigh-bours brought them swiftly into the fray. They had another incentive to confront the invader, for Severus intended to build a massive fortress at Carpow at the mouth of the River Earn on the southern edge of their heartlands. The new base was designed to accommodate an entire legion and, when completed, would have posed a major threat to native ambitions. A prolonged and bitter conflict seemed unavoidable until fate intervened to remove Severus from the equation. In February 211, at his military headquarters in York, he finally succumbed to illness. Caracalla became emperor, but no longer shared his father's enthusiasm for the northern campaign. He saw little gain in resuming it: the fighting was hard, the short-term rewards were meagre and the prospect of a lasting solution looked increasingly remote. Moreover, the drain on military resources was becoming acute and difficult to justify at a time when other parts of the Empire demanded urgent attention.

Foremost among Caracalla's anxieties was a bitter rivalry with his younger brother, Geta, whose growing influence at the imperial court was an irritation. Caracalla therefore called a halt to the war, made peace with the Maeatae and Caledonii and relinquished any serious claim on their lands. He returned to Rome to assert his authority and, within a few months, masterminded his brother's assassination. Meanwhile, in northern Britain, the forward bases occupied during the Severan campaign were evacuated. Construction at Carpow was halted and the soldiers withdrew. A token military presence lingered at Cramond on the Forth until it, too, was abandoned in the 220s. The imperial frontier again retreated to Hadrian's Wall, leaving only four outpost forts in the lands beyond: Risingham and High Rochester in the east; Bewcastle and Netherby in the west. With this retreat the Roman adventure in the Highlands finally came to an end.

Picts

Some Roman writers poured scorn on Caracalla's readiness to let the barbarians off the hook, but his treaties held firm and ultimately proved the doubters wrong. The third century passed in relative peace. No new outbreaks of trouble on the northern frontier are known from the surviving literary sources. Only in the century's last decade did the situation once again grow volatile. In 297, the poet Eumenius referred to a people called *Picti* ('Picts'), whom he named alongside the Irish as enemies of the Britons. He did not say where they came from, but they plainly lived outside the Empire. Their location was made clearer by an anonymous writer of the early fourth century who referred to 'the woods and marshes of the Caledones and other Picts'. This clearly identifies the Caledonii of earlier times as a component of the *Picti*. It also shows that Perthshire, the ancient Caledonian heartland, must have lain within Pictish territory. Later in the fourth century, the historian and ex-soldier Ammianus Marcellinus regarded the Picts as a fusion of two distinct peoples, the Verturiones and Dicalydones. The latter name relates in some way to *Caledonii* and indicates that this ancient grouping still functioned as a political force three hundred years after the Agricolan invasion. The Verturiones are previously unknown, but their name connects them to Fortriu, an area of importance during the second half of the first millennium AD. In the nineteenth century, the Scottish antiquary William Forbes Skene equated Fortriu with the later earldom of Strathearn and Menteith. This identification remained largely unchallenged until 2006, when its weakness was highlighted in a groundbreaking paper. Fortriu is now regarded as a more northerly territory centred on Moray. In another recent development, some historians have adopted the adjective 'Verturian' when referring to the land and people of this region.

Picti means 'Painted People' or 'People of the Designs'. When and why this name originated are questions to which several plausible answers can be offered. So far, no consensus has yet been achieved. The name may be derived from, or related to, a collective term used by the Picts of themselves, but it is equally possible that no such term existed until the Romans began to distinguish the peoples of northern Britain from one another. Sadly, the Pictish language vanished after c.900 and, as no Pictish writings have survived, there is now little hope of ascertaining whether or not a native precursor of Latin *Picti* ever existed. Historians are left instead to muse on the nature and purpose of the 'designs' that gave rise to the name. Did the Picts tattoo their skin, or did they merely daub their bodies with warpaint? Tattooing was regarded as archaic and primitive by the Romanised Britons living south of Hadrian's Wall, but it possibly lingered as a custom further north. If so, its continuing use far beyond the frontier might explain why the poet Claudian, writing in the late fourth and early fifth centuries, referred to Roman soldiers observing the decorative body-art of slain Pictish warriors.

Whatever the origin of their name, the Picts posed a major threat to Roman Britain throughout the fourth century. They were a numerous people whose lands encompassed a broad swath of territory stretching from the Western Isles to Fife and from Shetland to the Ochil Hills. Within this large area many communities shared cultural traits we now regard as essentially 'Pictish'. They shared a common language similar to, and no doubt once indistinguishable from, the language of the Britons. On a political level, however, the Picts were not a single entity but a patchwork of separate groups, each of which was probably ruled as a small kingdom. In early times, when they first came to Rome's attention, their most frequent foes were likely to have been fellow-Picts rather than people living south of the Forth–Clyde isthmus. Much of the slave-raiding and cattle-reiving undertaken by Picts in Roman times was surely conducted within their own homelands. Ambitious leaders would have had little incentive to act in unison against an external power unless persuaded or coerced to do so. Thus, although the notion of pan-Pictish unity might have simplified matters for Roman chroniclers, we should not feel tempted to run too far with it. Temporary pooling of military forces in response to Roman aggression perhaps occurred from time to time, but the Picts were not a homogeneous group. Their default political framework was rooted in local allegiances rather than in abstract concepts of nationhood. Although this pattern began to change in the sixth century, with the emergence of one or more Pictish overkingships, the marauding bands of 'Painted People' who troubled Roman Britain in 297 were almost certainly not acting in unison.

What distinguished the Picts from other indigenous peoples of the British Isles? The simplest answer to this question is that Pictish culture must have been unique, distinctive and recognisable to outsiders. It was sufficiently distinct for Roman writers to differentiate the Picts from the Britons and the Irish. All three were part of a Celtic cultural zone, but, despite this shared heritage, they each exhibited certain traits that set them apart from one another. One important difference was language: the Picts and Britons spoke variants of a Brittonic language of the 'P-Celtic' group, while the Irish used Goidelic or Gaelic speech which modern linguists define as 'Q-Celtic'. The Pictish and British varieties of Brittonic represented separate dialects which, although mutually intelligible, may have sounded quite distinct when spoken. The date at which the two diverged is unknown but their separation perhaps began in Roman times, when the influence of Latin south of Hadrian's Wall might have made northern dialects seem barbarous and different. By 297, when the Picts emerged into recorded history, it is possible that their speech already sounded sufficiently different to set them apart.

In ethnic terms the Picts of the third and fourth centuries were simply the most northerly of the Britons. There is no doubt that they were a 'Celtic' people. Like their southern cousins they had been exposed to Celticisation during the first millennium BC when cultural influences from Continental Europe spread throughout the British Isles. Unsurprisingly, the Pictish landscape contains a number of 'Celtic' features, the most visible being hilltop fortresses defended by concentric walls of unmortared stone laced with timber. Certain other structures are not found elsewhere in the Celtic world, or are encountered only rarely, and seem to be indigenous to the Pictish zone. Of these, the best-known are the brochs, the enigmatic towers found all over the Pictish area, with a major concentration north and west of the Great Glen. Isolated examples in southward districts such as Lothian suggest that the design was not confined to what is usually regarded as the main Pictish zone. As previously noted, archaeological study has dated their main occupation phase to the period 500 BC to AD 100 which means that they had probably fallen out of use when Roman writers first mentioned the Picts. The northern concentration of brochs has led to their builders being seen as 'proto-Pictish' ancestors of the later raiding bands. A simpler explanation is that the brochs were built by 'Britons' whose descendants in the early centuries AD remained largely untouched by Romanisation.

The *Picti* were none other than the Caledonii, Verturiones and other indigenous peoples previously recorded as separate entities but now appearing under a new collective name. Aside from this 'rebranding' of Rome's old enemies, the situation on the northern frontier remained largely unchanged for much of the fourth century, except perhaps for an increasing number of barbarian raids. Whether these incursions became as serious as those of the

Severan era in the early 200s is unknown, but they caused sufficient anxiety to provoke a Roman response. In 305, the respected general Constantius Chlorus marched from his base at York to deal with the Picts. He presumably defeated them. Likewise, his son Constantine, whom the frontier army proclaimed emperor in 306, took a break from civil war in Europe to wage a Pictish war in 312. Hostilities with the Picts continued up to the middle years of the fourth century when the emperor Constans, son of Constantine, came to Britain to oversee the imperial response.

Defence in Depth

Rome's strategy in dealing with the Pictish threat after c.340 was essentially defensive and reactive. Retaliatory strikes deep into the Highlands were no longer part of the plan. Instead, the prime objective was maintenance of a static frontier supplemented by covert military operations between the two walls and in the wild lands further north. In an effort to maintain the integrity of Hadrian's Wall the Romans were helped by Britons living in the lands beyond. The native population of this region between the Hadrianic line and the disused Antonine ramparts became a first line of defence. Such an arrangement suited the economic constraints and political uncertainties facing Rome at that time. It allowed a dwindling number of imperial troops to be redeployed elsewhere. At the hub of the new defensive network lay Hadrian's Wall with its forts and crossing-points. Behind the great barrier stretched an infrastructure of roads, forts and watchtowers providing both an early warning system and a capability for rapid response. In theory at least, this strategy of 'defence in depth' shielded the people of Britannia from hostile attacks by Picts, Saxons, Irish and other predators. North of Hadrian's Wall the four outpost forts garrisoned in the third century were still occupied at the dawn of the fourth. Although situated outside the Empire's boundary, none of the quartet lay more than twenty miles from the Wall. Their garrisons supervised the natives of the intervallate zone, a population whose status *vis-à-vis* the imperial authorities after 300 remains a matter of debate. In this region four large amalgamations of Britons already existed in the second century: the previously mentioned Damnonii, Votadini, Selgovae and Novantae. Whether these groups owed their origin to Rome's onslaught in the first century or were formed in spite of it we are unable to say. By c.300, they may have been in existence for two hundred years or more, but how much longer they endured is unknown. Ptolemy's map shows their positions relative to one another and identifies their chief centres of power. Although the map shows a snapshot of political geography as perceived by Roman geographers in the second century, the distribution of peoples in the intervallate region may have remained largely unchanged two hundred years later.

On Ptolemy's map we see the Novantae inhabiting the northern shorelands of the Solway Firth, in territory corresponding to present-day Dumfriesshire and Galloway. Although their lands were vulnerable to raids from Ireland and the Hebridean seaways, their main centres of power were sited on the western coast, in the vicinity of Loch Ryan and modern Stranraer. Here, the long peninsula of the Rhinns of Galloway, marked on the map as *Novantarum Chersonesus*, protrudes into the Irish Sea. The key settlements were *Rerigonium* (possibly Innermessan) and *Loucopibia* (possibly Gatehouse of Fleet). Directly north, in what is now the county of Ayrshire, lay territory associated with either the Novantae or with a people called *Damnonii* (or *Dumnonii*). Damnonian lands included the lower valley and estuary of the River Clyde, together with parts of what later became the medieval earldom of Lennox. An important centre of power in this area was the imposing mass of Dumbarton Rock, a volcanic 'plug' jutting into the Firth of Clyde and dominating the surrounding area. Traces of elite occupation on the summit indicate that it was used by high-status Britons as far back as pre-Roman times. Later, when local native leaders were apparently co-operating with Rome, the great Rock may have guarded imperial interests in the north-western seaways. Through the Damnonian heartlands ran the western extremity of the Antonine Wall, its turf ramparts and abandoned forts already falling into dereliction by c.300. Further east, in Stirlingshire and Lothian, the redundant barrier meandered through the northern borderlands of the Votadini, another of the four intervallate groupings. Votadinian territory extended south of the Firth of Forth to the River Tweed and perhaps even as far as Hadrian's Wall. Its hub was evidently the Castle Rock at Edinburgh, but other hilltop strongholds, such as a probable *oppidum* on Traprain Law, were also used in Roman times. The northern border-lands of the Votadini faced the Maeatae of Stirling-shire and the Picts of Fife. On the south-western flank lay the Selgovae ('Hunters'), another large amalgamation of peoples. Selgovan territory included the central and upper vales of Tweed together with vast tracts of uncharted forest. Unlike their neighbours, the Selgovan elites of the third and fourth centuries were closely super-vised by Rome. Within their territory lay the last of the outpost forts: Bewcastle and Netherby in the valleys north of Carlisle, and Risingham on the strategic Dere Street highway.

The nature of the relationship between the Empire and the intervallate Britons in Late Roman times is difficult to ascertain. It may have been sustained by regular payments from the imperial coffers to purchase the continuing goodwill of the four groups described above. One theory imagines their kings and chiefs as *foederati*, 'federates', of Rome, their domains constituting a buffer-zone between Hadrian's Wall and the northern barbarians. If these Britons did indeed serve as allies of Rome, they would have been expected to bear the brunt of raids on the imperial frontier. Thus, while nominally independent, they may have pledged to protect Roman interests against the Pictish menace. Nevertheless, to all but the most trusting Roman officials, the intervallate Britons would have represented a potential threat. Keeping an eye on them was arguably the main function of the *exploratores*, 'scouts', a class of troops whom we can envisage patrolling beyond the outpost forts. These men were perhaps similar to the colonial rangers of eighteenth-century North America, using local knowledge to gather intelligence and launching punitive raids on troublemakers. The outpost fort at Netherby became so closely associated with these 'special forces' that it was known along the frontier as *Castra Exploratorum* ('Fort of the Scouts'). Operating alongside the *exploratores* were the shadowy *areani* or *arcani*, members of a secret service responsible for covert operations, whose agents spied on the Picts and other barbarians. Historians sometimes regard them as a kind of 'Roman CIA' and the analogy may be broadly accurate.

Little is known of the kings and chieftains who ruled the inter-vallate Britons during the fourth century. Some appear to be named in genealogical texts preserved in medieval Wales but possibly drawing data from much older northern sources. The Welsh genealogies or 'pedigrees' show the lineages of a number of North British kings who lived in the sixth and seventh centuries. Each pedigree uses a sequence of patronyms ('X son of Y son of Z') to extend a royal ancestry back to the Late Roman period and, in some cases, to an even more remote time. Any hope of gleaning genuine fourth-century history is hindered by the stark fact that the texts containing the pedigrees were written no earlier than the ninth century. Most survive only in manuscripts of the twelfth century or later and none can be shown to be original creations by North Britons rather than by Welshmen. The pedigrees cannot therefore be regarded as storehouses of reliable information, especially for any period before the time of the historical North British kings. As repositories of genealogical data relating to the fourth century their value is even more limited. They require very careful handling if they are to be used at all.

Several pedigrees include figures whose chronological contexts seem to coincide with the final phase of Roman rule in Britain. Cinhil and Cluim, for instance, are two individuals listed as ancestors of a ninth-century king who ruled on the Clyde. We cannot be certain that these two are anything more than fictitious 'ghosts' inserted into the pedigree to give it a longer and more impressive lineage. If they existed, they probably belong to the second half of the fourth century and may have been members of the Damnonian elite. Another example is Padarn, apparently a Votadinian, to whom the genealogists gave the epithet or nickname

Pesrut ('Red Tunic'). Alongside Cinhil and Cluim, Padarn Pesrut is often regarded as a Briton of the intervallate zone in Late Roman times. It has been suggested that all three sprang from Romanised or pro-Roman families, their names being seen as medieval Welsh renderings of Quintilius, Clemens and Paternus. Upon this a more or less plausible scenario of loyal native *foederati* defending the Empire's northern frontier has been constructed, with Padarn's red tunic being interpreted as a Roman military garment, a gift from an imperial official to a trusted ally. Such theories are imaginative but need not be taken seriously. Regardless of whether or not the later Welsh names derive from Latin-sounding originals, we have no reason to believe that such naming was exclusive to the imperial authorities or to *foederati* in their service. Many non-Romans, friends and foes of the Empire alike, arguably bestowed Roman-sounding names on their children if it pleased them to do so. A young North Briton bearing a name such as Quintilius or Clemens was just as likely to develop anti-Roman sentiments as a compatriot who bore a non-Latin name. Nor is there anything uniquely Roman about the colour of Padarn's tunic, which could have been obtained from any competent tailor whose skills included the extraction of red dye from plants such as madder. There were no doubt many red tunics among Rome's friends in the lands north of Hadrian's Wall, but probably just as many blue or green ones. Indeed, it is easy to imagine the nickname *Pesrut* being bestowed on any Pictish warrior in the hostile country beyond the Firth of Forth who chose to wear a bright red garment on military expeditions.

The Crisis of 367

The effectiveness of security arrangements on the northern frontier was put to the test in the second half of the fourth century when barbarian attacks increased. As well as the ever-hostile Picts the imperial garrison also endured raids by Gaelic-speaking groups in the western seaways – the Irish and the 'Scots'. At this time the name *Scotti* seems to have been borne by, or bestowed upon, any marauding band from Ireland or Argyll. Indeed, it is likely that Roman observers regarded all the Gaels as one people. Like the Picts, these raiders from the West had taunted Rome since the time of Agricola. Three more groups now joined them: the Franks, whose descendants in the following century would leave their mark on Roman Gaul by turning it into France; the Saxons, who were soon to play a similarly important role in Britain; and a mysterious people called *Attacotti* who were perhaps of Irish or Hebridean origin. Eventually, the leaders of these hostile nations devised a *barbarica conspiratio*, a 'barbarian conspiracy', to co-ordinate their attacks on Roman Britain. Their plans came to fruition after crucial information was provided by traitors on the Roman side: corrupt officials, army deserters and rogue agents among the *arcani*. In 367, a huge barbarian assault was unleashed, its impact sweeping away the imperial defences. Seaborne raids from east and west drove far inland into the rich countryside of southern Britain, bringing death and destruction to the bewildered citizens. Towns were ransacked and villas were looted. Down from the north came the Picts, some to overwhelm the garrisons of Hadrian's Wall while others swarmed along the eastern coast in flotillas of boats. The outpost forts north of the Wall were either bypassed or overwhelmed. In a battle between the frontier army and Pictish marauders, Fullofaudes, the senior Roman general in Britain, was taken prisoner. Leaderless and demoralised, the entire imperial garrison was thrown into chaos. Some soldiers cast off their uniforms and deserted their posts, while others roamed the land in lawless gangs. Fearing the total loss of Britain, the emperor Valentinian despatched a strike force of elite regiments led by the renowned Count Theodosius. Two years of hard fighting eventually led to the expulsion of the barbarians and, after Theodosius issued an amnesty for deserters, stability was gradually restored. The soldiers returned to their forts and Hadrian's Wall was reinstated as the boundary of the Empire. In the wake of the crisis, however, the outposts beyond the Wall were finally abandoned. Theodosius redeployed what remained of their garrisons, disbanded the treacherous *arcani* and withdrew all Roman forces behind the Tyne–Solway line.

After the disaster of 367, the Britons beyond Hadrian's Wall were effectively cut off from their countrymen south of it. Both groups had suffered grievously during the barbarian onslaught, but there is no record of Theodosius driving Pictish raiders from the lands of the Damnonii or Votadini. The natives of the inter-vallate zone were presumably left to fend for themselves. One medieval Welsh legend tells of a Votadinian prince or chieftain called Cunedda who led a warband to North Wales to expel a colony of Irish pirates from Gwynedd. Cunedda's position in the genealogies makes him a figure of the late fourth to mid-fifth century and this chronology has led some historians to see him as a Roman federate transferred from Lothian during the Theodosian reorganisation. Much detailed speculation about Rome's rela-tionship with the Votadini has been woven around this scenario, but the data is too fragile to support it. A more sceptical, more objective view sees the story of Cunedda as a later Welsh attempt to create a fictional link between the kings of Gwynedd and their fellow-Britons of the North.

Among the repercussions of the barbarian conspiracy the most ominous development, at least for the native population of Roman Britain, was the recruitment of Germanic *foederati* to guard the southern towns. These were mostly Angles, Saxons, Jutes and Frisians from the North Sea coastlands of what are now Denmark and Germany. In northern Britain there were fewer towns and villas than in the south, but one area where Romanisation had taken root was the fertile Vale of York. There are archaeological hints that German warriors were settled in this district in the late fourth century, either by Theodosius after 367 or by the imperial usurper Magnus Maximus in 383. Serving Rome as mercenaries, the Germans initially performed a useful gatekeeping role against seaborne attacks by Pictish and Saxon pirates. Like all hirelings their services were not given freely, but were bought with regular gifts of cash from the imperial treasury. Any disruption to these payments was likely to turn friendship and service to ill-feeling and hostility.

In the 370s, the lands south of Hadrian's Wall returned to a position of watchfulness. The northern frontier remained on a high state of alert, as did the lines of forts and signal-towers along the western and eastern coasts. North of the Wall the independent Britons, almost certainly without Roman help, repelled marauding bands of Picts and regained control of their own borders. But the barbarians were not so easily cowed and their raids continued to gnaw Britannia from all sides. With the situation deteriorating once more, the conspirators of 367 may have watched in gleeful disbelief as parts of the imperial garrison began to leave the island in the period after 380. The first big troop-withdrawal came in 383 when Magnus Maximus, a high-ranking officer in Britain, resolved to make himself emperor. Ironically, he had previously inflicted heavy defeats on the Picts and Scots, but now he poured his energies into his personal ambitions. Supported and encouraged by other officers, he led a substantial army across the sea to Gaul, thereby depleting Britain of forces essential for her protection. The barbarians are likely to have taken full advantage of his departure, but this time there was no Theodosius to confront them. Troubles elsewhere in the Empire made it impossible to send reinforcements to Britain. Another famous general, the half-Vandal Flavius Stilicho, is depicted in a contemporary Latin poem leading an expedition against the Picts at the end of the fourth century. It seems, however, that this campaign existed only in the imagination of the poet Claudian who used it as a literary device to illustrate the far-reaching extent of Stilicho's fame. In reality, the Empire lacked the will to rescue Britain from the brink of catastrophe. To compound the situation, the Roman authorities now faced a peril much closer to home.

On the last night of the year 405, the imperial frontier in Germany was overwhelmed by a host of Vandals, Alans and other barbarians who crossed the Rhine to begin the dismemberment of Roman Gaul. In Britain the garrison reacted by rallying around Constantine, an ambitious officer with an auspicious name, and proclaimed him emperor. Leading a large force, Constantine sailed over to Gaul to assert his claim against forces loyal to the legitimate emperor Honorius. The loyalists were victorious and the usurper was executed. By 410, his henchmen in Britain were rooted out, but they bequeathed a desperate situation. With the depleted imperial troops struggling to stand firm against barbarian raids, the native elites of the southern towns seized control of the imperial administration. Taking the initiative, these Romanised Britons restored a semblance of order before appealing to the emperor for aid. But Honorius was grappling with the problems of a disintegrating Empire and had no help to offer to beleaguered subjects in a faraway land. Instead, he sent a letter urging the anxious Britons to organise their own defence. This had profound consequences for the remaining Roman troops, all of whom relied on wages issued by the imperial treasury. Their pay had probably been arriving erratically for some time, but now it ceased altogether. Without it the soldiers had no incentive or obligation to defend the Empire. On the northern frontier, groups of disillusioned men gradually abandoned their forts, taking their families with them and vanishing into the countryside. In the lands to the south, the last vestiges of imperial bureaucracy were swept away as power was seized by native leaders. By c.420, the Roman occupation of Britain was over.

CHAPTER 3

Britons, Picts and Scots

Independent Britain

Prior to the fifth century, the civilian population of Britannia grew accustomed to paying taxes to the imperial treasury and receiving protection from imperial troops. In towns and cities, where Romanisation was well-established, a wealthy elite of Latin-speaking Britons wielded power at local level. Members of this upper class held offices of authority as local representatives of the imperial government. Their homes were in the countryside on large agricultural estates worked by tenant farmers who themselves lived in scattered homesteads or small villages. This was how life had gone on for as long as anyone in Roman Britain could remember. The deeds of their forefathers in pre-conquest times already belonged to a remote past.

Everything changed after 410, when the emperor Honorius handed the reins of power back to the Britons. He is unlikely to have envisaged this as a permanent state of affairs. On the contrary, we have every reason to believe that he hoped one day to restore Britannia to the Empire. By refusing to send military aid he was simply appointing the native elites as temporary custodians of Rome's interests. Nevertheless, as the fifth century progressed, it became increasingly clear that the western half of the Roman Empire was collapsing. Barbarian attacks and internal strife continued to weaken imperial power until, in 476, the last emperor of the West was deposed. By that time, the Britons had been governing themselves for more than half a century. Few of those

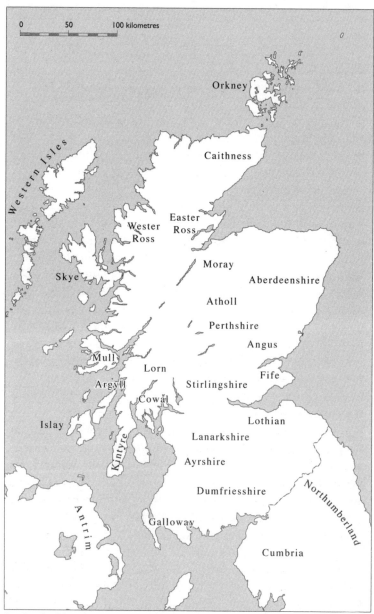

Scotland: old and new territorial divisions

living in 476 would have been able to recall the final years of Roman rule.

In the first half of the fifth century, what had once been Roman Britain was breaking apart. Rivalries among the Britons, coupled with continuing barbarian raids, made any semblance of unity impossible. Indigenous military forces proved inadequate for national defence and Roman armies were unlikely to come to their aid. Individual land-owners, worried by barbarian attacks, may have taken matters into their own hands by recruiting their own private militias. One group of leaders, apparently acting in unison, agreed upon a drastic course of action: they decided to use the barbarians against each other. This was not a new policy, for Rome had often used it to boost troop numbers. It had been employed in the late fourth century when German mercenaries were invited to settle in eastern parts of Britain. The descendants of these hirelings were still there when more of their kind were brought in by the Britons. The new arrivals came from three of the most dangerous raiding nations: the Angles, Saxons and Jutes. Attracted by offers of land, they eagerly accepted the invitation, settling with their families in areas deemed most at risk from attack. Their colonies were established in what are now the eastern midlands of England and East Anglia, and in some areas further west. For a time they performed their duties adequately, guarding the exposed North Sea shorelands. Sometime after c.430, however, the situation began to deteriorate. Having integrated with descendants of earlier Germanic settlers and with neighbouring Britons, the mercenaries already formed a substantial minority. When their demands for higher wages were refused, they rose against their paymasters and attacked their lands. In desperation, the Britons sent an urgent appeal to Flavius Aëtius, one of the last Roman generals in Gaul, begging for help. Their appeal was rejected, for Aëtius had other matters to deal with, the most serious being Attila and the Huns. No troops could be spared for the situation in Britain. After defeating Attila in 452, Aëtius became embroiled in politics in Rome and was eventually assassinated. His death, at the hands of a jealous emperor, deprived the Britons of the one individual who could have dug them out of their crisis. By then, the revolt of the Germanic mercenaries was gaining momentum. Its eventual outcome was the Anglo-Saxon conquest of southern Britain and the foundation of England.

The Post-Roman North

Between Hadrian's Wall and the Forth–Clyde isthmus the Britons had not lain under direct Roman rule since the third century. After 410, when Honorius gave autonomy to their southern countrymen, the northerners had been ruled by their own leaders for more than a hundred years. Some of them entered the fifth century with their old political identities still intact. At the head of the Firth of Clyde, the Damnonii continued to occupy their ancestral lands, eventually leaving their mark in local place-names such as Dowanhill and Cardowan. East of the Clyde, the Votadini still held sway over Lothian and the southern shore of the Firth of Forth. There is no evidence that the other two major groupings of intervallate Britons – the Selgovae and Novantae – retained their identities into the fifth century. They may have fragmented into smaller units before the end of the Roman period.

It is possible that native leaders in the lands north of Hadrian's Wall were calling themselves 'kings' before c.400. The previous chapter referred to medieval Welsh genealogical texts which seem to identify two mysterious figures – Cinhil and Cluim – as fifth-century kings on the Clyde. These men are frequently assumed to be leaders of the Damnonii, forefathers of an early medieval dynasty which ruled until 870 from the Rock of Clyde at Dumbarton. Although the assumption of their Damnonian ancestry is no more than an inference, it is more than can be said of the Votadini further east. No surviving source names any Votadinian ruler other than the mysterious Cunedda, nor is a Votadinian royal pedigree identifiable in the later Welsh genealogical tracts. The name of the people themselves was, however, remembered in literature. In the form *Gododdin* (pronounced 'Godothin'), a late rendering of earlier

Guotodin, a memory of the Votadini was preserved in medieval Wales. The name survived in Ireland, too, where it was rendered into Gaelic as *Fothudan*. Historians now use 'Gododdin' not only as a label for the post-Roman Votadinian kingdom but also in reference to an eponymous heroic poem which we shall encounter in Chapter 5. Modern maps accompanying studies of Scotland's early history usually place the name 'Gododdin' over a large area stretching from Stirlingshire to Tweeddale, but the true extent of the kingdom is uncertain. An ancient core or heartland of the Votadini possibly lay around Edinburgh where, according to the *Gododdin* poem, the imposing Castle Rock supported a major royal residence in the sixth century.

In erstwhile Roman territory south of Hadrian's Wall, in a region divided by the Pennine uplands, kings probably began to emerge during the fifth century. Some may have claimed royal status by constructing lineages reaching back to tribal monarchies in pre-Roman times. It is even possible that the royal pretensions of certain families had already been acknowledged by the Late Roman authorities. New monarchies owing little to the ancient past undoubtedly appeared as the century progressed. No kingdom preserved the name of the Brigantes who had formerly inhabited most of this area. Indeed, the name of only one post-Roman kingdom in the Pennines is known, a realm called Elmet or Elfed. Others are wholly invisible in the surviving sources, their names unknown and their kings unidentifiable among the North British pedigrees preserved in Wales. Even of Elmet we know little beyond a few contemporary references and some modern geographical inferences. It seems to have been broadly coterminous with the present-day county of West Yorkshire, possibly with a focus of power in the vicinity of Leeds. Its inhabitants were presumably descended from a constituent tribe of the Brigantes.

Under the imperial administration a Brigantian district or *civitas* had been created in what is now the county of North Yorkshire with a focus at *Isurium Brigantium*, a Roman town whose ruins lie beneath modern Aldborough. In the fifth century, this *civitas* supported substantial Germanic or 'Anglo-Saxon' settlement around a nucleus of older, long-established mercenary colonies. The new native kingdoms of the Pennines thus emerged alongside domains forged by Anglo-Saxon settlers in the wake of the revolt of the hirelings. These people called themselves *englisc*, 'English', and proudly nurtured their distinctive cultural heritage as well as their Germanic language. Intermarriage with local Britons produced a hybrid population which identified itself as English in terms of linguistic and cultural affiliations. How far such labelling held real importance in the fifth century is unknown, but an apparently widespread rejection of 'Britishness' by some native communities suggests that ethnicity was defined less by blood than by other factors.

The most northerly town in Roman Britain lay at Carlisle, nestling at the western end of Hadrian's Wall. Originally a military site, it had evolved into an urban centre in the second century to become the administrative focus of a district. It may have been the chief centre of the *civitas Carvetiorum*, a territory created by Rome for a group called the *Carvetii*. Little is known of this people, but their heartland was the rich vale of the River Eden and perhaps the area around Carlisle. In pre-Roman times they had probably been the most north-westerly of various Brigantian groups. Unlike their countrymen east of the Pennines, they had not seen large contingents of German mercenaries billeted on their lands and had relied instead on the Wall garrison for security. When the last of the frontier troops drifted away in the early 400s, Carvetian lands became vulnerable to raids from the Irish Sea and the Solway Firth. As the fifth century progressed, urban settlements in the region were gradually abandoned. Archaeological evidence at Carlisle suggests a continuing presence, perhaps by a religious community or a local warlord, but nothing more is heard of the Carvetii. On Hadrian's Wall itself we find scant evidence for occupation beyond the early 400s except at Birdoswald, a Roman fort in the Irthing valley east of Carlisle, where a timber hall was constructed on the ruins of a granary. This is the only clear evidence of a post-Roman phase on the northern frontier, but whether it implies unbroken continuity of habitation is unknown. Some historians envisage a partial remanning of the Wall by native militia, or even large-scale survival of the imperial garrison, but such ideas are unsupported by archaeology and are generally disregarded. It seems far more likely that the majority of forts on the Wall and in the Pennine hinterland were abandoned to dereliction long before c.450.

Scots

During the late Roman period, the Damnonii of the Clyde may have served as a bulwark against Rome's enemies in the north-western seaways. In the fifth century, after the collapse of the imperial administration, the main concern of these Britons was the defence of their own lands. They were ruled at that time by kings whose centre of power lay at Dumbarton. In their own language their descendants called this seat of ancient power *Alt Clut* (the 'Rock of Clyde'). How far their kingdom extended south and east is hard to say, but it may have encompassed parts of Clydesdale around modern Hamilton in Lanarkshire. Westward the kings of Alt Clut faced Gaelic-speaking neighbours in Argyll and the inner Hebridean isles. These were the Scots, a people whom Roman writers had recognised as being distinct from the Picts and Britons. In Roman military parlance the term *Scotti* was seemingly bestowed on any Gaelic-speaking group. These folk spoke a common language from which the later dialects of Irish and Scottish Gaelic both derived. In the early eighth century, the English monk Bede called the inhabitants of Argyll 'the Scots in Britain' and regarded them as descendants of Irish colonists. This vision of migration and colonisation eventually became a building block of early Scottish history. It almost certainly originated in Argyll, among the 'Scots in Britain' themselves, and may have been a fairly new tradition when reported by Bede in 731. According to a later version of this 'foundation-legend', the initial settlement by Gaelic-speakers in northern Britain was led by Fergus mac Eirc, also known as Fergus Mór, a mighty warrior-king who sailed over from Ireland with his sons. In Argyll he is supposed to have founded a kingdom called Dál Riata, borrowing the name from that of an ancestral domain in Antrim. This story has lain at the heart of Scottish origins since medieval times and, for that reason, it warrants a detailed examination here.

Prior to the alleged migration of Fergus and his sons, Argyll was home to an indigenous population. The Romans called these natives *Epidii*, this being the Latinised form of a Brittonic name meaning 'Horse Folk'. To Roman geographers, the most prominent landscape feature in Epidian territory was *Epidium Promontarium* ('The Promontory of the Horse Folk'), today's Mull of Kintyre. Because the name *Epidii* is recorded in a Brittonic form, historians have often assumed that the 'Horse Folk' themselves must have spoken a Brittonic dialect. This is not, however, a necessary deduction from the Latinised name which almost certainly came to the Romans via North Britons in their service. The form *Epidii* merely shows that the informants who relayed it to imperial officials spoke a Brittonic language. It carries no implication that Brittonic was the language of the Epidii themselves.

The conventional view of early Scottish history sees the Epidii as Britons whose leaders were overthrown by immigrants arriving from Dál Riata in northern Ireland at the beginning of the sixth century. This derives from the foundation-legend and provides a historical context for Fergus mac Eirc, who thus slots neatly into his role of conqueror in the years around 500 when invasion and migration were forming new political identities all over Western Europe. Any objection to the legend is a challenge to the testimony of Bede who is usually regarded as a reliable source. In fact, Bede is no more immune to our scepticism than any other eighth-century writer. We therefore need to look closely at what he says about the origins of the Scots. Interestingly, his version refers not to Fergus mac Eirc but to a different ancestor called Reuda. According to Bede:

> In the course of time, after the Britons and Picts, Britain received a third people, that of the Scots, who came from

Ireland under their leader Reuda and won among the others, either by agreement or by iron, the seats that they still possess; from this leader they are still called *Dalreudini*, for in their language *daal* signifies 'part'.

In Bede's account, Reuda replaces Fergus as the founder of an Irish colony in north-west Britain, but otherwise the two versions seem to present a broadly consistent view. Both portray the Scots as an immigrant population who came from Ireland to establish a new kingdom in Argyll. But how far should we accept their testimony as an accurate record of Scottish origins? It is possible, for instance, that they represent two separate attempts to create an Irish ancestry for Dál Riata, the land of 'the Scots in Britain'. The tale of Reuda as told by Bede might then be an early version, like the first draft of a fictional story, with the Fergus version supplanting it at a later date. This seems consistent with the first appearance of the Fergus story in the tenth century. Bede's contemporary and fellow-scholar, Abbot Adomnán, makes no mention of Fergus in his *vita* or 'Life' of Columba, the saint who founded the monastery of Iona in the sixth century. Nor does Adomnán hint at an Irish origin for the Scots, despite being himself an Irishman in close communication with Dál Riata's kings. Fergus in fact makes no appearance in literature until c.950 when his deeds were added retrospectively to earlier chronicles. The eponymous forefather Reuda is mentioned only by Bede, a singular reference which likewise makes his historical existence doubtful. Plausible reasons as to why the later kings of Scots felt compelled to devise a fictional Irish ancestry for their dynasty are not hard to find. Across the narrow straits between Kintyre and Antrim lay the territory of 'Irish' Dál Riata which was ruled by the Scots of Argyll for much of the seventh century. This landholding led to frequent involvement by Argyll-based kings in Irish dynastic wars which, in turn, provide a likely context for the creation of the foundation-legend. It is possible that the earliest version, the story of Reuda, was devised to strengthen a claim on Irish Dál Riata in a period of conflict and instability.

We may note at this point that the idea of an Irish colonisation of Argyll exists only in literature. It draws no support from archaeology, linguistic history or the study of place-names. Archaeologists expecting to find evidence of an indigenous population of Britons being supplanted by Gaelic-speaking newcomers find instead a rather different picture. There appears to be no break in the settlement history of Argyll during the first millennium AD, nor is there any archaeological hint of substantial immigration from Ireland. Such indications, if they are to be found at all, should be visible in the landscape as a change in the pattern of settlement or in the design of houses. In contemporary Ireland, the typical habitation site was the circular ringfort with surrounding walls of earth or stone. This type is so numerous that it should be expected to appear wherever people of Irish origin settled during the early centuries AD. It is not found anywhere in Argyll. On the contrary, the Argyll equivalent is the dun, a stone-walled enclosure, the design of which is not derived from the ringfort. Duns were constructed over a remarkably long period, from the Iron Age through the early Middle Ages. Their longevity suggests unbroken continuity in the pattern of settlement. Faced with such data it is difficult to imagine a significant Irish presence in Argyll at the time of the alleged migrations of Fergus and Reuda.

When an immigrant population displaces or subjugates an indigenous one, it often imposes its language, assuming, of course, that natives and newcomers do not already speak the same tongue. There are many examples of this process, from all periods of history and from all parts of the world: the Romans in Mediterranean Europe; the Spanish and Portuguese in Latin America; the French and English in nineteenth-century Africa. In the British Isles the prime example comes from England itself, where the Germanic language of the Anglo-Saxons supplanted an indigenous Celtic one. Similar linguistic displacement has traditionally been envisaged for Argyll, with historians viewing the dominance of Gaelic as evidence for an Irish takeover of Brittonic-speaking districts in the sixth century. In England, the linguistic aspect of the Anglo-Saxon conquest is plainly visible in the distribution of English, Brittonic and hybrid Anglo-Brittonic place-names. A simultaneous takeover of Argyll by Gaelic-speakers from Ireland should likewise be represented in modern toponymy. In other words, if the migration hypothesis is to be accepted, a mixture of Gaelic, Brittonic and hybrid place-names ought to be visible today. Instead, we find that the place-names of Argyll are almost wholly Gaelic. Thus, rather than supporting the idea of an Irish takeover, the toponymic evidence suggests that Gaelic was the language of the indigenous population.

The stories of Fergus and Reuda begin to seem less like folk-memories of real events and more like fictional legends. By setting them aside we gain a simpler, more plausible vision of Scottish Gaelic origins. The true beginnings of Gaelic speech among the Scots lie not in a mythical invasion but in social interactions among maritime communities on both sides of the Irish Sea. When the ancestors of the Gaelic and Brittonic languages began to diverge in the late Iron Age, the people of Argyll were sundered by geography from linguistic developments southward and eastward. The mountainous mass of the central Highlands, known in medieval times as *Druim Alban* ('The Spine of Britain'), isolated the people of Argyll from their landward neighbours. Sundered from the Roman province of Britannia, and separated from the eastern Pictish heartlands, they followed instead the linguistic trends of the western seaways. They adopted the Gaelic speech of their closest neighbours: the Irish of Antrim. With these folk they undoubtedly shared a perception that the narrow waters in between were not a barrier but a channel of trade and communication. When the Celtic dialects of the British Isles began to coalesce into two large groupings – Brittonic and Gaelic – it was to the latter that the spoken language of Argyll came to belong. Since Gaelic probably became distinct from Brittonic around the end of the Roman period, we may cautiously describe Argyll as an integral part of Gaeldom from c.400.

The Epidii or 'Horse Folk' should be regarded as a linguistic anomaly: a people eventually drawn into the Gaelic-speaking world despite living outwith its Irish heartlands. Identifying them as the indigenous population of Argyll rather than as Irish immigrants allows us to discard the later foundation-legends. In place of the migration hypothesis we thus have a more plausible vision of Scottish origins, namely the less dramatic scenario of a native people in mainland Britain – the Epidii – evolving into Gaelic-speaking Scots. Indeed, they are unlikely to have used the name *Epidii* when speaking of themselves in their own language. As mentioned above, most territorial and tribal names on Roman maps of Britain were Latinised forms of names given to Roman geographers by native informants. *Epidii* derives from a Brittonic or 'P-Celtic' form as spoken by a Briton or a Pict. If the informant had been a Gaelic speaker, the name would have taken a Goidelic or 'Q-Celtic' form such as *Echidii*, which retains the meaning 'Horse Folk'. Perhaps this was used by the inhabitants of Argyll as their own name for themselves in the centuries prior to 500? It is also possible that the personal name *Eochaid*, derived from a Gaelic word for 'horse' and borne by several later kings, was an acknowledgement of their 'Echidian' ancestry.

Pictish Kings

Alongside the Saxons, Scots, Irish, Franks and Attacotti the Picts played a key role in the barbarian conspiracy of 367 and continued their raids into the following century. In the early 400s, they posed a significant threat to the crumbling edifice of Roman Britain. Their attacks wreaked havoc among civilian communities in the lands south of Hadrian's Wall, highlighting the feebleness of whatever remained of the imperial garrison. In the sixth century, a British cleric called Gildas looked back upon these woeful times and saw the Picts as a major cause of destruction and distress. He envisaged their seaborne attacks intensifying after 410, when Honorius suspended imperial rule in Britain:

> As the Romans went back home, there emerged from the coracles that had carried them across the sea-valleys the foul hordes of Scots and Picts, like dark throngs of worms who

wriggle out of narrow fissures in the rock when the sun is high and the weather grows warm.

Gildas believed that this new phase of raiding was briefly resisted by the Britons before resuming in earnest around the middle of the fifth century. By then, the northern and western barbarians – the Picts and Gaels – had inflicted so much disruption that the Britons felt obliged to hire Germanic mercenaries as protectors. Although Gildas saw this policy as sowing the seeds of an Anglo-Saxon takeover, he did not deny that its initial objective was achieved. The raiders were successfully repulsed and made no further appearance for many years. Gildas then turned his attention to the revolt of the Germanic mercenaries and to the bitter wars that followed. His account does not say what became of the Picts at the time of the Anglo-Saxon revolt, nor does he take up their story at a later point. Pictish history in the years 450 to 550 is extremely vague, with only a handful of sources offering any kind of useful information, but among the various chronicles, legends and folk-traditions is a long list of kings.

The Pictish king-list survives in several versions, each displaying slight differences but all apparently deriving from a tenth-century original. The chronological span of reign-lengths runs from a remote prehistoric period to the end of the Pictish kingdom in the ninth century. Legendary material pushes the line of kings back to Cruithne, an eponymous ancestor whose name is simply the Irish word for 'Pict'. According to a ninth-century legend, Cruithne had seven sons, each of whom founded seven provinces or sub-kingdoms roughly encompassing the Pictish heartlands. The seven realms have frequently been matched to seven major earldoms of medieval Scotland, but the resulting 'fit' is not particularly neat and there is no ancient warrant for it. Leaving Cruithne and his sons aside, we see the king-list naming some sixty individuals, the last of whom reigned c.850. No king in the earliest or 'prehistoric' portion of the list can be securely identified as a real figure. The horizon of Pictish history, in terms of reliable information in the literary sources, lies therefore in the mid-sixth century. Prior to c.550 no information in the king-list can be confirmed by reference to other texts. This uncertainty means that any pre-550 king named in the list should be regarded as legendary until a case for his actual existence can be made. Only one of these early kings – the mysterious Wradech Uetla – seems to be mentioned in a source outside the list: he may be the Pictish ruler 'Feradach' who appears in Irish tradition as a contemporary of the fifth-century Munster king Conall Corc. Another possibly real figure from before 550 is Drust, son of Erp, whom the list assigns to the period of Saint Patrick's mission to Ireland in the fifth century. The long chronology of the list implies that the entire Pictish nation was ruled by a paramount monarch or 'overking' from Roman times to the mid-ninth century. Most historians would now regard such a scenario with scepticism. A more plausible interpretation envisages two or more regional overkingships developing in the sixth century, these being contested by powerful families within each region.

A striking feature of the king-list is the rarity of patrilineal inheritance, a system of succession in which authority passes from father to son. Although each king's patronym is given, in the form 'X son of Y', the fathers seem not to be succeeded by their sons until the final century of Pictish kingship. This is a feature of 'matriliny' or matrilineal succession, a method of inheritance practised in various parts of the world in various periods. When applied in royal contexts, it usually transfers a king's authority to his nephew ('son of the king's sister') or to his brother ('son of the king's mother'). According to Bede, who probably had contacts among the Pictish clergy, the Picts were unusual among the peoples of the British Isles in choosing their kings from the female royal line. He stated that they used this method only when the succession was in doubt. A brief glance at the king-list seems rather to suggest that matriliny was the rule rather than the exception: before the ninth century, no Pictish overking is shown being succeeded by his son. Some historians therefore believe that Bede was mistaken in believing that matrilineal succession was used only in special circumstances. They take the view that Pictish royal inheritance was regularly determined by matriliny, at least in so far as the election of overkings was concerned. Other historians disagree by suggesting that the system was conventional and patrilineal and that the king-list is a flawed document, or that it reflects an alternating or rotating overkingship which transferred power to a different family when the sovereign died. In this book the matrilineal hypothesis is tentatively supported, although the point is nowhere pressed too strongly.

Whatever their arrangements in matters of royal succession, the Picts were largely indistinguishable from their neighbours in most aspects of society and culture. They were one of several barbarian nations inhabiting the fringes of Late Roman and early medieval Britain. Like the Scots and North Britons they entered the sixth century under the rule of kings, some of whom claimed superiority over others. Beneath the kings stood a landowning aristocracy, itself perhaps graded according to wealth and lineage, which provided manpower for royal warbands. Of the latter there were perhaps a considerable number at any one time, each serving the king of a small kingdom. How far these kings and their retinues saw themselves as members of an abstract Pictish 'nation' is impossible to assess, but the king-list implies the existence of at least one large regional hegemony or overkingship by c.550. With dubious and incomplete information at our disposal we can do little more than suggest one overkingship in the North, between Orkney and the Grampian mountains, and a southern counterpart in Perthshire. At times, these two may have been ruled as a single realm by a very powerful monarch. At other times, each or both may have divided into smaller realms which were more or less independent. One feature which arguably bound all Pictish communities within a defined identity was their common language, a form of Brittonic. This was sufficiently distinct from the speech of the adjacent North Britons by c.500 to warrant the modern labels 'Pictish' or 'Pictish-British'. Thereafter it may have become receptive to Gaelic influences.

CHAPTER 4
Christian Beginnings

Paganism in Northern Britain

On the eve of their exposure to Christianity in the early centuries AD, the peoples of ancient Scotland worshipped a pantheon of gods and goddesses. A handful of these deities appear in the archaeological record, but the rest are invisible. Of the identifiable ones we know little or nothing. In most cases we can only suppose that they represented aspects of the natural world or of human experience. The total number of native deities at the time of the Roman invasion of Britain is unknown, but some continuity from much older religious beliefs can probably be assumed. Survival of very ancient cults is likely to have depended on their relevance to contemporary needs at local level, especially in areas affected by environmental change and population movement. Thus, although ancestral sacred places remained in the landscape, the dwindling importance of stone circles and other large monuments as ritual sites before 1000 BC suggests that pagan Celtic Britain developed its own patterns of worship. Identifying the cults behind these practices is no easy task. There are few archaeological hints of pre-Christian religion and almost no textual clues. Roman writers occasionally referred to Celtic religious practices in Gaul, but concentrated on the most gruesome rites, such as human sacrifice, to conjure vivid images of barbarian savagery. These accounts, whether accurately reported or wildly exaggerated, shed almost no light on what was happening in Britain at the time.

During his Gallic campaigns, Julius Caesar encountered native priests called 'druids', whom he described as a religious order of British origin. Their role in society was not only spiritual, but also judicial and political. If Caesar's description of this pan-Celtic priesthood is accurate, the presence of druids in early Scotland should be regarded as very likely, at least in the first century BC – when Caesar campaigned in Gaul – and in the following century when Roman troops attacked the headquarters of British druidism on Anglesey. Whether any druids in Britain, Ireland or Gaul actually regarded themselves as members of a religious institution spanning large parts of Europe, rather than as loose groups of holy men, is extremely doubtful.

The gods and goddesses venerated in the northern parts of pre-Roman Britain are difficult to trace. A female deity worshipped in the middle of the first millennium BC is apparently represented by a large figure, crudely carved in wood, found buried in peat at Ballachulish in Lochaber. Traces of wicker unearthed from the site might be the remains of a wooden shrine in which she once stood as the centrepiece. Her identity is unknown, but she may be an early example of a Celtic nature goddess. How widely she was venerated is likewise impossible to deduce, but her cult was perhaps fairly localised to the area where her image was unearthed. One Celtic deity venerated more widely was the warrior-god Camulos whose cult originated in Gaul before spreading to the British Isles by the first century AD. Later, after the Romans conquered a large part of Britain, they adapted the native names of sites associated with him to produce the Latinised place-name *Camulodunum* ('Fort of Camulos'). Colchester in Essex bore this name in Roman times, as did Almondbury in Yorkshire, while in Scotland the unlocated place-name *Camulosessa* apparently means 'Seat of Camulos'.

Other deities venerated in Britain were indigenous rather than imported. Brigantia, for instance, was the mother-goddess of the Brigantes of northern England and southern Scotland. Her name means 'High One' or, if a geographical analogy is preferred, 'Highland Goddess'. In Celtic society it was not unusual to find the name of a deity being adopted as the name of a people, but, in this case, the deity seems to have personified the main topographical characteristic of the Pennine zone. Another figure associated with the northern regions of Britain was Maponus or Mabon ('The Divine Son'), whose name survives today in the Dumfriesshire place-name Lochmaben. A few miles further south, on the shore of the Solway Firth, stands the Clochmabenstane, 'The Stone of Mabon', which presumably served as a focus for ancient rituals connected with this god. Mabon's strong link with Dumfriesshire suggests that he was a favoured local deity in pre-Christian times. Later traditions from fragments of pagan mythology preserved in medieval texts refer to him as 'Son of Modron' which means 'Son of the Mother'. Modron or Matrona represents an image of immense antiquity rooted in prehistoric notions of a universal mother-goddess associated with fertility and protection. Similar notions of a divine ancestress or 'queen of the gods' are, of course, found in many different religions and appear in the British Isles in various forms: Modron, Brigantia, the Irish mother-goddess Danu and – in Christian times – the Virgin Mary.

Less widely known are local deities whose names appear only in particular districts. These were probably gods and goddesses venerated by individual communities and worshipped by fairly small numbers of people. In Scotland this category includes such figures as Magusanus, a deity commemorated west of Edinburgh along the shore of the Firth of Firth. Nothing is known of him, but he may have been especially venerated in Lothian. On the other hand, the lone occurrence of his name on a Roman inscription might equally mean that his cult was imported from further afield, perhaps even from outside Britain, by travellers or traders. Uncertainty of another kind surrounds the god Manau whose name survives today in the landscape of Stirlingshire and Clackmannanshire. In the town of Clackmannan the boulder known as the 'Stone of Manau' suggests a northerly equivalent of the Dumfriesshire 'Stone of Mabon' and might point to a god who subsequently gave his name to the lands around his cult-centre. It has been suggested that Manau might be northern Britain's equivalent of Manannan mac Lir, the Irish sea-god, but this is based on little more than a superficial similarity between the two names.

The gods and goddesses named above represent only a small sample of the pantheon of deities worshipped by the peoples of ancient Scotland. Others, such as the enigmatic female figure discovered in the peat at Ballachulish, are identifiable archaeologically but not by name. Analogy with southern Britain suggests that many northern deities originated in specific localities where they were worshipped by individual tribes, or by sub-groups within a tribe. In Caithness a people called Cornavii bore a name incorporating the Brittonic word for 'horn' or 'horned'. It has often been assumed that the 'horn' in this instance was the promontory of Caithness and that the tribal name therefore denotes 'People of the Promontory'. An alternative theory is that the name means 'People of the Horned God', the latter perhaps a local variant of the ubiquitous horned deity of the Celtic world.

South and west of Caithness the Epidii ('Horse Folk') of Kintyre were perhaps so called because of religious devotion to a local equivalent of Epona, a Gaulish goddess who gave protection to horses. Divine protection of animals was an important part of pagan religious beliefs and would have been the chief function of many other deities whose names are now unknown. A later echo of goddesses who protected herds of wild deer in pre-Christian Scotland is perhaps represented by the *cailleach* or 'hag' who appears in the medieval folklore of many districts. Similar localised veneration may have been bestowed on features in the landscape. The inhabitants of a particular valley, for instance, might have worshipped a deity associated with a well or spring on a nearby upland watershed, or with an artificial feature such as an ancient burial mound. Thus, the ancient fort on Loudoun Hill in Ayrshire apparently owes its name to pre-Christian traditions of the universal Celtic god Lugus or Lugh. It seems likely that this place was called *Lugudunon* ('Fort of Lugus'), a name borne also by the original Gaulish settlement underlying the French city of Lyons. Another *Lugudunon*, perhaps a hillfort on Arthur's Seat overlooking modern Edinburgh, might have given its name to the place-name Lothian.

Roman Religion

Like the Britons whom they conquered, the Romans practised a polytheistic religion which venerated a multiplicity of gods and goddesses. Many Roman deities had parallels in the Celtic world, thereby providing the conquerors with a ready-made link between their own patterns of worship and those of the native population. Identification of a Roman god with a Celtic counterpart often resulted in a melding of the two to produce a hybrid deity who could then be venerated by native and Roman alike. This went hand in hand with an ongoing process of Romanisation and provided an additional means of turning a conquered people into amicable, peaceful subjects. The practice was known in Latin as *interpretatio Romana* and mirrored the much earlier *interpretatio Graeca* by which the gods of ancient Greece had been absorbed into the Roman pantheon. In those parts of northern Britain under direct or indirect Roman rule – the military zone behind Hadrian's Wall and the intervallate region stretching to the Forth–Clyde isthmus – a number of indigenous deities were matched to Roman equivalents. Thus, the Celtic warrior-god Cocidius was linked to Mars, the Roman god of war, to produce the composite figure 'Mars Cocidius' whose name was inscribed on objects found at the Roman fort of Bewcastle a few miles north of Hadrian's Wall. Another native deity associated with war was Camulos, already mentioned above, who appears in Romanised guise as 'Mars Camulos' on an altar from Bar Hill in Dunbartonshire. Maponus ('Son of the Mother') was viewed by the conquerors as an equivalent of Apollo. Dedications in Latin on Roman monuments show not only this god's native name but also the compound 'Apollo Maponus'. At the Dumfriesshire fort of Birrens, the native name was carved on a sandstone slab in the misspelt form *Mabomi*, this being the only Maponus inscription known from Scotland. In the Wall area slightly to the south his name appears on four stone altars dedicated by Roman soldiers at Brampton and Corbridge. His widespread popularity among fort garrisons further afield from the presumed cult-centre near the Solway Firth is indicated by an inscription from Ribchester in Lancashire. The cult's influence evidently faded further north: at Inveresk in Midlothian the soldiers chose Grannus, not Maponus, as the local equivalent of Apollo. Not all native deities found a match in the Roman pantheon. Those who had no obvious equivalent were generally tolerated, their cults being allowed to continue under imperial rule. One of these was Brigantia, the eponymous mother-goddess of the Brigantes, whose likeness was carved on a stone at Birrens. The devotee who commissioned this particular carving was Amandus, formerly a military architect, who perhaps had a kinship link or some other affinity with local natives. Brigantia is represented on the Birrens stone as a spear-wielding figure reminiscent of Victoria, the Roman goddess of victory, although the two deities were not fused as one under the *interpretatio Romana*. A plethora of lesser gods was undoubtedly encountered by the Romans as they pushed north towards the Highlands, but few are identifiable in the archaeological record. One of them might be the mysterious Grannus, apparently a pan-Celtic protector of thermal springs, whose commemoration at the fort of Inveresk indicates his popularity among Britons and Romans alike.

Soldiers on the northern frontier had access not only to those native deities whom they adopted and adapted but also to a range of imported figures whose cults were popular with the army. Into the latter category fall the major gods and goddesses of the Classical world, such as Jupiter, Mars, Mercury, Neptune, Juno and Minerva. In the last quarter of the second century, on the Antonine Wall, at the fort of Castlecary, a group of Italians and Austrians – all of them soldiers of the Sixth Legion – dedicated an altar to Mercury. On the same frontier, a centurion of the Second Legion commissioned several altars at the fort of Auchendavy, dedicating them to a dozen gods and goddesses who were presumably his personal favourites. Further south, at Newstead, another centurion marked his devotion to the huntress Diana. Lesser Roman gods venerated in the Antonine region include the forest deity Silvanus, commemorated at Bar Hill. Abstract military concepts such as Discipline and Victory were also adopted for religious purposes, as at the fort of

Bertha near Perth where an inscribed stone was dedicated to 'the Discipline of the Emperor'. Even more specific to the army were the *Campestres*, the protective mother-goddesses of the parade ground, who were particularly venerated by cavalry regiments. Today, however, the most well-known god of the Roman military is Mithras, a deity of eastern origin whose cult became popular among soldiers in all parts of the Empire. Many Roman forts in Britain would have contained a *mithraeum*, a temple of Mithras, in which the cult's tough initiation rites and other arcane rituals were practised. On the northern frontier, *mithraea* have been discovered at three forts on Hadrian's Wall, the best-preserved being at Carrawburgh where the remains can still be seen, but none have so far been found in Scotland. Also of eastern origin and adopted by the army was the cult of Jupiter Dolichenus, a storm-god whose popularity increased under the patronage of the Severan emperors. At Corbridge on the Tyne this armoured, axe-wielding deity was named alongside Brigantia in an inscription commissioned by a centurion of the Sixth Legion. Dolichenus, like Mithras, has yet to appear on inscriptions unearthed at Roman sites further north, but it is more than likely that both deities were worshipped along the Antonine Wall and at the outpost forts in the intervallate region. Their cults, along with the rest, swiftly disappeared after pagan worship was outlawed by imperial decree in the late fourth century. Only one exotic eastern cult was allowed to survive. This was Christianity, a set of beliefs embraced by the emperor Constantine the Great in the early 300s and promoted thereafter as the official religion of the Empire. In the British Isles, its subsequent impact on native populations cannot be overstated.

Christianity

Early medieval society in Britain was more stratified than its Iron Age precursor. By c.500, many folk descended from the free farmers of pre-Roman times seem to have constituted an underclass of agricultural peasants who sustained the privileged lifestyle of an aristocratic elite. Another key difference between the two periods lay in the character of the relationships between secular and religious leaders. Pre-Roman rulers had been supported by a pagan clergy whose origins lay in local cults associated with specific places or with particular tribes and kin-groups. A typical pagan priest, although undoubtedly a figure of great power within a local context, was nonetheless subservient to the authority of his local chieftain. By contrast, the spread of Christianity brought a new type of priesthood whose international links transcended local loyalties and whose personnel frequently intervened in the business of government.

Like their peers in other parts of Western Europe, the kings who arose in fifth-century Britain were increasingly exposed to a vision of Christian monarchy based on Biblical and Classical models, the prime exemplars being the Israelite kings of the Old Testament and pious Roman emperors such as Constantine the Great. This idealised tem-plate of kingship was actively promoted by the Christian clergy to the 'barbarian' kings who emerged in Britain, Gaul and other erstwhile provinces of the decaying Empire after c.400. It was presented as an attractive package to heathen rulers, many of whom aspired to portray themselves as the true heirs of Rome. Such men eagerly embraced the vision and willingly converted to Christianity in ceremonies presided over by their new 'high priests' – the bishops and abbots whose churches and monasteries had recently been established by royal gifts of land. Conversion created a symbiotic relationship between a king and his chief bishop or abbot, with clear advantages for both parties. Literate, Latin-speaking Christian clerics offered ambitious barbarian kings the high-status trappings of imperial pomp, sanctioned by rituals in which the language of Rome was a sacred tongue. In return, the clergy were permitted to spread the Faith across the king's domain, conducting their missionary labours under royal protection. Successful missions led to mass conversion of the populace, thus creating a constant need for more churches and monasteries, all of which enhanced the status of the bishop or abbot who stood beside the king's throne.

Patrick and Coroticus

The beginnings of Christianity in Scotland seem to lie in the fifth century. Further south, in former Roman territories nestling behind Hadrian's Wall, the retreat of paganism had begun before the end of imperial rule. In the lands north of the Wall, far from the urban centres where the new religion gained its first major footholds in Britain, Christian influence was barely felt before c.400. The earliest literary evidence for what we might call 'Scottish Christianity' comes from the writings of Saint Patrick whose ecclesiastical career belongs to the second half of the fifth century. In his own words, Patrick described himself as a Briton from a Christian family of considerable wealth and status. His grandfather had been a priest and his father a deacon in a town called *Bannavem Taburniae*. This place cannot now be identified, but historians generally agree that it lay near the west coast, in an area easily accessible from Ireland. During his youth Patrick was captured in a raid by Irish pirates and taken back to their homeland as a slave. At that time Ireland was still a pagan country, a patchwork of heathen kingdoms ruled by warrior-kings whose fleets frequently plundered British shores. While in captivity there, Patrick nurtured a desire to bring the Irish into the Christian fold. When he eventually escaped, he returned to Britain to train as a priest before going back to Ireland to preach the Faith. It was during his time as a bishop to a thriving community of Irish converts that the district was attacked by a marauding band of Britons. The raiders cruelly slew many of their victims and abducted the rest, taking them back to Britain to be sold as slaves to the heathen Picts. This savage deed so enraged Patrick that he sent a stern letter to the perpetrators. To him these Britons were not 'my fellow-citizens', still less 'fellow-citizens of the holy Romans', but a bloodthirsty gang whom he scorned as 'fellow-citizens of demons'. Their leader, on whose orders the raid on Ireland had been launched, was a king called Coroticus. Seventh-century Irish tradition associated this ruler with a stronghold called 'The Rock', almost certainly the imposing citadel of Alt Clut ('Clyde Rock'), where Dumbarton Castle now stands. Patrick's words imply that Coroticus and his warriors were Christians, even if they showed a tendency to slide into wickedness and brutality. He distinguished them, for instance, from the heathen Picts, 'a foreign people who do not know God'. To him, the Clyde Britons were a predominantly Christian nation ruled by a nominally Christian king.

Nowhere in Patrick's writings is there any clue as to how, when or by whom Coroticus and his people were evangelised. The saint's reference to 'fellow-citizens of the holy Romans' is a rhetorical description carrying no implication of a Christian presence on the Clyde in late imperial times. Its purpose was probably to draw a contrast between 'civilised' Romans and 'barbarian' Clydesiders, especially if the latter and their king considered themselves in some way to be the heirs of Rome in north-west Britain. In fact, the earliest evidence for Christianity in this area belongs not to the Roman era but to the fifth or sixth century. The relevant data comes from the old parish church at Govan, an ancient religious site situated ten miles east of Dumbarton. Taken together, the archaeological data and Patrick's writings suggest that the Clyde Britons had only recently embraced the new religion when Coroticus held the kingship. It is even possible that Coroticus was the first king of Alt Clut to turn away from paganism.

Galloway

Archaeological evidence testifies to the presence of Christian communities in southern Scotland in the fifth-century, but only on the Clyde do we have corresponding literary data. No first-hand observations of the kind recorded by Patrick emerge from other regions. We can, nonetheless, make some useful deductions from archaeology. Our attention is drawn first to Galloway, where a series of inscribed stone memorials commemorates Christian Britons of the fifth and sixth centuries. These monuments were commissioned by local elites who wanted the names of their dead to be carved in Latin. This need not imply a knowledge of written or spoken Latin among high-status families, but it does suggest what modern historians call 'Romanitas' – an aspiration to Roman ideals. Who these families were, and what status they held within the secular hierarchy, are unanswerable questions. We do not even know the name of the kingdom or kingdoms to which the Galloway sculptors and their patrons belonged. Early medieval centres of power in the region are identifiable archaeologically, but their relationship to the communities represented by the stones is uncertain.

The earliest of the Galloway Christian monuments commemorates a man called Latinus and his young daughter, both of whom must have belonged to a prominent local kindred. Their memorial stone was erected at Whithorn where it can now be seen in the museum. In its original position it may have been a grave-marker, perhaps serving an additional purpose in the local landscape as the conspicuous display of one family's wealth and religious affiliation. This family was certainly prosperous enough to commission monumental stonework for its departed members and keen to display its quasi-Roman aspirations. In addition to commemorating the deceased, the stone refers also to Barrovadus, a kinsman – possibly a grandfather – of Latinus. Barrovadus was arguably an important ancestral figure for the family, a man whose name when inscribed on a stone would have conveyed special meaning to the local community. Archaeologists usually date the stone to the second half of the fifth century, making Latinus a contemporary of Coroticus on the Clyde. His memorial is the oldest surviving Christian monument from Scotland.

Twenty miles west of Whithorn another religious community flourished at Kirkmadrine in the Rhinns of Galloway. A memorial stone, probably erected in the early sixth century, commemorates two of Kirkmadrine's most important clerics, the *sacerdotes* ('priests') Viventius and Mavorius. Another stone mentions Florentius who was either a clergyman or a secular benefactor of the church, while a third bears the Christian phrase *initium et finis* ('The Beginning and the End'). All three monuments were carved with a chi-rho, a monogram formed from the first two letters of the Greek name *Christos*. A fourth stone, found in the Rhinns but now lost, was the memorial of Ventidius, a *subdiaconus* ('sub-deacon') who perhaps belonged to the same religious community as Viventius and Mavorius. No structural traces from this early period are visible at Kirkmadrine, but any ancient remains presumably lie beneath the foundations of the present church which was built in 1889. Archaeological investigation would no doubt shed light on the history of the site and might also reveal evidence of a relationship between the religious communities of Kirkmadrine and Whithorn. The latter, as we shall see, remained important long after the sixth century and appears in later textual sources from Britain and Ireland. By contrast, Kirkmadrine's complete absence from the documentary record suggests that it played little or no role outside the Rhinns. Perhaps it possessed no famous shrine or tomb around which a devotional cult and pilgrimage centre could be developed?

The date when Christianity first arrived in Galloway is unknown. The earliest church at Whithorn appears to have been founded at the end of the fifth century or at the very beginning of the sixth. Archaeologists have unearthed its remains on a site subsequently occupied by the medieval priory and cathedral. The form of lettering on the Latinus stone, together with stylistic features on other sculptured monuments at Whithorn and in the Rhinns, suggest an ecclesiastical link with Gaul. Whether this went beyond an exchange of sculptural influences to include a transfer of Gaulish clergy to Galloway we cannot say. As far as we can tell, the earliest Christian activity at both Whithorn and Kirkmadrine was indigenous rather than imported. In other words, Christianity took hold in these places through the efforts of native clerics who spread the Word among their own communities.

Ninian

Many holy men and women played important roles in the birth of Scottish Christianity, but two figures stand out from the rest. Both were active in the sixth century, in different parts of northern

Britain. Long after their deaths they were remembered as key players in the destruction of paganism, as founders of important religious settlements and as focal points of devotional cults. In our modern era they are frequently seen as patriarchs of the so-called 'Celtic Church'. Their names were Ninian and Columba. Although their careers had no point of intersection, they are linked by their respective roles in the conversion of the Picts.

In the early eighth century, Bede included in his *Ecclesiastical History* a brief synopsis of Ninian's accomplishments, placing them 'a long time before' those of Columba. The principal events of Columba's life are securely dated, from his birth in Ireland c.521 to his death on Iona in 597. Bede was aware of this chronology and therefore had an accurate perception of Columba's dates, but the imprecision of 'a long time before' suggests that he was unsure of Ninian's. We can infer that Bede did not really know when Ninian lived beyond a vague understanding that he had preceded Columba.

Bede is more precise about Ninian's origins and career, identifying him as a Briton who undertook missionary labours among the 'Southern Picts'. The latter were presumably those who dwelt south of the Mounth, the eastern section of the Grampian range separating Perthshire from Moray. After converting Pictish pagans to the Christian faith, Ninian sought a final resting-place at Whithorn. There, according to Bede, he built a church of stone called *Candida Casa* ('The White House'). There, too, he was eventually interred alongside other saints. During Bede's own lifetime, Galloway lay under direct Northumbrian control and English bishops held sway at Whithorn. The first of these was Pecthelm who was consecrated in or before 731. He became, for Bede, an important source of data on Whithorn's early history. To what extent this information was Northumbrian propaganda rather than reliable tradition is unknown, but it was duly incorporated into the *Ecclesiastical History*. Another text of English origin is the Latin poem *Miracula Nynie Episcopi* ('The Miracles Of Bishop Nynia'), composed in the eighth century. The *Miracula* uses a variant spelling of the saint's name and includes various additional details, such as the claim that a certain King Tudwal, ruler of the area around Whithorn, sent 'Nynia' into exile. In the same poem a Pictish group converted to Christianity by Ninian is called the *Naturae*, an otherwise unknown ethnonym.

Much later than Bede and the *Miracula* is the twelfth-century *Vita Niniani* ('Life of Ninian'), written by Ailred, abbot of the monastery at Rievaulx in Yorkshire. The *Vita* belongs to a literary genre known as hagiography, the art of writing about holy men and women, which has little in common with modern biography. A medieval hagiographer, unlike a modern biographer, was less concerned with the facts of his subject's life than with promoting him or her as a worker of miracles and therefore as a figure worthy of devotion. A hagiographical text was essentially a marketing brochure produced by, or on behalf of, the primary cult-centre of a long-dead saint. It could be used to enhance the status of the cult by attracting pilgrims to its principal church and to satellite churches. In Ninian's case, the *Vita* written by Ailred served as a promotional tool for the main cult-centre at Whithorn. Neither its lateness nor its literary objectives invalidate it as a source of potentially useful data, but, like all hagiography, it has to be approached with caution.

Supplementing the written sources for Ninian is the rich Early Christian archaeology of Galloway, already mentioned above. Excavations at Whithorn have unearthed evidence suggesting that the religious settlement began around AD 500, perhaps in the last years of the fifth century. The first church, constructed of wood, served a community of farmers and traders and was built on the site now occupied by the medieval priory. At some point in the sixth century the church became known as *Candida Casa*, either because it was rebuilt in stone or because the original timber walls were whitewashed. It was around this time that Ninian may have been appointed as the first bishop. After his death, his tomb became a shrine and focus of veneration, and tales of his deeds began to be told locally. These stories depicted him as a worker of miracles and as a missionary to the Picts. Eventually, the fame of his real or imagined accomplishments made him the focus of a cult which was subsequently adopted by English priests arriving at Whithorn after the Northumbrian conquest of Galloway in the late seventh century. It is generally assumed that Whithorn's religious elite prior to the English takeover were Britons, like Ninian himself, and this is probably an accurate assumption. An obscure tale from Ireland, preserved in an eleventh-century text, implies that the religious community at sixth-century Whithorn included Irish monks of whom Abbot Mugint was the most senior. The tale reports an incident in the early career of Saint Finnian of Moville, a Briton who undertook missionary work in Ireland and whose death in 579 was noted in the Irish annals. Despite the prominence given in this story to Mugint and his countrymen, we should be wary of imagining Whithorn as a predominantly Irish monastic settlement. More plausible is a recognition that the reputation of *Candida Casa* in the late sixth century was sufficient to attract clerics from Ireland. The most interesting aspect of the Irish tale is its mention of Finnian, a real figure of history whose connection with Whithorn might be genuine. A recent theory about Ninian proposes that he and Finnian were in fact one and the same and that both names derive from an original form *Uinniau*.

Forth and Tweed

Having looked at two areas of south-west Scotland, our focus moves east to Lothian and Tweeddale, respectively the lands of the Votadini and Selgovae in Roman times. Somewhat west of Edinburgh, on the southern shore of the Firth of Forth near Kirkliston, a distinctive natural boulder bears a Latin inscription carved in the fifth century. This is the Catstane, a monument within a cemetery of 'long cist' burials. Cist-graves are so called because they are lined with stone slabs and, when orientated on an east–west axis, might indicate that the deceased were Christians. The inscription on the Catstane commemorates Victricius and his daughter Vetta, members of a prosperous Christian family which, like the kin of Barrovadus at Whithorn, commissioned Latin memorials for its dead. In the context of a wider community,

Victricius and his daughter were Votadinian Britons, just as Latinus and Barrovadus and the Kirkmadrine priests were probably members of, or descended from, the Novantae people of Galloway.

South of Lothian in Selgovan territory a Briton called Coninia was commemorated on a stone bearing a small cross alongside her name. This monument, carved in the late fifth or early sixth century, was discovered near the site of an ancient church dedicated to the obscure Saint Gordian. The site itself lies within the valley of Manor Water, a small tributary of the Tweed running through lands that today seem quite remote and isolated. In Coninia's time, this area evidently supported one or more prosperous Christian families whom we may cautiously identify as a local aristocracy descended from Selgovan ancestors. A similar family seemingly held power and influence to the south-east, in Liddesdale, where Carantius, the son of Cupitianus, was buried in a grave marked by a Latin-inscribed stone. Further east still, in the valley of the River Yarrow, a family claiming royal status entombed two of its princes together. These men or boys were Nudus and Dumnogenus, the sons of Liberalis. What peril or pestilence caused their deaths is unknown, but their father was presumably a local king. One reading of the inscription seems to call the two princes 'famous', a label hinting at martial renown. Perhaps they died together on one of their father's military campaigns?

Pictish Christian Origins

Bede credited Ninian with bringing Christianity to the 'Southern Picts', who, as we have already noted, presumably dwelt south of the Mounth. Their core territories can thus be envisaged as Perthshire and Fife, and it is in these areas that we may tentatively locate the mysterious Naturae people of the *Miracula* poem. Other traditions report other saints undertaking missionary campaigns in Pictish territory. In the foundation-legends of Abernethy, for example, we find references to a sixth-century evangelising mission from Ireland. Here on the northern coast of Fife stood an important

Pictish royal church which retained its status in later times. One legend credits its foundation to disciples of the renowned Saint Brigid, abbess of Kildare, who died in 526. It tells of a visit to Britain by Darlugdach, Brigid's successor, during the reign of a certain Nechtan Morbet as overking of the Picts. According to this story, Nechtan bestowed upon Darlugdach a gift of land for the building of a church, in gratitude for hospitality received during his exile in Ireland. Another legend tells of Brigid herself participating in Abernethy's foundation and receiving a land-grant from the Pictish king Gartnait, the son of Domelch. Extricating a kernel of truth from these traditions is almost impossible, not only because they tell different stories but also because they appear in manuscripts no older than the fourteenth and fifteenth centuries. As works of literature these legends belong to a period eight or nine hundred years after the events they claim to describe. As repositories of genuine history their value is therefore dubious. Brigid and Darlugdach, and their alleged Pictish patrons, belong to the sixth century, but whether they really co-operated in the foundation of Abernethy is uncertain. A better guide to Abernethy's Christian origins is the archaeology of the town and the surrounding area. At the base of the eleventh-century round tower, the most famous local landmark, a carved stone bearing Pictish symbols stands on a plinth. The stone seems to be a work of the late sixth or early seventh century and, while it has no obvious Christian associations, it might relate in some way to the earliest church. There is, in fact, nothing inherently implausible about a Kildare connection, especially if we acknowledge the possibility of high-level contacts between Pictish kings and the heads of Irish monasteries at a time when the former were still pagan.

Away from the uncertainties of ecclesiastical folklore the period of transition from pagan to Christian beliefs among the Picts of Fife may be visible archaeologically. Burial in stone-lined graves or 'long cists' has already been noted as a possible indicator of Christianity at the Catstane cemetery in Lothian, where a community of Britons interred its dead in the fifth century. At Hallow Hill on the Fife coast, eighteen miles east of Abernethy, on the outskirts of St Andrews, a large cemetery of long-cist graves has been found. Medieval documents refer to the nearby place-name *Eglesnamin*, now no longer extant, which contains a word derived from Latin *ecclesia* ('church'). No such church has yet been identified, but the presence of an 'eccles' place-name points to a Christian foundation of very early date, possibly of the sixth century and perhaps even contemporary with the alleged activities of Kildare missionaries at nearby Abernethy.

CHAPTER 5
Celt and Saxon

Cenéla

In the opening chapter of this book the main textual sources for the early history of Scotland were briefly described. One group of texts mentioned as being of special importance were the chronicles and year-tables known collectively as the 'Irish annals'. Of these the most reliable are the *Annals of Ulster* and the *Annals of Tigernach*, both of which were partly compiled from earlier texts written contemporaneously with the events they recorded. We now turn to these annals as our principal guide through the second half of the first millennium AD. Our journey resumes in Argyll, ancient Dál Riata, the ancestral homeland of the Scots.

The annalists noted retrospectively the death, in 506, of a king called Domangart. Although written one or two centuries after the event, this entry marks the beginning of authentic history in Dál Riata. Domangart ruled the long peninsula of Kintyre and was given the patronym 'son of Ness' by the annalists. Ness is an otherwise unknown figure whose name is absent from the various king-lists. Instead, we find Domangart's father being identified there as Fergus Mór mac Eirc of the Scottish foundation-legend. Some historians suggest that Ness was the name of Domangart's mother, but this seems unlikely as matronyms did not usually replace patronyms in the annals. A more credible explanation is that Ness really was Domangart's father but lost his true place in Scottish history when later tradition created the fictional ancestor Fergus Mór. The king-lists give Domangart a reign of five years, after which he was succeeded by his son Comgall who was in turn followed by another son Gabrán. Little is known of Comgall other than his name, but Gabrán's reign was marked by an event of no small significance: the earliest recorded clash between Scots and Picts. This was noted by the annalists under the year 559:

> A flight before the son of Maelchon. And the death of Gabrán, son of Domangart.

Other versions of the annals reverse these two items of information by placing Gabrán's demise before the battle, but it is possible that the events were linked and that Gabrán perished in the 'flight' before Maelchon's son. The latter was Brude, a powerful Pictish overking whose domains stretched from Moray to Orkney.

Neither the site of the battle nor its causes are known. One suggestion is that the defeated Scots were pioneers or colonists seeking new settlements in the fertile East. Another envisages Gabrán holding a portion of Pictish territory by right of inheritance, perhaps via his mother if she was a Pict, and defending it against Brude's aggression. This theory derives from a belief that Gabrán gave his name to the Perthshire district of Gowrie, itself an unproven hypothesis based on a superficial similarity between the names *Gabrán* and *Goverin*, the latter being a fourteenth-century form of *Gowrie*. An alternative etymology could be sought for the modern place-name, just as an alternative and more plausible context should be sought for the conflict of 559. If the notion of Gabrán's alleged landholdings in Perthshire is disregarded, a likelier cause of the battle was raiding by one party in a shared frontier zone among the central Highland glens. In any case, we should be wary of thinking in terms of a simple 'Scots versus Picts' scenario. Ethnic boundaries in early medieval Britain were undoubtedly blurred rather than clear-cut, and might not have seemed as significant to the people of those times as modern historians formerly believed.

Within two or three generations of Gabrán's death his family adopted the name *Cenél nGabráin* ('Gabrán's kindred') to distinguish themselves from other *cenéla* or royal dynasties. Their domains lay in Kintyre, probably at the peninsula's southern tip where the coastal fortress of Dunaverty may have been their main centre of power. They became the most powerful kindred in Argyll and played a major political role for the next three centuries. During this period the homeland of the Scots was not a single, unified realm but comprised a number of small kingdoms. The *cenéla* or principal kindreds of these realms competed with each other for the overkingship of all Dál Riata, a position of dominance that only a strong and charismatic individual could hope to attain. When an overking died, his paramount status was not automatically inherited by a designated heir unless he, too, was strong enough to push other contenders aside. At the time of Gabrán's death the main rivals for the overkingship were his own sons and those of his brother Comgall, together with ambitious princes from other *cenéla* in various parts of Argyll. Cenél Comgaill, the descendants of Comgall, ruled the Cowal peninsula and the Isle of Bute. They became a major power in the Firth of Clyde, competing against the neighbouring Britons of Alt Clut with whom they shared territorial ambitions and a land frontier.

Beyond the northern fringe of Cenél nGabráin territory lay the kingdom of Lorn, the heartland of the Cenél Loairn kindred. In later centuries its rulers claimed descent from Lorn, an eponymous and almost certainly fictional ancestor identified as a brother of Fergus Mór. Another alleged sibling of Fergus was Óengus Mór, forefather of the Cenél nÓengusa kindred of Islay. Unlike their neighbours in Kintyre and Lorn, the leaders of Cenél nÓengusa took little part in the contest for overall supremacy in Argyll or, to put it another way, whatever part they played is not visible in the sources. They were, however, the masters of a large and fertile Hebridean island straddling the western sea-routes. That they had access to substantial military resources cannot be doubted, but they presumably saw benefits in absenting themselves from the struggle for regional supremacy, if this was indeed the path they chose. On the other hand, their territorial ambitions may have been repeatedly thwarted by those of Cenél nGabráin and Cenél Loairn, or simply excised from the documentary record by writers affiliated to these two *cenéla*.

Across the narrow strait between Kintyre and Antrim lay Irish Dál Riata, a south-western outlier of the extensive maritime overkingdom ruled in the sixth and seventh centuries by Argyll-based monarchs. Later legend repackaged the Irish territory as the ancestral land of Fergus Mór and his descendants. By the twelfth century it was firmly established in Scottish pseudo-history as the true homeland of the Scots and as the base from which their forefathers migrated to Britain. Looking behind the legends we encounter a different story, a more realistic account of relations between peoples living on either side of the Irish Sea. We see both Cenél nGabráin and Cenél Comgaill competing for power in Irish Dál Riata in the seventh century, both kindreds having become entangled in a complex web of Irish politics. At the centre of this web lay the Uí Néill, a powerful royal family whose northern and southern branches respectively ruled large overkingships spanning much of Ireland. An early instance of contact between the Uí Néill and the Argyll Scots came after Gabrán's death when the kingship of Kintyre was held by his nephew, the Cowal prince Conall mac Comgaill. The annals show Conall raiding the Inner Hebrides in 568 and joining the southern Uí Néill king Colman Bec for an attack on Seil and Islay. The latter island was ruled at that time by the ancestors of Cenél nÓengusa, but the reason for its targeting by Conall and Colman is unknown. Their combined assault implies a political relationship based on shared ambitions in the Hebridean seaways.

On Conall's death, in 574, the kingship of southern Argyll fell vacant. Contenders undoubtedly emerged among the descendants of his grandfather Domangart, each with a valid claim. A system of alternating kingship may have been in place to deal with such uncertainty, perhaps in imitation of practices in contemporary Ireland. Succession systems of this type were designed to minimise the risk of internecine strife by allowing different branches of a large extended family to share high-kingship in rotation. Succession in Kintyre and Cowal was perhaps decided in this way, with Gabrán having been succeeded by his nephew Conall, who was followed in turn by Gabrán's son Áedán. It is equally possible, however, that Áedán gained the kingship by force, by defeating his rivals on the battlefield. Whatever the circumstances of his succession, he is rightly regarded as one of early Scotland's greatest kings.

Áedán mac Gabráin

The annals and other sources portray Áedán as a belligerent monarch whose reign was punctuated by frequent conflict, much of it driven by personal ambition. He was undoubtedly a strong ruler at home and an effective war-leader abroad. The beginning of his reign coincided with a battle in Kintyre at an unidentified place called *Delgu* or *Teloch* where, according to the annalists, the casualties included a son of Conall and 'many allies of the sons of Gabrán'. If Áedán participated in this battle, it may have been the key event in his rise to power. Alternatively, it may have been a defeat for his and Conall's kinsmen at the hands of external foes, perhaps from Ireland. An Irish connection at least seems plausible when we recall Conall's recent dealings with the southern Uí Néill, which may have invited resentment from their northern rivals and a punitive response. Colman Bec had been slain in battle by the northern Uí Néill within a year of the Hebridean campaign of 568 and a similar showdown might have been sought with his Dál Riatan allies six years later. Conall was already dead when the battle of Delgu took place but the annals name his son Donnchad among the slain. Curiously, there is no mention of Áedán. The latter's participation can nevertheless be envisaged: he was a prince of Kintyre and probably led a warband to the battlefield, either standing alongside Donnchad as a loyal kinsman or fighting against him as a rival for kingship.

After his succession, Áedán became deeply enmeshed in Ireland, primarily because of his family's longstanding claim on Irish Dál Riata. During the early part of his reign he supposedly swore an oath of submission to Báetán mac Cairill, king of the Dál Fiatach people of Ulster, at Island Magee on the Antrim coast. Báetán was an aggressive king whose predatory interests in the Irish Sea probably brought the Isle of Man under his rule. He may even have been the unnamed victor at Delgu in 574 if the battle was not indeed an Uí Néill venture or an internal squabble. Áedán's formal submission to Báetán acknowledged the latter's supremacy over Irish Dál Riata and may also have laid Kintyre under tribute. The submission would have placed specific obligations on Áedán, among which was a pledge of service to Dál Fiatach military campaigns. Only when Báetán died in 581 was the burden of vassalage lifted from Áedán's shoulders. By then, he was already pursuing his own ambitions.

In 580, Áedán led a plundering expedition to Orkney, leading his war-fleet around the furthest tip of Britain to attack these northern isles. This was a direct challenge to the Pictish overking Brude, Maelchon's son, who counted the Orcadian kings among his subordinates. Brude's response is not known, but a period of hostilities with Áedán can perhaps be envisaged, involving raids and counter-raids by both sides. Áedán was evidently attracted to the wide lands east of Druim Alban and scored a major victory there against the Britons of Stirlingshire in 582. His opponents, the Maeatae of Manau, inflicted a grievous blow by slaying two of his sons, but defeat on the battlefield probably forced them to recognise him as overlord. Such a development would not have been pleasing to Brude, whose own overkingship – at its greatest extent – may have reached as far south as Perthshire on the frontier of Maeatae territory.

Áedán's wars with the Britons were not confined to Stirlingshire. Subjecting the Maeatae to vassal status gave him a valuable foothold in the Forth Valley and nudged his ambition towards their fellow-countrymen on the Clyde. In 590, he fought a battle at *Leithreid* against foes whom the sources do not name. If, as several historians have suggested, the location was Leddrie in Strathblane or Letter near Killearn, then Áedán's foes were probably the Britons of Alt Clut. The king at Dumbarton Rock at that time was Rhydderch Hael ('the Generous') who will be encountered again later in this chapter. In traditions preserved in medieval Wales, but referring to what Welsh poets called *Hen Ogledd* (the 'Old North'), a fragment of heroic literature lists the 'Three Unrestrained Ravagings Of The Island Of Britain' and tells of:

> . . . the third Unrestrained Ravaging, when Áedán the Treacherous came to the court of Rhydderch Hael at Clyde Rock and left neither food nor drink nor living beast.

This snippet of folklore may have originated on the Clyde long after Rhydderch's time but might preserve some garbled memory of a historical event. Perhaps Áedán really did launch a raid on Alt Clut? Why the Britons subsequently regarded him as treacherous is not known, but he perhaps broke a peace treaty with them. If the battle of Leithreid has been correctly identified as an assault on the borderlands of Alt Clut, it may have formed part of a sustained campaign which led ultimately to an 'unrestrained ravaging' of Rhydderch's stronghold.

In Ireland, meanwhile, a formidable power had arisen during the 580s in the shape of Áed mac Ainmerech, high king of the northern Uí Néill. Áed's principal enemies were his Ulster neighbours the Dál Fiatach, whose kingdom adjoined both his own domain and Irish Dál Riata. Seeing an advantage in surrounding Dál Fiatach territory, Áed invited Áedán mac Gabráin to attend a meeting to discuss terms for a military alliance. The two kings met at *Druim Cett*, the Ridge of Cett, now the Mullagh or Daisy Hill on the edge of Limavady. In the annals, this important event is misplaced under the year 575, ten years before Áed attained the paramount kingship of the northern Uí Néill. A more plausible date for the meeting lies within the range 586 to 594, between Áed's first recorded war as high king of Ireland and the time when Saint Columba, who also attended the meeting, became too old to travel far from Iona. The royal conference has become entangled in an intricate web of folklore, legend and dynastic propaganda, while Columba's role has been embellished with a plethora of later stories designed to enhance his reputation. Within this web we find such oddities as a detailed debate about whether or not poets should be expelled from Ireland. Only by scraping away the layers of bogus material do we see the event in a more realistic historical context: a meeting of two ambitious Gaelic kings, each of whom stood at the height of his power. The most likely result of their discussions was a military agreement between Áedán's kin and the northern Uí Néill, probably at the expense of Dál Fiatach interests.

If Áedán undertook any joint military campaigns with Áed, there is no mention of them in the sources. Instead, we see his warbands heading not west to Ireland but east into Pictish territory. Brude, son of Maelchon, had died in 584, his departure removing a significant obstacle to Áedán's ambitions. With the Maeatae still subjugated as tribute-paying clients, Áedán was able to use Stirlingshire as a springboard for raids against the Picts. Rich pickings awaited him in the valleys of Earn and Tay, but, in 598, he over-reached himself while venturing deep into the Pictish heartlands. On a battlefield in the ancient province of Circinn, the present-day district of Angus, he sustained a heavy defeat which claimed the lives of two of his surviving sons. This setback may have dented his eastward ambitions and could partly explain why, as the curtain drew down on the sixth century, he turned his eyes elsewhere. Leading his army south of the Firth of Forth he encountered a new and powerful foe, a recent arrival on the northern political stage.

Britons and Anglo-Saxons

While Aedan mac Gabráin was striving to impose his supremacy over Picts and Scots alike, a similar contest was being played out among the North Britons. In the lands between the two Roman walls a number of kingdoms had arisen during the late fifth and early sixth centuries. The largest of these, as we saw in Chapter 3, were two realms located respectively on the firthlands of Clyde and Forth. On the west lay the kingdom of Alt Clut, successor realm of the Damnonii, centred on the imposing bulk of Dumbarton Rock. Eastward in Lothian stood the great citadel of

Din Eidyn, chief stronghold of Gododdin, the post-Roman kingdom of the Votadini. By the mid-500s, these two realms were competing for land and resources, not only with each other but with neighbouring kingdoms whose origins are unknown. Like Alt Clut and Gododdin, some of these other realms might have begun as fifth-century manifestations of Iron Age 'tribes' whose indigenous elites had been suppressed but not completely extinguished by Rome. If so, their emergence is invisible in the documentary record. No surviving source tells us how these Britons made the transition to independent kingship before or after the Romans departed.

South of the headwaters of the River Clyde, in what are now Dumfriesshire and Galloway, the tribal cohesion of the Novantae was a distant memory by 500. After the fall of Roman Britain, this group is not heard of again, despite modern attempts to identify its name in later poetry. Its constituent parts probably developed into small kingdoms whose names have not been remembered, although their existence is implied by a scatter of literary references. One modern theory proposes that the erstwhile Novantian lands reappeared in the sixth century as part of a kingdom called Rheged. Supporters of this idea point to the Galloway place-name Dunragit, recorded in 1535 as *Dunregate*, and suggest that it might mean 'Fort of Rheged'. Additional support is drawn from a widespread belief that Carlisle lay in Rheged, an idea prompted by the casual mention of both city and kingdom in a poem written in Wales in the twelfth century. Earlier poems, apparently composed by the North British bard Taliesin, describe a warrior-king called Urien ruling Rheged in the late sixth century. Modern historians have attempted to equate place-names in the Taliesin poetry with various locations in Cumbria, Dumfriesshire and Galloway, thereby providing additional support for the notion that Rheged lay near the Solway Firth. Closer examination, however, reveals the theory's shaky foundations. At Dunragit, the site usually proposed as the Fort of Rheged lacks the imposing character of other early medieval citadels. Its setting, on a rather small hillock overlooking the Piltanton Burn, makes it a poor candidate in any search for Urien's primary residence. Being an ambitious warrior-king, he would have regarded himself as sharing equal status with his peers at Alt Clut and Din Eidyn. The unimpressive height at Dunragit is unlikely to have attracted his attention. In fact, the entire 'Fort of Rheged' theory begins to look like a red herring. References to Carlisle and Rheged in a twelfth-century Welsh poem likewise contribute nothing of value to an objective search for the kingdom's actual location. It is extremely doubtful that a Welshman of c.1150 had any special knowledge of sixth-century North British political geography, nor would he have been particularly interested in such a topic. Rheged's fame in Welsh heroic poetry, due largely to the popularity of Taliesin's poems, has understandably created a modern desperation to place the kingdom on a modern map. Unfortunately, when the limitations of the Carlisle-Galloway identification are highlighted, the only geographical certainty about Rheged is that it lay somewhere south of Alt Clut and Gododdin. This means that the sixth-century political geography of Cumbria, Dumfriesshire and Galloway is likewise unknown. The lands around the Solway Firth surely supported one or more realms of substantial wealth and power – presumably founded by descendants of the Novantae and Carvetii – but their names and histories are not retrievable from the sources.

In Roman times, the eastern neighbours of the Novantae were the Selgovae whose heartland lay in Upper Tweeddale. When the kingdoms of the North Britons began to emerge in the early 500s, the name *Selgovae* had already disappeared. Its demise as a collective term for a population group indicates that it was no longer relevant to contemporary political identities. This suggests that the Selgovae were held together by subservience or affiliation to a dominant sept whose authority held firm in Roman times before unravelling after the fourth century. Like the Novantae, the Selgovae eventually dissolved into sub-groups to whom local allegiances seemed more important than regional ones.

One Selgovan sub-group or sept may have established a centre of power at Kelso, a place formerly known as *Calchow* ('Chalk Hill'). Today, the old name still exists in the street-name Chalkheugh Terrace, although the feature it once described is hidden beneath the modern town. It is possible that Kelso was once the chief stronghold of a kingdom called *Calchfynydd* ('Chalk Hill'), whose rulers held authority in Tweeddale. If so, then the actual site probably lay at the confluence of the rivers Tweed and Teviot, immediately to the west of the town, where a castle was erected in the twelfth century. Little is known of the kings of Calchfynydd, but, if their power-base has been located correctly, their realm nestled in a crucible of sixth-century political ambitions. Northward beyond the Tweed lay the frontiers of Gododdin; westward, a ribbon of native kingdoms extended back along Tweeddale towards the watershed where both Tweed and Clyde spring from the hills. East of Kelso, the Tweed skirted the high fells of Cheviot to enter the heartland of Bernicia, a kingdom ruled by a dynasty of 'Anglo-Saxon' kings.

Bernicia is a Latinisation of the Brittonic name *Berneich* which seems to be an ethnonym meaning 'People of the Gap'. The 'gap' in question was presumably a major topographical feature, perhaps the wide trough of Lower Tweeddale between the Cheviot and Lammermuir Hills. In simple terms, the native inhabitants of Berneich were Britons who, by c.550, were ruled by English-speaking kings. Behind this ethnic and linguistic labelling lies a much more complex process: the Anglo-Saxon takeover of an indigenous population. How this process was achieved – whether by war or invitation or gradual assimiliation – we are unable to say. Our lack of knowledge is largely due to an apparent reticence by Bede, himself a Bernician, to give us the origin-story of his ancestors. Remarkably, his vagueness on the topic suggests that he and his contemporaries knew little more than we do.

The beginnings of Anglo-Saxon Bernicia should probably be sought among the Germanic mercenary colonies of the fourth and fifth centuries. In the previous chapter we noted the existence of a cluster of these settlements in Yorkshire. From here a kingdom called Deira subsequently emerged, with an English-speaking elite holding power. Deira's kings ruled a population of mixed Anglo-British stock among whom a shared sense of 'Englishness' developed during the sixth century. This common identity was expressed in a widespread adoption of the English language as the preferred medium of communication. A similar process began further north, in Berneich, perhaps with Deiran encouragement or military support. By the middle of the century, an 'English' royal dynasty was in residence at the coastal fortress of *Din Guayroi*, which was subsequently renamed *Bebbanburh*. This stronghold occupied the imposing crags where Bamburgh Castle perches today. The native Britons of Berneich, like their compatriots in Deira, seem to have willingly embraced the new order. 'Britishness' went out of fashion and 'Englishness' became not only the route to social advancement, but also, perhaps, a preferred ethnic affiliation. Old cultural identities were discarded and new ones were adopted and assimilated.

This process of cultural modification or 'acculturation' was well underway when Ida, the first Bernician king of whom more is known than a name, fought a war against neighbouring Britons. The leader of Ida's foes was Outigirn, one of a number of kings whose domains cannot now be identified. If Outigirn was not himself from Bernicia he possibly ruled Calchfynydd or some other Selgovan sept, or his centre of power may have lain further north in Gododdin. His conflict with the English can be tentatively dated to the period 547 to 559, the span of Ida's reign according to Bede, but not even Bede can be completely trusted on sixth-century events. Neither Bede nor any of his contemporaries had access to accurate records relating to the period before c.625. They had to rely instead on orally preserved folklore, recitations of heroic war-poems, tales of old saints and casual scribblings in the margins of ecclesiastical texts.

Bede showed little interest in the Britons and viewed them with scorn. His antipathy sprang from a disdain for their clergy whose apparent refusal to evangelise the pagan English he regarded as unforgivable. Thus, although the North Britons played an important role in the birth of his own nation, they receive few citations in the *Ecclesiastical History*. For instance, Bede mentions the great fortress of Alt Clut, but does not name any of the native kings who ruled there. Like their clergy, they were beneath his contempt and unworthy of attention. Had he chosen any of them for detailed scrutiny he would almost certainly have cast them in a demonic role, as he did with the Welsh warlord Cadwallon. The Irish annalists took a little more interest in the Clyde kings but not until the 600s and only briefly thereafter. Historians must search elsewhere for detailed information on the North Britons and find themselves turning to sources of far less reliability than Bede and the Irish annals. Three genres of literature come to the fore, each purporting to offer useful insights into the North British kingdoms of the sixth century. One genre includes folktales of uncertain provenance, often embedded in works of hagiography written no earlier than the twelfth century. Another genre is heroic verse allegedly composed in the sixth century by bards such as Taliesin who plied their trade at the courts of northern kings. Small portions of this poetry survive today among a large corpus of medieval Welsh literature, either as complete poems or as enigmatic fragments scattered among works of much later composition. It is an inevitable consequence of this kind of haphazard preservation that none of the presumed sixth-century poems has survived in unaltered form. The third literary genre providing North British information is genealogical, being represented by the pedigrees or 'family trees' of a handful of kings. One of these pedigrees, by far the longest, gives the lineage of a ninth-century king of Alt Clut. It was briefly encountered in Chapter 3 during a discussion of the names *Cinhil* and *Cluim* ('Quintilius' and 'Clemens') and will appear from time to time throughout this book. Like the heroic poetry, the genealogical texts containing the North British pedigrees survive only in manuscripts written in Wales hundreds of years after the lifetimes of the people they describe.

Among the poems are two famous collections of verses, both of which are widely regarded as genuine compositions of the period 550 to 650. One is *Y Gododdin* ('The Gododdin'), a long poem or sequence of poems describing a sixth-century battle waged by a Votadinian army against Anglo-Saxon foes. The battle occurred at a place called *Catraeth* and was depicted by the poet as a major defeat for the Britons. Despite its subsequent fame in medieval Wales as an episode in the long struggle between Englishman and native, Catraeth receives no mention outside the poetic milieu. The battle was not noted by the Irish annalists, nor by Bede, nor indeed by any chronicler of the period, but the silence of the sources has not deterred modern observers from seeing it as a defining moment in early North British history. A scholarly consensus has grown around the suggestion, first made in 1853, that it took place at Catterick in Yorkshire. This has arisen not from geographical clues within *Y Gododdin* but from a guess based on the similarity between two place-names which happen to sound alike. A hint that the battle was fought in the Gododdin borderlands appears in the poem and might be a more useful signpost to the actual location if it was not routinely ignored by supporters of the Catterick hypothesis. A lengthy discussion of this issue is not appropriate here, but, if the poem itself has anything useful to say about the battlefield, it surely directs our search to the southern fringes of Lothian rather than to Yorkshire. The unanswered questions surrounding Catraeth are encountered again in this chapter, in a slightly different context, but otherwise they lie beyond the scope of this book. Dating the battle is likewise a matter of controversy, but the last quarter of the sixth century, perhaps its final decade, seems to broadly fit the political context envisaged by the poet. How far the defeat affected the political and military fortunes of Gododdin is unknown, but there is no reason to regard it as a fatal blow to the kingdom. Likewise, it should probably not be seen as a significant moment in Scotland's early history. The perceived importance of the battle is due to the fame of *Y Gododdin* among medieval Welsh poets rather than to what actually happened at Catraeth c.600.

The other major collection of North British heroic verse consists of nine poems attributed to Taliesin, the bard of King Urien of Rheged. Despite uncertainty about Rheged's location, the Taliesin poems are often used by historians to construct elaborate theories about history and political geography. The resulting hypotheses have little real value as long as the fundamental question 'Where was Rheged?' remains unanswered. Two theories in particular are now so widely accepted as hard facts that they constantly hinder objective discussion of the question, even though both are still unproven. One is the previously mentioned belief that Rheged lay on the shorelands of the Solway Firth, with a possible headquarters at Dunragit in Galloway. The other proposes that Catraeth, mentioned by Taliesin as a place ruled by Urien, is identifiable as Catterick and therefore a district of North Yorkshire within the hegemony of Rheged. As noted above, the *Gododdin* verses hint that Catraeth was not Catterick but a place in the Votadinian borderlands, thereby directing us to southern Lothian or Tweeddale. This area was a long way from Catterick, a former Roman settlement within what had become 'Anglo-Saxon' territory by c.500. Taliesin likewise describes Urien campaigning in Bernicia, Manau, Clydesdale and Ayrshire, but gives no indication that Rheged's core territory included any part of Yorkshire or indeed any other place so far south. If the Catterick hypothesis is set aside, Urien's main sphere of activity seems to be placed by Taliesin not south but north of Hadrian's Wall. In this book, Catraeth is cautiously envisaged as a district on the fringes of the Gododdin kingdom, perhaps in southern Lothian, while Rheged is left in limbo as a realm without a precise geographical context.

Upper Tweeddale, or at least a part of it, lay within a kingdom whose sixth-century rulers have left traces of their presence in the modern landscape. The kingdom's name is not known, but the names of three members of its royal family were inscribed on the Christian memorial stone described in Chapter 4. This monument stands near Yarrow Kirk in one of the tributary valleys of the Tweed. It was erected in the sixth century and, according to its Latin inscription, marks the grave of 'the most famous princes Nudus and Dumnogenus, sons of Liberalis'. Several figures bearing the name Nudd, a later Welsh form of Nudus, appear in the royal genealogies of the North Britons. Any or none of these might be the prince commemorated at Yarrow. The name Dumnogenus, which in medieval Welsh might be rendered 'Dyfnyen', is not found in the genealogical texts, nor indeed in other sources. We can, nevertheless, cautiously assume that Liberalis called himself a king, and that he regarded the area around Yarrow Kirk as holding ritual significance for his family. Attempts have been made to link him with the royal dynasty of Alt Clut, by interpreting *Liberalis* as a Latin translation of *Hael* (Old Welsh: 'Generous'), an epithet borne by a number of sixth-century figures associated with the Clyde. To modern historians, the best-known bearer of the epithet is Rhydderch Hael, whom we have already encountered in this chapter. It is clear, however, that whoever carved the Yarrow memorial regarded Liberalis as a personal name, not as an epithet or nickname. There is thus no need to associate his family with Alt Clut, nor is there any support for the suggestion that his son Nudd is an obscure sixth-century character called Nudd Hael. The latter appears in the genealogies as Rhydderch's contemporary but remains a shadowy figure. A more objective approach to the Yarrow stone leaves the question of the names aside and examines instead the possible funerary context as a burial-marker for two brothers. The implication of the double inhumation is that both princes perished around the same time, perhaps in battle, and were brought back to Yarrow. Their family clearly regarded the valley as a suitable place for royal burial, but the main centre of power has not yet been located, nor can the extent of the kingdom ruled by Liberalis be deduced. We might hazard a guess that its heartland nestled among the tributary valleys of the Tweed, west of the presumed location of Calchfynydd and south of Gododdin.

In the upper reaches of Tweeddale, or perhaps further west in Clydesdale, lay a kingdom or district called *Goddeu*. This name, in the language of the Britons, meant 'Trees' or 'Forest'. Hints in Welsh tradition and in ecclesiastical folklore imply that sixth-century Goddeu had dynastic links to Rheged, Calchfynydd and Alt Clut. It has been suggested that a memory of this lost kingdom might survive today in the place-name Cadzow which occurs around the town of Hamilton in Clydesdale. This theory rests on an unproven hypothesis that *Cadyow* – an older form of the place-name – might derive from a spoken form of *Goddeu*. An alternative suggestion is that Goddeu was located in the area later known as The Forest, a district straddling the uplands from which the rivers Clyde, Tweed and Annan arise. To the west of Clydesdale lies Ayrshire whose eponymous River Ayr has been equated with *Aeron*, another kingdom mentioned in Old Welsh poetry. It was evidently associated with Urien of Rheged whom Taliesin described as a 'defender' in Aeron, while a prince called Cynon 'of Aeron' is mentioned in the *Gododdin* verses. Further south, where the long valleys of Eskdale and Liddesdale point towards the Solway Firth, lay a realm whose centre of power was *Arfderydd*, the scene of a great battle in 573. To the court-poets of medieval Wales this clash of arms was renowned as one of three pitifully tragic encounters fought by Briton against Briton. It was supposedly waged over a lark's nest, a trifling issue which led to the slaughter of a king called Gwenddoleu and all his warriors. The victors were Gwenddoleu's fellow-countrymen, a coalition of warlords led by the brothers Gurci and Peredur. Neither of these two, nor their equally obscure allies Dunod the Stout and Cynfelyn the Leprous, can be assigned to any particular region of northern Britain. Only Gwenddoleu has a specific geographical context, namely the lands around the old parish of Arthuret, formerly Arfderydd, near the village of Longtown on the River Esk. Somewhere in the vicinity stood *Caer Gwenddoleu* ('Gwenddoleu's Fort'), a stronghold located either at the Roman fort of Netherby or on a site later occupied by the medieval motte of Liddel Strength. Various theories have tried to recreate the political context of the battle of Arfderydd by associating the victorious allies with places in southern Scotland or northern England, but none seem convincing. The cause of the battle is likewise unknown, despite misguided modern notions about a struggle between Christianity and paganism. Competition for resources provides a more plausible scenario and may have prompted a combined assault on Gwenddoleu at his *caer* near the head of the Solway Firth.

The preceding paragraphs give an insight into the many uncertainties surrounding the kingdoms of the North Britons. An accurate political map of southern Scotland in the sixth century is impossible to reconstruct. Only two kingdoms – Gododdin and Alt

Clut – can be located with even the slightest measure of confidence. South of these lay an unknown number of realms whose geographical contexts largely elude us. Gwenddoleu's lands seem to be identifiable today, but those of Gurci, Peredur, and their allies are not. The equation of Calchfynydd with Kelso looks plausible, despite being based on a guess, and so is the tentative identification of Aeron with Ayrshire. Even the famed kingdom of Rheged which is commonly – and perhaps erroneously – regarded as straddling the Solway Firth, cannot be assigned a location more precise than 'somewhere in southern Scotland or northern England'.

If the geography of the North Britons in the sixth century is a cloudy picture, then so is their political history. The first dated event occurs in the middle of the century when Ida, king of Bernicia, waged war against the mysterious Outigirn. Bede's date of 547 for the start of Ida's reign seems to be an eighth-century guess, but might be roughly correct. It gives historians a chronological anchor to which an outline narrative of northern Anglo-British wars can be attached. Unfortunately, it is the only such anchor offered by Bede who says nothing more of Ida and not very much about the fortunes of Bernicia in the period prior to 600. Three dated sixth-century events involving the North Britons appear in the Welsh annals, but all relate to the Arfderydd protagonists and the entries were inserted retrospectively by later scribes. The entries note the famed battle in 573, the deaths of Gurci and Peredur in 580 and the death of Dunod the Stout fifteen years later. Gurci and his brother perished, according to medieval Welsh tradition, at the hands of Eda Big-Knee. If their slayer's name represents a shortened form of an English name such as *Ead*wulf or *Ead*berht, he presumably belonged to Bernicia or Deira. The circumstances of Dunod's death are similarly vague, but the poems attributed to Taliesin name him among a group of British kings who attacked Rheged in the wake of Urien's death. Taliesin composed an elegy on the passing of Urien's son Owain whose most praiseworthy deed was the slaying of an enemy, probably a Bernician, who bore the nickname *Fflamddwyn* ('Flame Bearer'). Urien's own death-poem has not survived, but, according to the ninth-century

Historia Brittonum, a 'History of the Britons' written in Wales, he was assassinated while on a military campaign. The slaying was ordered by Morcant, a rival British king, whose envy of Urien's prowess turned to bitterness. It came at a time when Urien's attacks on Bernicia had forced Theodoric, a son of Ida, to take refuge on the island of Lindisfarne. Morcant may have been an ally or vassal of Rheged in these wars, but this is not a necessary deduction from the sources. His kingdom, like the mysterious Rheged, cannot be placed on a modern map, but it presumably lay somewhere between the two Roman walls. The *Historia Brittonum* counts Morcant and Urien among four British kings who fought Ida's sons, the other two being Rhydderch Hael of Alt Clut and a certain Gwallawg whose realm is unlocated. Some historians associate Gwallawg with the kingdom of Elmet around Leeds in Yorkshire, but the supporting data – a single line of Welsh poetry – is far too slight to sustain the hypothesis. Gwallawg's appearance among a quartet of Bernicia's enemies suggests rather that his domains lay further north, either in the hinterland of Hadrian's Wall or in the lands beyond.

By the end of the sixth century, Anglo-Saxon Bernicia was the dominant power north of the Humber and south of the Forth–Clyde isthmus. The military successes by which this ascendancy was achieved are not reported in the sources, but there can be little doubt that one or more native kingdoms were swept aside. The chief architect of this early phase of Bernician expansion was Aethelfrith, Ida's grandson, whose reign began in 592 or 593 and who, according to Bede, 'ravaged the Britons more extensively than any other English ruler'. Casualties of Aethelfrith's aggression are likely to have included realms along the southern borderlands of Gododdin, one of which may have been Calchfynydd, but those further west apparently remained unconquered. Bernician power had reached as far north as the Lammermuir Hills during the first quarter of the seventh century, probably as a result of Aethelfrith's campaigns in the preceding generation. He almost certainly laid the Gododdin heartlands around Edinburgh under tribute and may have reduced Rheged and Alt Clut to a similar status. Rheged's ruling dynasty eventually forged a political marriage with Bernicia in the 630s, but at the beginning of the century its leaders were undoubtedly under Aethelfrith's dominance. Neither they nor any of their neighbours could stand against him while he remained at the height of his power. The only real threat to his northern overlordship came not from the Britons but from the Scots, among whom a strong challenger arose in the person of Áedán mac Gabráin of Kintyre.

Degsastan

By 600, the expanding hegemonies of Aethelfrith and Áedán were inching closer towards a collision. A clash of swords and ambitions became inevitable as both kings sought dominion in the North. The most likely interface of their respective interests lay in the region of Manau at the head of the Forth estuary. This was an area inhabited by Britons, principally the Maeatae in their ancestral lands between the rivers Avon and Forth. They had been defeated by Áedán some years previously and probably still acknowledged his authority as the seventh century dawned. Their neighbours in Gododdin were under constant pressure from Bernicia and had most likely submitted to Aethelfrith, possibly as a consequence of their defeat at Catraeth. Both Athelfrith and Áedán were therefore in a position to demand military service from British clients in, respectively, Lothian and Stirlingshire. With the various pieces duly in place, the chessboard was set for a decisive contest.

It was Áedán who made the first move. In 603, he marched south through Manau to cross the River Avon into Votadinian territory. Leading his army through Lothian he eventually halted at a monument called Degsa's Stone. If this was a site of special significance to the Bernicians, it may have been symbolically 'captured' by Aedan as a provocative act. A brief account of the ensuing battle was given by Bede who gives two names for the setting: *Lapis Degsa* in Latin and *Degsastan* in Old English. He regarded it as *locus celeberrimus*, 'a very famous place', but gave us no hint of its precise location. To our profound frustration we are left with no clue as to where this important event took place. A guess made by one seventeenth-century writer highlighted a slight resemblance between the modern place-name Dawston and Bede's Degsastan, but the two have different etymological origins and are unlikely to be connected. Dawston, in Liddesdale, is in a remote part of the Anglo-Scottish border country and seems most unsuitable as a candidate. The wild guess associated with it has nevertheless enjoyed a surprisingly long life and still makes frequent appearances in scholarly publications. Somewhat remarkably, this repetitive theorising means that 'Dawston', a place-name borne today by nothing more significant than a windswept moor and a minor stream, is now a regular entry in the indexes of modern books on Anglo-Saxon and early Scottish history. What began as a shot in the dark has grown into a serious hypothesis which, in turn, seems to be accepted in some quarters as historical fact. A more rational approach rejects Dawston's candidacy in the search for Degsastan. Rather than allowing ourselves to be distracted by 'sounds like' etymology, we should look instead for a suitable monument in some district where Áedán and Aethelfrith were more likely to clash. Degsa's Stone was almost certainly a large monolith, a prominent feature in the landscape, perhaps erected by human hands or deposited by natural forces. We could picture it either as an upright standing stone or as a large glacial boulder of the type known as an 'erratic'. A number of suitable candidates are still extant in Lothian and Tweeddale, most of them within easy reach of Dere Street, the Roman road linking Bernicia to the Forth–Clyde isthmus. Both armies may have used this ancient highway *en route* to the battlefield. The Catstane, an ancient monolith now located within the environs of Edinburgh Airport, is one candidate. It bears an Early Christian inscription and a modern name that might mean 'Battle Stone'. This by no means makes it a front runner in the search for the lost Stone of Degsa, but its character and setting make it just as worthy of consideration as Dawston, if not more so.

Although the location of the great battle of 603 is unknown, it was trumpeted by Bede, who left his readers in no doubt of the outcome: Áedán was defeated and the Scots were discouraged from making an enemy of Bernicia. Any hope of imposing Dàl Riatan authority south of the Forth was extinguished for a generation or more. The defeat shattered Áedán's remaining ambitions and forced him to withdraw to his domains in the West. He died there in 608, five years after Degsastan, bequeathing the Kintyre kingship to his son Eochaid Buide. Despite successfully retaining overall sovereignty in Argyll, the new monarch sought no new showdown with Aethelfrith and may have submitted to him as a client. It may also have been during Eochaid's reign that Domangart's descendants separated into the two distinct kindreds of Cenél nGabráin and Cenél Comgaill. The two *cenéla* maintained close links throughout the seventh century, although their relationship was not always amicable.

In the meantime, the effects of Degsastan were profound. The Celtic nations of the North – Scots, Picts and Britons – were compelled to accept the English victor's supremacy. None were capable of toppling Aethelfrith from his dominant position. For the Britons, whose lands lay closest to Bernicia, the outlook after 603 probably seemed especially bleak. With Gododdin already under Aethelfrith's heel and Rheged apparently in decline, the only British kings with any real power were those of Alt Clut. There is, however, no record of any challenge from the Clyde. The king at that time was Rhydderch Hael, upon whom Áedán mac Gabráin had probably made war in the recent past. Rhydderch wisely chose not to pick a fight with the conqueror of his old Gaelic adversary and presumably followed other kings into a submissive relationship with Bernicia. This effectively gave Aethelfrith a free hand to extend his domains at the expense of whichever native elites still remained *in situ* along the Tweed and its tributaries. Bernician noblemen who had fought at Degsastan rightly expected an appropriate reward in the form of lands that they could rule as their own. Aethelfrith duly fulfilled his obligations to these men by expelling aristocratic Britons from rich estates and granting the vacant landholdings to his followers. By this process, the elites of small realms such as Calchfynydd would have been quickly replaced by Bernician counterparts. Whether or not the new masters were of English or hybrid Anglo-British stock was immaterial in a period when ethnic affiliation mattered less than political allegiance. We can assume, nonetheless, that the incoming 'Anglo-Saxon' landlords spoke English as their primary tongue, regardless of their ancestry. The prospect of a Bernician warrior-nobility settling in lands perilously close to their own must have caused concern among the Clyde nobility and in other unconquered native kingdoms. The rulers of these last remaining enclaves of North Britons were right to feel afraid: Áedán's failure in 603 had left them vulnerable to subjugation by an English king whose power they could not hope to defy. As the seventh century progressed, they and their descendants now faced the true legacy of Degsastan: the permanent Anglicisation of the eastern Lowlands.

Bernicia and Deira

Aethelfrith ruled for a further fourteen years after his great triumph over the Scots. During that time he consolidated his hold on the northern English by forcing the Deiran prince Edwin into exile in 604. By annexing Deira he unknowingly laid the foundations of 'Northumbria', a single kingdom unifying all English communities north of the Humber Estuary. Until the late seventh century this was not so much a political aspiration based on a communal identity as an outward reflection of royal ambitions in Bernicia and Deira. Nevertheless, although the name 'Northumbria' seems to have been invented by Bede c.730, it provides modern historians with a useful collective term for all the northern English from the sixth century onwards. Its application to Bernicia and Deira as far back as c.605 is thus a convenient shorthand for Aethelfrith's enlarged domain between Humber and Tweed.

For the first time, then, both 'Northumbrian' kingdoms were united under one king, a situation that inevitably drew Aethelfrith's ambitions beyond his Deiran frontier. Mercia, the land of the midland English, now shared a border with his realm and its kings were his new southern neighbours. A kingdom of the Britons still endured in Elmet, in the South Pennines around modern Leeds, but it may have been subject to Aethelfrith after his annexation of Deira. Further north, Aethelfrith's supremacy remained unchallenged. Rhydderch of Alt Clut died in 612 or 613, but we do not know who succeeded him. It has been suggested that the kingship eventually passed to Neithon, who belonged to a different branch of the Dumbarton royal kindred. The sources say nothing of Neithon's reign and, if he ruled at all, it is possible that he had few ambitions beyond his borders. The Scots were similarly quiet at this time, with Áedán's son Eochaid fully occupied with the task of maintaining his family's superiority in the face of challenges from other kindreds. Later developments hint at an amicable relationship between Kintyre and Bernicia, but this was probably rooted in Eochaid's recognition of Aethelfrith's overlordship. On the eastern side of Druim Alban a number of Pictish groups acknowledged the authority of one or possibly two overkings. In the early 600s, one of these paramount rulers was a certain Nechtan whom some historians equate with his Dumbarton namesake Neithon. It is unnecessary, however, to see these two figures as a single individual ruling Britons and Picts simultaneously. The name Nechtan in its various forms was fairly common in the early medieval period and would have raised few eyebrows when it was borne by two kings who happened to rule different kingdoms at the same time.

In 616, with the northern peoples still subdued, Aethelfrith's expansionism brought him into conflict with the Britons of North Wales. The result was a battle at Chester and another decisive victory on a par with Degsastan. Contrary to a suggestion voiced in the twentieth century, the result of this battle did not drive a wedge between the Welsh and their northern compatriots. The fusion of ethnic and political identities implied by such theorising did not exist in the early seventh century, nor was it ever a feature of relations between the Britons of Wales and those of the North. The Welshmen who fell at Chester in 616 were not fighting to preserve ancestral links with fellow-Britons in Lothian or on the

Clyde. On the contrary, they stood against Aethelfrith of Bernicia because his ambitions clashed with those of their own kings. His victory had few direct consequences for the North, but it sent a clear message to the Welsh and to the southern English. A response from the latter came in the following year when Redwald, king of the East Angles, seized an opportunity to advance his own position. At his court resided the exiled Deiran prince Edwin whose existence continued to gnaw Aethelfrith's pride. In rising wrath the Bernician king sent envoys to Redwald, urging him to surrender Edwin or face annihilation. Redwald rebuffed the repeated threats and began mustering for war. His primary objectives were the defeat of Aethelfrith, the toppling of his dynasty and the installation of Edwin as king of a united Northumbria. Redwald foresaw that a grateful Edwin would then acknowledge him as a patron and liege-lord deserving of homage and tribute. The great showdown between East Angle and Bernician came in the English midlands, at Bawtry, where a major Roman road crossed the River Idle. Aethelfrith was slain, his death liberating the northern Celtic kingdoms from the Bernician yoke. To those same realms his family now fled in fear, seeking protection from a vengeful Edwin. Sanctuary was duly offered by Aethelfrith's former clients. To the Picts came Eanfrith, the eldest son and heir, while the younger children found refuge with Cenél nGabráin at the court of Eochaid Buide. As will be seen later in this chapter, the exile of Aethelfrith's offspring ultimately gave the Gaelic monastery on Iona a major role in the Christianisation of Bernicia.

Edwin quickly secured his position as ruler of a united Northumbria. He gained the support of the Bernician elites and strengthened his authority over them by constructing a palace in their territory. This new focus of royal power was established below *Gefrin* ('The Hill of Goats'), upon the summit of which stood the crumbling ramparts of an old British fort. Today this hill is known as Yeavering Bell, but no trace of Edwin's palace is visible in the fields at its foot. The site has, however, been excavated by archae-ologists and much fascinating data has been unearthed. It was clearly an important centre in the northern part of Edwin's kingdom, serving not only as a royal dwelling but also as a venue for secular and religious ceremonies. Unlike Bamburgh, the rugged coastal stronghold of Aethelfrith's dynasty, the palace of Gefrin was unde- fended by walls or earthworks. If Edwin did not expect it to be attacked by hostile neighbours, he may have been on friendly terms with the local Britons of Lothian and Tweeddale, or their kings may have been his vassals. On the latter point, Bede's claim that the peoples of the Celtic North paid homage to Edwin implies that they were subdued by military force or by the threat of it. It is possible, however, that the claim was a retrospective one, and that Edwin undertook no major campaigns against the northern powers. Indeed, the North Britons, Picts and Scots seem not to have been the main targets of his ambition. His well-documented dealings with the southern English – especially the Mercians and West Saxons – show quite clearly where his political objectives lay. In 633, in the district of Hatfield near the Mercian-Deiran border, his life came to a violent end at the hands of a combined Welsh and Mercian army. His conqueror was Cadwallon, probably a king of Gwynedd, who consolidated the victory by ravaging Northumbria for a whole year. In Bernicia, the nobles now saw an opportunity to reinstate their exiled royal dynasty. They rallied around Eanfrith, Aethelfrith's eldest son, who returned to claim his birthright. Eanfrith had lived among the Picts for many years as a guest of a Pictish overking, probably with the special status of foster-son. There he had received Christian baptism and there, too, he had sired a son called Talorcan on a Pictish princess. Upon hearing the news of Edwin's death, Eanfrith hastened back to his homeland and was immediately proclaimed king of Bernicia. Flushed with pride, he renounced Christianity and embraced instead the paganism of his forefathers. He then sought a face to face meeting with Cadwallon who was still engaged in plundering Northumbria. With his military repu- tation riding high, the Welsh warlord had little incentive to engage in diplomatic discourse with Aethelfrith's heir. His contempt for Northumbrian royalty was duly demonstrated when he ordered Eanfrith to be slain during their discussions.

The assassination of Bernicia's new king was another of those seemingly distant events, the repercussions of which would soon be felt keenly by the northern Celtic realms. Its most profound effect was the elevation of Oswald, the victim's brother, as king of Bernicia. Oswald had spent his own exile among the Scots, learning the art of war from Cenél nGabráin kings and riding with their warbands. His foster-kin were Eochaid Buide, son of Áedán mac Gabráin, and Eochaid's son Domnall Brecc ('Freckled Donald'). With their encouragement, he and his younger siblings received Christian baptism. Eanfrith's death in 634 led Oswald to attempt a second restoration of the Bernician dynasty with support from his Gaelic patrons. By then, Eochaid Buide was dead, but it seems likely that Domnall Brecc lent a contingent of Kintyre warriors to the Bernician cause.

Oswald

After the death of Áedán mac Gabráin in 608, the Scots seem to have stayed within their own borders for a time. No external wars involving their kings are recorded in the sources until the third decade of the seventh century when Áedán's heirs became entangled in Ireland. Links between Argyll and Irish Dál Riata had led Áedán himself along a similar path, but the royal conference at Druim Cett c.590 may have curbed his territorial ambitions. His son, Eochaid Buide, seems to have aligned Cenél nGabráin with the southern Uí Néill against their northern cousins. In 624, Eochaid's son Domnall Brecc fought in Ireland at the battle of Cenn Delgthen where the northern Uí Néill were defeated. The site is unknown, but it probably lay in Meath, perhaps near the present-day village of Kildalkey. It occurred at a time when Cenél nGabráin may have had alliances not only with the southern Uí Néill but also with the northern Dál nAraidi people. The latter sent a warband to Argyll in 626 or 627 to assist Eochaid Buide against dynastic rivals, but its leader was slain by a Pict or a Briton, presumably an ally or hireling in the ranks of Eochaid's foes.

In 628, the Dál nAraidi were defeated in Ireland by the neighbouring Dál Fiatach, but the latter were themselves routed a year later by the Argyll king Connad Cerr. Connad was a member of the Cenél Comgaill kindred and seems to have ruled Cowal and Bute while his kinsman Eochaid Buide held Kintyre. When Eochaid died c.630, the overkingship of Cenél nGabráin and Cenél Comgaill, if not the sovereignty of all Dál Riata, was seized by Connad Cerr. In 631, Connad's reign ended on the unidentified battlefield of Fid Eoin in Ulster, his enemies being a faction of the Dál nAraidi. At his side perished a son and nephew of his predecessor Eochaid together with Osric, a son of Aethelfrith of Bernicia, who commanded a retinue of English warriors under the banner of Cenél nGabráin. Like his brothers, Osric had lived in exile among the Scots and repaid the gift of hospitality by fighting in defence of his foster-kin's Irish interests. In fulfilling this obligation and by paying the ultimate price he surely helped to secure military aid for Oswald's eventual restoration.

When Oswald returned to Bernicia in 634, his retinue included Bernician noblemen who had accompanied him in exile. These veterans now returned to their homeland as a personal bodyguard with, no doubt, a force of Scots to bolster their numbers. Against them stood the fearsome Cadwallon, supported by his many allies. The Welsh king was a formidable adversary who led the largest army of occupation ever seen in northern Britain since Roman times. Beneath his war-banner marched an array of subordinate lords, many of whom were themselves kings, together with their own armed retinues. Among them was an ambitious English king called Penda, a Mercian and a pagan, of whom more will be said later.

Having ravaged Northumbria for a full year, Cadwallon was still there when news of Oswald's return reached him. Alongside Oswald marched his fellow-exiles, their ranks no doubt strengthened by other Bernician noblemen who relished a chance to expel the Welsh king. Contingents of North Britons may have joined the fray on Oswald's side if it suited their interests to do so. They would have felt no obligation to support Cadwallon merely because he was a compatriot: alliances forged along ethnic lines were less common in the seventh century than those created for short-term political gain.

The opposing armies met near Hexham in the shadow of Hadrian's Wall. There, a fierce battle ensued, a mêlée that spilled southward across the River Tyne. Oswald emerged victorious to declare himself king of Bernicia. His triumphant warriors raged across the field, scattering their enemies, before trapping Cadwallon on the banks of the Rowley Burn. Thus was the slayer of Edwin and Eanfrith finally destroyed. The dispirited remnants of his once-mighty army surrendered or fled back to their own lands. In one decisive stroke, the balance of power in the North returned to Bamburgh. Oswald now found himself in a dominant position, having proved his worth as a war-leader by vanquishing a mighty king. The English elites of Bernicia and Deira duly acknowledged him as paramount sovereign of all Northumbria.

To consolidate his authority, Oswald had to deal with potential enemies outside the Bernician heartlands. In the North, his nearest neighbours were the surviving British kingdoms of what is now southern Scotland. With the exception of Alt Clut, little is known of the fate of these realms after the end of the sixth century, other than the likelihood that most of them had been subjugated by Aethelfrith. The latter's death had freed them from homage to Bamburgh and they may have remained independent until Oswald's reign. Although Bernicia's rapid expansion had reduced their territories, the remaining native realms seem to have suffered no major aggression by Edwin. The latter's death in 633 heralded a year of uncertainty in which Cadwallon's occupation of Northumbria meant that the native kings now saw a Briton rather than a Bernician prowling along their borders. Cadwallon's presence was hardly reassuring to the North British kings. He probably regarded them not as natural allies but as potential competitors in the dismemberment of English territory. Long after his demise, a Welsh poem portrayed him as the avenger of Catraeth, the battlefield where the men of Gododdin had fallen. This surely reflected the bardic rhetoric of Wales rather than Cadwallon's own view of himself. Instead of bringing the North Britons into an ethnic alliance as brothers-in-arms he is more likely to have approached each king individually, securing neutrality or co-operation with a mixture of incentives and threats. In the case of Gododdin he seems to have failed, for Oswald and his henchmen may have marched through Lothian on their return from exile in 634. If this was indeed the Bernician prince's homeward route, then the Votadinian elite in their citadel at Edinburgh presumably allowed him to pass unhindered. Such acquiescence would have been given either because Gododdin was too weak to confront Oswald and his powerful Cenél nGabráin allies or because Cadwallon was viewed by the lords of Din Eidyn as a greater menace.

After destroying the invaders, Oswald turned his attention to the Britons of the North, dealing with them in a manner which was far from conciliatory. According to Bede, a series of military campaigns regained much of Aethelfrith's former hegemony. Not all of Oswald's policies towards the Britons involved such raw aggression. In the case of Rheged, for instance, he may have adopted a less hostile stance, using a dynastic marriage to secure the support of Urien's descendants. At that time, Rheged's king was Urien's grandson Royth, son of Rhun, who had a daughter called Rieinmellth. She became the bride of Oswiu, younger brother of Oswald, perhaps to seal a political accord between Bernicia and Rheged. This need not imply that the two kingdoms were on friendly terms. Their relationship may have been unequal, involving an oath of homage by Royth as the price of immunity from Bernician aggression. Contrary to a view held by some modern historians, the marriage is unlikely to have delivered Rheged into English hands as a marriage dowry. As far as we can tell, such an occurrence would have been unprecedented in the British Isles at this time. Oswald's dealings with other North British kingdoms are largely unknown. There is no record of his relationship with the kings of Alt Clut but they may have acknowledged him as their overlord after his destruction of Cadwallon. A similar strategy may have been directed at Gododdin but, if so, the Votadinian response was seemingly deemed inadequate. It is generally believed that Oswald, within six years of his return from exile, launched an attack deep into Lothian. In the Irish annals an entry for 638 notes the siege of *Etin*, generally assumed to be Din Eidyn on Edinburgh's Castle Rock. The date may be awry and should probably be corrected to 640. If the place-name identification is correct, the event represented a military catastrophe for the Votadini and a devastating strike at the heart of their domain. It would have dealt a mortal blow to any lingering hope of maintaining British independence in Lothian. Even if Etin and Eidyn are not one and the same, the kingdom of Gododdin undoubtedly lay on the brink of extinction during Oswald's reign. Its royal dynasty was eventually dispossessed and its territory became a Bernician province. By the middle of the seventh century, and for the next four hundred years, the southern shore of the Firth of Firth lay firmly in English hands.

CHAPTER 6

The Struggle for Power

The Fall of Domnall Brecc

By 640, the North British kingdoms had been reduced to a rump comprising Rheged, Alt Clut and a handful of realms in Ayrshire and Galloway whose names we do not know. Most, if not all, were under Oswald's dominance, and none was capable of refusing his overlordship. They had little choice but to bide their time, waiting for a suitable opportunity to offload the burden of vassalage. This came in August 642 when a decisive battle in the English midlands brought Oswald's death at the hands of Cadwallon's former ally Penda of Mercia. The disaster shattered the Bernician hegemony and divided Northumbria into two constituent kingdoms. In Deira, Edwin's kinsman Oswine claimed the throne, while in Bernicia the crown passed to Oswald's younger brother Oswiu. With little hope of flexing their ambitions in Penda's shadow, both Northumbrian kings were obliged to stay within their own borders. In Oswiu's case this meant postponing a restoration of Bernician supremacy over his Celtic neighbours. He had to watch from the sidelines while other northern powers picked over the bones of his brother's hegemony. New rivalries soon emerged in the borderlands of the Forth–Clyde isthmus, reaching a climax in December 643 at Strathcarron near present-day Falkirk. On one side stood the Scots of Cenél nGabráin under their king Domnall Brecc, a frustrated warlord hoping to end an unlucky run of military defeats. On the other stood an army of Britons led by Owain, son of Bili, the king of Alt Clut.

Kingdoms and kindreds, sixth to eighth centuries AD

Ever since succeeding Connad Cerr in 629, nearly all of Domnall's political manoeuvrings had been thwarted. Despite leading the most powerful kindred in Argyll, he struggled to maintain his position and faced stiff competition from Connad's heirs in Cowal. Although frequently regarded as an overking of Dál Riata, like his renowned grandfather Áedán, Domnall's authority may not have extended very far beyond Kintyre. There is no reason to assume, for instance, that he was accepted as overlord by other *cenéla*, some of whom may have been strong enough to reject him by force of arms. Cenél Loairn defeated him in the district of Calathros, within their own territory, and other groups perhaps resisted him in similar fashion. His ill-judged meddling in Ireland was likewise unsuccessful, ending disastrously in an encounter with the northern Uí Néill on the plain of Moira in 639. Bad fortune continued to follow him when he decided to direct his ambitions eastward across Druim Alban. In 640, at a time when his foster-brother Oswald was menacing the Gododdin Britons, Domnall lost a battle against unknown foes at *Glind Mairison*, an unidentified Highland glen. Three years later, with his military reputation in tatters, he saw an opportunity to reverse the trend when a power-vacuum appeared in the wake of Oswald's death. Gathering his forces, Domnall set out from Kintyre in the final weeks of 643, marching east along the line of the River Forth from its headwaters among the mountains. Along this route he summoned to his banner the few loyal chieftains who still regarded him as their sovereign lord.

Awaiting him on the banks of the River Carron stood the Clyde Britons under their king Owain ap Bili. Like his Cenél nGabráin adversary, Owain hoped to profit from Oswald's recent demise. In the ensuing battle the question of overall supremacy in the North was decisively resolved when the Britons defeated and killed the luckless Domnall. Whatever remained of his family's authority east of Druim Alban evaporated. Landowning noblemen along the corridor of the Forth Valley who had formerly answered to Kintyre-based overkings now switched their homage to Owain, whose victory made him the most powerful figure in northern Britain.

The repercussions of the battle of Strathcarron were felt far and wide. In Argyll, the Scots of Kintyre mourned Domnall's passing, but those of Lorn and elsewhere knew that the power of Cenél nGabráin was diminished. Meanwhile, in distant Bamburgh, tidings of the battle reached the ears of Oswiu and would have done little to lighten his mood. With his Gaelic friends and foster-kin now languishing in defeat, and with a Briton of Dumbarton wielding supremacy over the North, the Bernician king knew that he had little hope of advancing his own position. His most immediate problem lay with Penda, his brother's nemesis, whose power over the southern English kingdoms mirrored Owain's newly forged northern hegemony. Releasing himself from the Mercian king's stranglehold became Oswiu's key objective in the years that followed.

Northumbrian Ascendancy

Owain of Alt Clut remained, for a time, the most powerful player on the northern political stage. Fearing no challenge from Bernicia or Dál Riata, he was able to strengthen his position in the region between Clyde and Solway, even as Penda was carving a similar hegemony much further south. With a cowed Bernicia nestling in the middle, these two overlords set about unravelling many of Oswald's territorial gains and laying them under tribute. In Owain's case, this meant seizing control of English-held estates on the western fringe of Lothian, either by ousting incumbent lords or by taking a tribute of cattle. Key beneficiaries of any redistribution of land would have been his own Clydeside henchmen rather than remnants of the old Gododdin aristocracy. The nature of his relationship with Penda is unknown, but some mutual agreement was no doubt forged at the interface of their respective hegemonies. There is no hint that Alt Clut was subservient to Mercia at this time. Penda's clients and subordinates included several British kings, but these are more likely to have been Welshmen rather than northerners and there is no particular reason to place Owain ap Bili among them.

Although somewhat constrained by Penda's supremacy, Oswiu of Bernicia quietly nurtured his own ambitions and began to strengthen his position. By the end of 643, his British wife, Rieinmellth of Rheged, was no longer his queen. She either died an untimely death or was pushed aside for personal or political reasons. Oswiu took a new wife, a teenage English princess called Eanflaed. She was a daughter of Edwin of Deira, a parentage undoubtedly seen as advantageous by Oswiu and his counsellors. Eanflaed's subsequent bearing of male children posed a serious threat to her husband's older offspring by Rieinmellth, especially to the latter's son Alchfrith whose succession to the Bernician kingship was no longer guaranteed. In the meantime, Oswiu issued a challenge to King Oswine of Deira who hesitated to give battle against a resurgent Bernicia. Oswine was subsequently captured and murdered by Oswiu, who declared himself the new sovereign of all Northumbria. At around the same time, Alchfrith married Cyneburh, Penda's daughter, a union perhaps ordered or sanctioned by the Mercian king. Alchfrith himself was instrumental in arranging the marriage of his sister Alchflaed to Penda's eldest son, no doubt with strategic political alliances in mind. His ambition would soon set him on a collision course with his father.

The main focus of Penda's Northumbrian policy was no doubt directed at stifling any attempt by Oswiu to gain influence in the southern English kingdoms. He frequently led his warriors on plundering forays in Bernicia, effectively depriving Oswiu of the resources necessary for mounting a serious military expedition across the Deiran-Mercian frontier. These destructive raids eventually forced Oswiu to seek respite by offering a huge tribute-payment which, according to Welsh tradition, was accepted by Penda and distributed among his British allies. The distribution is said to have taken place at *urbs Iudeu* ('The City of Iudeu'). A different account was given by Bede who reported that Oswiu's offer was summarily rejected. Historians are uncertain as to which account is closer to the truth. The city of Iudeu is usually identified as Stirling, which Bede called *urbs Giudi*, but such a northerly site seems to lie outside the range of Penda's territorial interests. A location in southern Northumbria would fit the circumstances rather better and it is indeed possible that the Iudeu referred to here lay in Deira. It might even have been the mysterious *Iudanburg*, a royal site mentioned in later English tradition as a place where a tenth-century Northumbrian bishop was imprisoned by his West Saxon overlord. Whatever the outcome of Oswiu's offer, he swiftly set aside his policy of appeasement. Hostilities with Penda erupted and the two sides met in battle at the unidentified River Winwaed, somewhere near modern Leeds, in November 655. Against all odds the seemingly invincible Mercian king was killed and his extensive hegemony collapsed around him. At the Northumbrian court, Alchfrith's insecurity may have been alleviated when Oswiu appointed him as sub-king of Deira in the aftermath of Winwaed. Nevertheless, the relationship between father and son deteriorated in the following decade and eventually broke down, its collapse being marked by a revolt which resulted in Alchfrith's exile or execution. In the meantime, with the menace of Penda removed, Oswiu was at last able to emulate his brother's achievements by becoming an overlord in his own right. After imposing his authority on the beaten Mercians and securing the homage of Penda's erstwhile allies, he turned his gaze upon the northern Celtic kingdoms.

Even before Winwaed, the balance of power in the North had already started to shift. Owain, the victor of Strathcarron, died c.650 and an obscure figure called Guriat became king at Dumbarton, perhaps seizing power by force during a period of doubt. In the aftermath of Owain's death, the Clyde Britons seem to have lost their dominant position and other groups stepped forward to grasp the initiative. Among the Scots, the Cenél nGabráin kindred rekindled its ambition to rule all of Dál Riata. Led by Conall Crandomna, a brother of Domnall Brecc, it became once again the strongest power in Argyll and proceeded to flex its military muscle. Cenél nGabráin forces attacked Skye in 649, seeking to despoil or subjugate a possibly indigenous, probably Gaelic-speaking kindred called Cenél nGartnait who may have been of Pictish origin. This marked the beginning of a conflict that continued intermittently for the next fifty years before passing into a haze of legend and folklore. It did not involve the Picts of the eastern Highlands, although they, too, clashed swords with Cenél nGabráin in the middle years of the seventh century. The Pictish king Talorcan, a son of Eanfrith of Bernicia, defeated an army of Scots in the valley of Strathyre in 654 and slew there a cousin of Conall Crandomna. Talorcan's presence in a battle on what must have been his eastern border implies territorial ambitions towards Argyll, although these need not have been prompted or encouraged by his English uncle's rise to prominence after the death of Penda. The sources give no hint that Oswiu sponsored or supported his half-Pictish nephew, nor do they imply the existence of friendship between them. If Oswiu had amicable links with any of his Celtic peers, the likeliest was Talorcan's enemy Conall Crandomna, a son of the king who had willingly fostered the exiled children of Aethelfrith. Perhaps a more likely scenario is that Oswiu demanded homage from every northern power in the wake of his great victory at Winwaed in 655. This is what Bede wanted his readers to believe when he said of Oswiu that he 'overwhelmed and made tributary even the tribes of the Picts and Scots who inhabit the northern parts of Britain'. Thus Talorcan, notwithstanding his English ancestry, and also Conall Crandomna, despite his family's hospitality towards the exiled Bernician princes, may have been obliged to accept Oswiu as overlord.

Within three years of his victory over the Scots, Talorcan was dead. The next couple of years saw the passing of both Guriat of Alt Clut and Conall Crandomna. At Dumbarton Rock, the new king of the Clyde Britons probably became a tribute-paying vassal of Bernicia. In Argyll, the kingship of Cenél nGabráin passed to Domangart, a son of Domnall Brecc, but he issued no challenge to Oswiu. While the latter remained alive, the northern Celtic realms could do little except wait for another shift in the balance of power. This seemed to arrive in 670, when Oswiu died peacefully in his bed, but the wind of change ushered in by his death was no breeze of good fortune for the client kings under his heel. He was succeeded by Ecgfrith, perhaps his eldest surviving legitimate son, a man who had no intention of letting the hard-won Bernician supremacy slip away.

The Rise of the Picts

Ecgfrith inherited from his father not only the kingship of Bernicia but that of Deira too. With the resources of a unified Northumbria at his disposal, he had the capability to maintain the extensive hegemony established by Oswiu. His chief trouble in the early part of his reign came from Mercia where Penda's sons were eager to shake off the dominion imposed upon their lands in 655. In the North, the Scots and Britons accepted Ecgfrith as overlord, recognising him as a worthy heir of mighty forebears. Their regular tribute payments to the Bernician royal coffers continued, renewed by oaths of submission to the new sovereign. In return, they received assurances that he would not plunder their lands. When he demanded the same homage from the Picts, he found them rather less compliant and sent an army to remind them of their obligations. At that time, the southern Pictish region of Fife probably lay under English control. It may have been conquered by Oswiu sometime after 655, becoming thereafter a Bernician province. Beyond its northern border, in the fertile river valleys of Earn and Tay, lay the heartlands of the Picts: Strathearn, Strathmore, Atholl and Moray. Around the time of Ecgfrith's punitive raid, the Picts in one of these regions expelled Drust, an overking, and installed in his place an ambitious prince called Brude, son of Bili. The new monarch was a half-Pict whose father had ruled the Clyde Britons and whose half-brother Owain had destroyed Domnall Brecc at Strathcarron in 643. Brude's ambitions may have included a determination to hurl the English settlers and tribute gatherers back across the Forth. If so, he had first to establish himself as a viable challenger to Ecgfrith by carving out a martial reputation of his own.

After gaining the overkingship in 672, Brude spent the next ten years imposing his authority on outlying districts. Rivals and rebels were besieged in their centres of power and forced to submit. Frontier lords were brought to heel by punitive raids on their strongholds at places such as Dunnottar on the Aberdeenshire coast, Dundurn on the western land-route to Argyll and perhaps Dunbeath in the northern province of Caithness. Nor were the offshore territories immune from Brude's consolidation of a wide hegemony: the Picts of Orkney were attacked in 682, their kings thereafter acknowledging him as liege-lord.

There is no record of conflict between Brude and the Scots or Britons, both of whom were more than distracted by troubles of their own. Strife had broken out in Dál Riata after the slaying of Domangart, son of Domnall Brecc, in 673. Domangart's death came at a time when his family's hold on the regional overkingship was under threat from ambitious challengers in Lorn. A vigorous king called Ferchar Fota ('the Tall') had emerged among Cenél Loairn to compete with Cenél nGabráin rivals. Whatever remained of the latter's grip on the overkingship was tenuously retained by Maelduin, a son of Conall Crandomna. Neither Maelduin nor Ferchar Fota mounted a revolt against Ecgfrith's northern supremacy, nor did either king seek a showdown with the Picts. In 678, Ferchar found himself in conflict with the Clyde Britons and suffered a heavy defeat, but the sources attribute no further warfare to him and none at all to Maelduin. The Scots were perhaps so preoccupied by internal strife that they posed little or no threat to their neighbours. Cenél nGabráin was in any case unlikely to stir against Ecgfrith because of its longstanding friendship with his family, while Cenél Loairn lacked the military resources to mount an effective challenge. The initiative lay rather with the Pictish overking Brude, whose power had grown considerably during these years. By c.684, the northern political arena was set for another mighty clash of ambitions.

The countdown to war began with a seemingly unrelated conflict on a distant southern battlefield. In 679, beside the River Trent in north-east Mercia, Ecgfrith led his forces against Aethelred, a son of Penda. The result was inconclusive, but tensions remained high and a further outbreak of hostilities looked inevitable. Among the casualties in the battle was Ecgfrith's young brother Aelfwine, the last recorded king of Deira, whose death placed a burden of vengeance on Ecgfrith. With grievances on both sides threatening to erupt into bloody feud, the archbishop of Canterbury intervened to broker an uneasy peace. Despite ecclesiastical mediation, it is unlikely that the protagonists regarded the truce as anything more than a pause allowing them to regroup their forces. In the meantime, Ecgfrith vented his belligerence and frustration on other targets. Five years after the Battle of the Trent he ordered a trusted lieutenant, an ealdorman called Berht, to launch a raid on Ireland. The reason behind this campaign is unclear. With neither Bede nor the Irish annals offering an explanation, modern historians are left to muse on various possibilities. One theory imagines Irish kings secretly planning a *coup d'état* to replace Ecgfrith with his half-brother Aldfrith. The latter claimed to be Oswiu's son by an Irish princess and had spent his childhood in Ireland before becoming a monk. Perhaps Ecgfrith sought to discourage Irish support for Aldfrith's claim on the Northumbrian throne, if indeed the pious cleric nurtured any such ambition. Alternatively, Berht's raid may have been prompted by an unrecorded disagreement between Ecgfrith and an Irish king. Whatever the motive for the assault, its repercussions were extremely damaging for Ecgfrith. His reputation at home and abroad suffered a major blow. Reports of English warriors plundering Irish churches and committing atrocities caused widespread revulsion, even in Northumbria itself. Bede, who was about eleven years old at the time, would have heard tidings of the raid. Many years later, he presented it to his readers as a deeply shameful incident, a dark stain on Ecgfrith's character. Meanwhile, in the Celtic lands of the North and West, disapproval and dismay soon gave way to a demand for retribution.

Events drew towards a climax in the following year. The first few months of 685 saw Ecgfrith making plans for a new military campaign against the Picts, who had probably defaulted on tribute payments. By mid-April he was ready to march north to deal with these recalcitrant vassals, putting aside his desire for renewed hostilities with Mercia. Penda's sons were still his arch-foes, but the Pictish situation now posed an imminent threat and could no longer be ignored. On 23 April 685, he celebrated Easter Sunday at the newly built monastery of Jarrow, where a contemporary inscription marking the event still bears his name. Within a few days he began the long northward march, leading his army through Bernicia and Lothian to the Forth borderlands and the Pictish frontier. Crossing the rivers Earn and Tay, he advanced into the heart of Brude's kingdom, striking north-east along the fertile vale of Strathmore. On 20 May, he engaged the Picts in battle near Dunnichen Hill, a site four miles east of Forfar. Heavily outnumbered and caught between high ground and swamp, the Northumbrians were cut to pieces and their mighty king was slain. Such was the completeness of the Pictish victory that Bede regarded it as a major turning point in the fortunes of his people. 'From that time,' he wrote mournfully, 'the hopes and strength of the English kingdom began to ebb and fall away.'

The battle of Dunnichen released the Picts from three decades of Northumbrian dominance. It likewise freed the Scots and North Britons from the burden of homage to an English overlord, but left them at the mercy of Ecgfrith's Pictish conqueror. Supremacy in the North was now held by Brude, Bili's son, and he showed little hesitation in wielding it. Quickly following up his victory, he led his army across the Tay to liberate Fife by expelling its English settlers. The great northern hegemony forged by Oswiu and maintained by his son now shrank back across the Firth of Forth to the old Gododdin lands around Edinburgh. Ecgfrith had died childless without an obvious heir and the vacant Northumbrian kingship passed to Aldfrith, his scholarly half-brother, who relinquished a monastic career in Ireland to take the reins of secular power. There can be little doubt that Aldfrith's elevation to the throne was approved or facilitated by Brude. It may have been additionally supported by interested parties in the Gaelic West, such as the southern Uí Néill – whose lands had been ravaged by Ecgfrith's soldiers in 684 – and the religious community on Iona who counted Aldfrith among their brethren.

Brude reigned a further nine years after Dunnichen, dying

peacefully in 694 and receiving burial on Iona. He was the last of the great warlords of the seventh century and is widely regarded as one of the prime movers in Scotland's early history. The modern fame surrounding his triumph in 685 makes him the best-known of all Pictish kings. His achievement was matched only by one other of his countrymen, another ambitious individual whose exploits are described later in this chapter. In the meantime, Brude's overkingship seems to have passed to Tarain, who was perhaps his nephew. Tarain's reign turned out to be brief: he was deposed in 697 and sought exile in Ireland two years later. The faction that ousted him installed as his successor another Brude, the son of a man or woman called Derile. Whether Tarain and the two Brudes originated from a southern Pictish kingdom in Perthshire or from a northern one in Atholl or Moray is unknown. A northern and a southern overkingship probably existed simultaneously and both were arguably under the sway of the elder Brude after his great victory at Dunnichen. A reference in the annals to his raid on Orkney in 682 might even suggest that his original power-base lay north of the Mounth. The activities of his younger namesake, Derile's son, seem rather to have been directed southward, perhaps from a core domain in Atholl or Angus. The younger Brude's reign coincided with a period of dynastic strife that would reach a bitter climax in the following century. In the meantime, he rekindled the old feud with Northumbria by defeating her forces in 698. The English commander in this battle, named in the sources as Berhtred, was among the high-profile casualties. It is possible that he was the ealdorman 'Berht' who had led the notorious raid on Ireland fourteen years earlier.

Kin-strife in Dál Riata

Meanwhile, in Argyll, Ferchar Fota of Cenél Loairn pursued his ambition to wrest the overkingship of Dál Riata from Cenél nGabráin hands. In 695, he defeated Maelduin's brother Domnall Donn ('Brown Donald') to briefly seize the paramount sover-

Eildon Hill North, Tweeddale: an ancient stronghold of the Selgovae.
Photograph: Barbara Keeling

The Broch of Mousa, Shetland. © Historic Scotland. Licensor www.scran.ac.uk

Early Christianity in Galloway: the memorial to Florentius at Kirkmadrine. Photograph: Barbara Keeling

Early Christianity in Galloway: the memorial to the *sacerdotes* at Kirkmadrine. Photograph: Barbara Keeling

Pictish symbol stone from Dingwall, Easter Ross (from Allen & Anderson 1903).

Alt Clut: Dumbarton Rock, royal fortress of the Clyde Britons.
Photograph: Barbara Keeling

Iona Abbey. © British Geological Survey/NERC. All rights reserved.

The Rock of Dunaverty at the southern end of Kintyre. Photograph: Barbara Keeling

Above. Urbs Giudi: Stirling Castle Rock. Photograph: Barbara Keeling

Right. Pictish symbol stone from Tullich, near Ballater, Aberdeenshire (from Allen & Anderson 1903).

Above. Strathyre, near Lochearnhead, site of a Pictish victory over the Scots in 654.
Photograph: Barbara Keeling

Left. Reverse of the Pictish cross-slab in Aberlemno kirkyard.
Photograph: Barbara Keeling

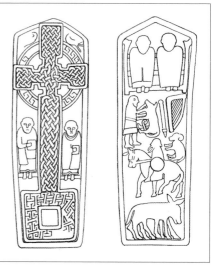

Pictish symbols on the reverse of a cross-slab from Rosemarkie, Easter Ross (from Allen & Anderson 1903).

Pictish cross-slab from Aldbar Castle, Angus (from Allen & Anderson 1903).

Kirk Hill, St Abbs Head, site of a Northumbrian monastery founded by St Aebbe. Photograph: Barbara Keeling

The Dupplin Cross, a Pictish royal monument of the early ninth century. © Royal Commission on the Ancient and Historical Monuments of Scotland. Licensor www.scran.ac.uk

The St Andrews Sarcophagus: an elaborate Pictish shrine or tomb of c.800.
Photograph: Barbara Keeling

The Moot Hill, Scone, an important ceremonial venue in the tenth and later centuries.
© Crown Copyright reproduced courtesy of Historic Scotland.
Licensor www.scran.ac.uk

eignty before perishing himself within a couple of years. Cenél nGabráin regained its former status after Ferchar's death, but his son Ainfcellach launched a new claim on the sovereignty. Ainfcellach was initially successful, but ruled as overking for less than a year before being ousted by Lorn-based enemies. These probably sprang from Cenél Cathbach, a royal kindred who appear in the sources as the main rivals of Cenél Loairn in the district around modern Oban. The leaders of Cenél Cathbach apparently seized the great fortress of Lorn at Dunollie, holding it until 701 when they were ejected by Selbach, another son of Ferchar Fota. At the same time a new conflict broke out on Skye, probably a resumption of the earlier strife between Cenél nGabráin and Cenél nGartnait. A Skye leader called Cano, son of Gartnait, had been slain in 687, but the long-running feud continued to claim lives into the next century. Cano's son Conamail was slain in 705 and an otherwise unknown Óengus lost his life on Skye five years later. After the killing of Óengus, the sources make no further mention of the struggle, their silence perhaps suggesting that it was over. The final outcome is unknown but, given the resources available to the lords of Cenél nGabráin, it is likely that Cano's heirs fell under the sway of Kintyre-based kings.

Cenél nGabráin's military ventures at this time were not confined to the Hebridean seaways. In 704, this ever-ambitious kindred sent an army down the west side of Loch Lomond to harass the borderlands of Alt Clut. Their reward was a bloody slaughter at the hands of the Britons who, despite dwelling in the shadow of Northumbria, were still capable of defending their lands. Two further encounters, in 711 and 717, resulted in defeats for the Clydemen, but produced no long-lasting effect beyond a clear signal that the ancient dynasty on Dumbarton Rock was unwilling to submit to a new overlord. Indeed, subsequent events around the middle years of the century would soon reaffirm Alt Clut's status as a major northern power.

The rivalry between Cenél nGabráin and Cenél Loairn escalated dramatically in 712 when Selbach of Lorn led an army into the northern districts of Kintyre to attack the fortress of Tarbert. This strategic stronghold lay on the narrow isthmus between Loch Fyne and the Atlantic seaways, guarding the overland portage-route which allowed light vessels to traverse the Kintyre peninsula. In a vivid display of destructive power it was burned by Selbach's warriors. A few months later, the war-fleet of Cenél Loairn sailed around the Mull of Kintyre to besiege Dunaverty, an important Cenél nGabráin citadel. In 714, Selbach rebuilt the Lorn fortress of Dunollie, presumably repairing damage inflicted during his family's contest with Cenél Cathbach at the beginning of the century. He no doubt added improvements and adornments befitting his new status as the paramount king of Dál Riata. Within five years he received a challenge from his own kin when his brother Ainfcellach raised an army against him. The two siblings met in battle at Finglen near Loch Avich in September 719. There Ainfcellach was killed and Selbach emerged victorious with his position at home considerably strengthened. Barely three weeks passed, however, before he again had to take up arms. This time the enemy was a seaborne force from Kintyre under the command of Donnchad Bec, king of Cenél nGabráin. Selbach sailed forth at the head of his own fleet to engage Donnchad in battle, the first recorded naval encounter in the history of the British Isles. The two sides fought in the choppy waters off an unidentified promontory called *Ardae Nesbi*, most likely one of the many headlands jutting into the Sound of Jura between mainland Argyll and the inner isles. Wherever the mêlée took place, it resulted in a defeat for Cenél Loairn and was a major setback to Selbach's ambitions. For a while he chose retirement from the stress of kingship, withdrawing from the secular world to become a monk. Before entering monastic life he passed the mantle of power to his son Dungal, a man whose misguided ventures would soon plunge Dál Riata into catastrophe.

Some sources imply that Dungal received not only the kingship of Lorn but also the overkingship of Dál Riata. This seems an unlikely scenario in the wake of his father's defeat at Ardae Nesbi, but the shifting fortunes of those times mean that it cannot be ruled out. What does seem certain is that the strife between the Lorn and Kintyre kindreds continued after Selbach's retirement. In 726,

Dungal suffered a heavy defeat at the hands of Eochaid, the new king of Cenél nGabráin and a great-grandson of Domnall Brecc. Eochaid then claimed the regional overkingship and defended it in the following year at *Rosfoichne*, presumably a sea-cape or promontory like *Ardae Nesbi*. His opponent was Selbach who, having chosen to return to the maelstrom of secular affairs, now took up the reins of war-leadership in an attempt to recover the initiative for Cenél Loairn. The outcome of the battle is unknown, but it marked the penultimate mention of Selbach in the annals, his final appearance being an entry noting his death in 730.

Dungal refused to give up the struggle and led an army into Kintyre within a year of his father's passing. Imitating Selbach's earlier campaign he attacked and burned the fortress at Tarbert, no doubt as a gesture of defiance against Eochaid. It was around this time, however, that a new bout of internecine fighting broke out in Lorn among Ferchar Fota's descendants. A challenge to Dungal's kingship was mounted by his cousin Muiredach whose father Ainfcellach had been slain by Selbach's forces at Finglen in 719. Muiredach made his move while Dungal was away on a military campaign along the Irish coast, the main thrust of which seems to have been a series of raids on isolated settlements. It was during one of these, a cowardly assault on the monastery of Tory Island, that Dungal's men found a young Pict called Brude dwelling among the monks. He was quickly identified as a prince of royal blood, his father being the Pictish overking Óengus son of Fergus, but his high status gave him no immunity and he was dragged out of the monastery in chains. Dungal took him back to Argyll as a trophy, perhaps in the hope of parading a high-status captive to enhance his own reputation among the Lorn elite or to score points against his cousin. Muiredach nevertheless held on to the Cenél Loairn kingship, leaving Dungal with few options. Unfortunately for Brude, the rivalry between these ambitious cousins did nothing to ease his plight and he remained Dungal's prisoner. By then, however, news of his abduction had reached his father's court in the East. The tidings set in motion a chain of events that would eventually bring a full-scale Pictish invasion of Argyll.

The Pictish Ascendancy

Brude's father Óengus was the most powerful Pictish king of the eighth century. He had fought his way to power by vanquishing a series of rivals in a long and bloody contest. Like the struggle for sovereignty in Dál Riata, the Pictish rivalry involved a small group of ambitious individuals and was fought at roughly the same time. At stake was the paramount kingship of a substantial territory encompassing lands north and south of the Mounth. The contest began with the death of Brude, son of Derile, in 706 and the succession of his brother Nechtan. This sidelined other claimants but spawned resentment towards Nechtan and his surviving brother Cináed. Rivalry simmered among the various royal factions, but no formal challenge was issued to Nechtan for several years. He was a strong king whose position was fairly secure in the early part of his reign. His rivals bided their time before moving against him in 713, two years after a serious defeat at the hands of Northumbrian forces on the plain of Manau weakened his reputation. A *coup d'état* was attempted, its aim being to replace Nechtan with one of his kinsmen, a man called Talorcan son of Drostan. Hostilities erupted and the ensuing battle claimed the life of Nechtan's brother Cináed but was otherwise indecisive. Nechtan eventually managed to defeat and capture Talorcan but the seeds of discontent had been sown and would soon yield a bitter harvest.

After holding the overkingship for eighteen years, Nechtan retired from secular life to join a monastic community. It is not known whether this was a voluntary act or the result of coercion by rivals. Becoming a monk was certainly in keeping with his reputation as a scholar and religious zealot, a facet of his character examined in the next chapter, and he was not the first warrior-king to relinquish his crown by personal choice. Nor was he the first to enter holy orders: Selbach, king of Cenél Loairn, had already followed the same path. Like Selbach, Nechtan was ultimately destined to return to the cut and thrust of secular politics. In the meantime, however, the overkingship passed to Drust, an obscure figure who evidently harboured no great fondness for his predecessor. At Drust's command, Nechtan was hauled out of his monastic refuge and imprisoned, for reasons not explained in the sources. This vengeful deed precipitated a move against Drust by rivals who promptly deposed him in favour of their own candidate Alpín. Within a couple of years Alpín also faced troubles and had to defend his position against another competitor, a ruthless and energetic prince called Óengus, son of Fergus, whom he fought in 728. This event marks the first appearance of Óengus in the sources and heralds the beginning of his illustrious career. Little is known of him before his encounter with Alpín. His power-base may have lain north of the Mounth, in the region called Fortriu, but his ambition drew him southward in the 720s. If matrilineal succession was the key to eligibility, he may have owed part of his claim to his mother who can perhaps be envisaged as the daughter or sister of a previous overking. It is possible that her brothers – the maternal uncles of Óengus – were Brude and Nechtan, the sons of Derile.

When Óengus fought Alpín in 728, their conflict was played out in southern Perthshire, in the shadow of Moncrieffe Hill upon whose summit lay the ruins of an Iron Age fortress. The clash brought victory to Óengus and death to a son of Alpín. Having survived the defeat, Alpín refused to give homage to the victor and quickly regrouped his forces. At this point Nechtan returned to the political fray, having escaped from Drust. He promptly sought a showdown with Alpín. The ensuing battle occurred in the vicinity of *Caislen Credi*, an unidentified fortress, and brought victory to Nechtan. In the aftermath, Alpín was forced to endure a humiliating surrender which ended his ambitions: the lands under his lordship, together with the remnant of his army, were placed in Nechtan's hands. With Alpín no longer a contender, the struggle for power was played out by Nechtan, Drust and Óengus. All three may have been rivals, or Nechtan and Óengus may have acted in unison against Drust. What happened next is unclear, but it may be that Nechtan claimed the overkingship for himself. The annals mention what appears to be a battle between him and Óengus in the shadow of 'Mount Carno', an unidentifiable hill, where Nechtan's army was utterly routed. Among the casualties were Nechtan's *exactatores*, perhaps 'tax gatherers' sent by him to demand a tribute payment from Óengus. A wholly different interpretation translates *exactatores* as Nechtan's 'oppressors' and sees them not as men in his service at Mount Carno but as foes whom Óengus vanquished on his behalf. Drust was finally slain in a battle against Óengus at *Druimm-Derg-Blathuug* ('The Red Ridge of Blathuug'), in August 729. Of Nechtan nothing more is heard until his death in 732. Whether he spent his final years in a power-sharing relationship with Óengus, or in monastic retirement, the sources do not tell. In any case, it seems beyond doubt that a very substantial Pictish overkingship eventually passed solely to Óengus.

Within two years of his triumph, Óengus came into conflict with Dál Riata when his son Brude defeated a force of Scots under the command of a man bearing the Pictish name Talorc. The latter's father, Congus, seems to have been a member of the Cenél nGartnait kindred of Skye, formerly the enemies of Cenél nGabráin but now perhaps their vassals. The circumstances behind Talorc's skirmish with Brude are impossible to discern and might have involved nothing more than a cattle raid or border dispute. In the aftermath, Talorc fled the battle-field and returned to his own lands. Brude also went home but was soon venturing westward again, this time much further afield and without an army at his back. His destination was the Irish monastery on Tory Island off the coast of Donegal, where he dwelt for a time among the holy brethren. It was while residing in this place of peace and sanctity that he was captured in a raid led by Dungal of Cenél Loairn.

Brude's abduction was an affront to Óengus and demanded an appropriate response. Having risen to power through a series of bloody conflicts, the Pictish overking was not afraid of tackling the Scots. Muiredach, the king of Cenél Loairn, awaited the inevitable onslaught. When the Picts invaded in 734, their principal target was Muiredach's kingdom, but other parts of Argyll were also at risk of being drawn into the conflict. In Kintyre, the same Talorc who had been defeated three years earlier by Brude, son of Óengus, tried to curry favour with the invaders by offering his own brother as a high-status hostage. The gift was accepted by Óengus who ordered the unfortunate captive to be ritually drowned. A different Talorc or Talorcan, an exiled Pictish prince living as a guest of Cenél Loairn, was captured by Óengus near the fortress of Dunollie and imprisoned to await his fate.

Dungal, the main villain of the piece, was wounded while defending a minor stronghold in Lorn. Evading capture, but no doubt terrified of falling into Pictish hands, he fled to Ireland, seeking refuge with friends or kinsmen. There he remained for a time until the lure of ambition drew him back to Argyll. Joining his brother Feradach he made a last stand at Dunadd, an iconic centre of royal power. Óengus stormed the fortress and took both brothers alive, binding them with chains while considering what should be done with them. Dungal's chances of avoiding a grim fate are unlikely to have been improved by the death of Brude, son of Óengus, in the days following the fall of Dunadd. Feradach was mercifully spared to be kept alive as a hostage, ending his days in the land of the Picts.

The Cenél Loairn leadership now stood on the brink of anni-hilation, but the war was not yet over. Muiredach, son of Ainfcellach and cousin to Dungal, gathered an army at the southern end of Loch Awe. In this district, near the present-day village of Ford, he encountered a Pictish force led by Talorcan, brother of Óengus. Muiredach lost the battle and many of his warriors perished before he himself was chased off the field, never to be heard of again. With the power of Cenél Loairn utterly broken and its lands laid waste, Óengus turned his attention to other parts of Dál Riata. As conqueror of one major kindred he was in a position to demand homage and tribute from others. Since the sources give no hint of opposition by Cenél nGabráin, the traditional rivals of Cenél Loairn, we may assume that Kintyre and possibly Cowal submitted to him. In 741, the annalists noted 'the smiting of Dál Riata by Óengus, son of Fergus'. At first glance this looks like a reference to Pictish forces rampaging indiscriminately through Argyll, but its scope might have been limited to Lorn.

With the Scots subjugated, Óengus returned home as the

undisputed master of a broad swath of territory stretching from the Moray Firth to the Mull of Kintyre. He knew that the supreme overlordship of the North lay within his grasp if he could sweep aside two remaining obstacles. One of these was Anglo-Saxon Northumbria, now a more or less unified kingdom ruled by a Bernician dynasty which had ousted Aethelfrith's descendants in 716. The other was Alt Clut, the kingdom of the Clyde Britons at Dumbarton Rock. Neither of these two powers was likely to submit to Óengus without a fight. In 744, Óengus tested the resolve of the Britons in a preliminary skirmish but the outcome is unknown. A more significant battle took place six years later when his brother Talorcan marched across the River Forth to assail the northern frontier of Alt Clut. The Britons, led by their valiant king Teudebur, met the Picts at Mugdock and gained a great victory in which Talorcan was slain. Never before had the power of Óengus been resisted so fiercely, nor had his army previously endured such a setback. His fearsome military reputation, honed by more than two decades of fighting, began to look less secure in the aftermath of his brother's failure. The battle of Mugdock had shown his neighbours, not least the still-subjugated Scots, as well as rivals within his own country, that he was not invincible after all. In the meantime, however, the hopes of his enemies at home and abroad were thwarted by a swift resurgence of his fortunes. The catalyst was an attack on Clydesdale in 750 by the Northumbrians under their ambitious king Eadberht. Part of Ayrshire was wrested from the Britons and annexed to Eadberht's domains. Two years later, Teudebur of Dumbarton died and was succeeded by his son Dyfnwal. Seeking to exploit the situation, Óengus entered into negotiations with Eadberht to plan a joint operation against the Britons. The two kings agreed to launch a two-pronged assault which would bring a Pictish army down from the north while a Northumbrian one attacked from the south. In 756, the allied forces drove deep into British territory to threaten Dumbarton itself, their combined strength forcing Dyfnwal to surrender on 1 August after a brief siege. The allies took a hefty tribute payment before leading their armies back to ther respective homelands. On

10 August, while marching away from the ancient church at Govan on the banks of the Clyde, Eadberht was ambushed and his forces sustained heavy loss. The identity of the attackers is not known, but they were either Picts or Britons. Given that the latter had recently been beaten into submission, the assault may have been mounted by Óengus, although it is hard to see why he should have turned against his English ally. If the ambush was indeed his doing, it was his last known act of aggression. No more foreign wars are attributed to him in the sources, nor did he apparently face further challenges from Pictish rivals. He died in 761, as paramount king of the Picts and overlord of Dál Riata. In Northumbria he later received a disparaging obituary, probably derived from a Gaelic source, which stated that 'he perpetrated bloody crimes, like a tyrannical slaughterer'. This negative view was by no means universal among his English contemporaries, some of whom regarded him as worthy of remembrance in the prayers of Bernician monks at Lindisfarne. He was indeed the first Pictish king to be accorded this honour, even if his positive image among Eadberht's people eventually turned sour.

CHAPTER 7
The Northern Churches

Columba

To Bede and his contemporaries in eighth-century Northumbria, the evangelisation of the southern Picts had been undertaken by Saint Ninian of Whithorn. Bede believed that the northern Picts had received Christianity from a separate mission conducted by Columba, an Irish monk who came to Britain in 563. Columba founded a monastery on Iona, a small island off the Hebridean isle of Mull, which became his base of operations for missionary work. Iona's location placed it within the bounds of Dál Riata and brought it into contact with the Scots, but it lay also within reach of Pictish communities further north in the Western Isles and on the adjacent mainland.

Bede gives a few brief facts about Columba's career, but the main source of information is a Latin *vita* or 'Life' produced by Adomnán a hundred years after the saint's death. Adomnán held the abbacy of Iona in the final quarter of the seventh century and was a major figure in the ecclesiastical affairs of northern Britain and Ireland. His *Vita Sancti Columbae*, while being rightly regarded by historians as a valuable source, was first and foremost a work of hagiography. It sought to highlight Columba's holiness by crediting miracles to his God-given powers. Being a fairly substantial work – by comparison with other *vitae* – it certainly provides a fascinating glimpse into Iona's early history. Its testimony, however, cannot be accepted at face value. Thus, although Adomnán lived far closer in time to Columba than did Ailred of Rievaulx to Ninian, not

Major centres of Christianity

everything he wrote was necessarily true or accurate. As abbot of Iona he had direct access to the monastery's own written and oral traditions about its founder, but these were unlikely to have been genuine fossils preserving unaltered snapshots of sixth-century history. Between Columba's death in 597 and the publication of the *Vita* c.700, the old traditions passed down by the monks were undoubtedly amended and embellished to suit the monastery's needs in an ever-changing world. Adomnán himself had very specific political interests and deliberately tailored parts of his work accordingly, most obviously by projecting the concerns and anxieties of his own age backwards into the sixth century. This does not mean that we must view everything he wrote with scepticism, but we should nevertheless keep in mind that he was, after all, a hagiographer rather than a historian. Notwithstanding this, he remains our best source of information on Columba. His testimony is supplemented by *Amrae Coluimb Chille* ('The Praise of Columb Cille'), a poem supposedly composed around the time of Columba's death. A preface giving biographical details about the saint was added to the *Amrae* c.1000, no doubt incorporating older traditions that – in some cases – may have preserved accurate information. Other texts are generally deemed less reliable and must be approached with even more caution. Among them is another *vita*, in Gaelic rather than in Latin, written in Ireland in the twelfth century. Its author presented it in the form of a sermon or homily, but its content is essentially biographical and includes many details not found in Adomnán's work. Because it incorporated stories known to be circulating in Ireland in the tenth century – some of which, by inference, must have been even older – it can be cautiously used alongside *Vita Sancti Columbae*. A much later hagiographical text, also in Irish Gaelic, appeared in the sixteenth century. This was a compilation of data from various sources, including Adomnán's *vita* and the 'Homily', but its value as a commentary on events from a thousand years earlier is doubtful.

Taking the various sources together, and making judgments about their respective merits, we can draw what may be a broadly accurate picture of Columba's life. At its core stands Adomnán's *vita*, with additional data cautiously selected from the *Amrae* prefaces and other Irish texts. There seems to be no doubt that Columba was born in 521 to aristocratic parents in Donegal. His father was a nobleman of the Cenél Conaill kindred, a branch of the northern Uí Néill, and therefore a man of royal blood. This kinship embroiled Columba in dynastic politics and ultimately led to his departure – or expulsion – from the land of his birth. As a young man he trained as a priest in Ireland, probably at a number of monasteries, where he earned the respect and friendship of some of the greatest ecclesiastical figures of his day. In 561, at around forty years of age, his family background drew him into a bitter strife between rival branches of the Uí Néill, a struggle which culminated in a bloody battle at Cul Dreimne near Sligo. In the aftermath, a finger of blame was pointed at Columba and he was accused of involvement in the conflict. A synod of churchmen duly assembled to consider the accusation and, despite earnest pleading on Columba's behalf, he was penalised with temporary excommunication. Perhaps feeling aggrieved at the harshness of the judgement, he gathered a small group of monks and sailed across the sea to Britain, seeking voluntary exile in the land of the Scots.

When Columba arrived in Argyll in 563, the paramount regional ruler was Conall mac Comgaill, king of Cowal and Kintyre. Conall welcomed the Irish exiles and offered them the hospitality of his court, recognising in Columba not only a distinguished guest but also a man of high royal lineage. When Columba expressed a wish to establish a monastery, Conall granted him the small island of Iona, a place remote enough to satisfy an ascetic craving for isolation but not too far from the centres of royal power. Such a location was eminently suited to Columba's purposes: he had no real desire to shut himself away from the world of secular politics, a world in which he had already become involved during his time in Ireland. King Conall thus became his protector and patron, the first in a long line of kings to seek the friendship of Iona. In Bede's alternative version of the story it was not Conall who bestowed the gift of land but the Pictish monarch Brude, son of Maelchon. This can be dismissed as eighth-century propaganda devised by the Picts or, quite possibly, by Bede's Pictophile colleagues among the Northumbrian clergy. Iona's own version of its beginnings, namely the story of King Conall presented by Adomnán, should be regarded as being much closer to the truth.

According to Adomnán, one of Columba's first ventures into Argyll politics came in 574, after Conall's death, when he anointed Áedán mac Gabráin as the next king. This was presented in the *Vita* as a ritual performed on Iona and as a sacred rite of ordination by which Columba placed his hands on Áedán's head to bless him. Another ritual, not mentioned by Adomnán but perhaps nonetheless performed at Áedán's kingmaking ceremony, owed more to the customs of the pagan past. It required the new king to place his foot in a shallow footprint carved out of living stone. Such a footprint can still be seen today on the summit of the fortress at Dunadd and might have been used during Áedán's royal ordination. An alternative setting is St Columba's Chapel, at the southern tip of the Kintyre peninsula, which also has a footprint carved in stone. From the site of this ancient ruined church the Cenél nGabráin stronghold of Dunaverty is clearly visible. Curiously, Adomnán portrayed Columba as initially reluctant to anoint Áedán as Conall's successor. For reasons left unexplained we learn that Eóganán, another of Gabrán's sons, was Columba's first choice. Only when a whip-wielding angel appeared to the saint in a dream was he persuaded to switch his support to Áedán who thus became the first Iona-ordained ruler of Kintyre. In his role as Iona's abbot, Columba was able to present himself as spiritual mentor to Áedán, thereby occupying a position formerly held in heathen times by the high priest or chief druid. It was in this guise of royal patriarch that he accompanied the king to Ireland for a meeting with Áed mac Ainmirech at Druim Cett near Limavady, probably c.590. Áed was king of the northern Uí Néill and shared close kinship with Columba, who was therefore ideally placed to be an intermediary. The political circumstances surrounding the convention at Druim Cett have already been discussed in the previous chapter.

Columba's missionary work among the Picts began with a

visit to their northern overking, Brude, son of Maelchon. The date of this meeting is unknown so it could have occurred anytime between the founding of Iona and Brude's death in 584. It took place at a royal fortress near the River Ness, possibly the hilltop stronghold known today as Craig Phadraig or some other site in the vicinity of Inverness. Accompanied by his companions, Columba ascended the steep path to the fort's entrance but found the gates barred by order of the king. This, at least, is the story as told by Adomnán. It gave him an opportunity to describe a miracle by which Columba, with divine assistance, opened the gates and passed through. Behind this and similar hagiographical motifs we are probably seeing a formal embassy from Iona to the pagan north-east. A political aspect may also have accompanied the religious one, with Columba taking on an additional role as Áedán's representative to a Pictish counterpart, or perhaps facilitating a truce between the two kings. It is likely that he had already performed a similar function at Druim Cett. Adomnán provides enough anecdotes and miracle tales about the meeting with Brude to suggest that a positive outcome was by no means guaranteed. He portrays the obstinate druid Broichan, the Pictish king's foster-father and spiritual mentor, as a hindrance to Columba's mission. A far greater obstacle to peace was surely the sporadic warfare between Áedán and Brude, a simmering rivalry which had brought, or was soon to bring, a raid on Brude's vassals in Orkney. In the longer term, the religious side of the negotiations paved the way for the establishment of churches in Pictish territory, each of which became an eastern outpost of Gaeldom. Most, if not all, were founded after Columba's lifetime and provided Iona with an additional source of secular patronage. Through Columba's labours at the end of the sixth century his successors gained a foothold among the Picts in the seventh. Whether or not his contact with Brude yielded a positive outcome on the political front can only be surmised. If dialogue took place after Áedán's Orcadian venture in 580, it might explain why the annals report no further hostilities between the two kings during Brude's reign.

Columba's mission evidently achieved no mass evangelisation

of the Picts. According to Adomnán, some members of the landowning class willingly adopted Christianity, but the number of converts appears to have been small. We cannot even be certain that King Brude was one of them. Those who converted to Christianity must have thought it a more attractive package than paganism, for a variety of spiritual and non-spiritual reasons. The new religion's international links made its personnel seem sophisticated and cosmopolitan, while its Latinity and literacy had strong 'imperial' associations with the Roman past. For an ambitious pagan king on the edge of the known world, baptism gave immediate entry to an exclusive club of Christian monarchs headed by the Byzantine emperor in Constantinople. How far Brude was tempted along this path is unknown, for Adomnán is silent on the issue. Nevertheless, even if the king kept faith with the old gods, he allowed the new religion to be practised within his realm. Columba's Pictish mission, while probably not the resounding success described by Bede, can therefore be credited with sowing the seeds of Christianisation. The main evangelising achievements should, however, be credited to his successors in the abbacy of Iona. The first of these was his cousin, Baithéne, who served as abbot for three years until his death in 600. Both Baithéne and his own successor, Abbot Laisren, presumably oversaw the continuing Pictish mission, but neither of them is commemorated in place-names in the East. Instead, we find the names of the fourth and sixth abbots, Fergna and Cumméne, remembered in the Pictish landscape. Both men may have taken a keen interest in bringing Christianity to the Picts, either in person or by sending their chief disciples. Before Cumméne's death in 669, an Iona-trained clergy was flourishing in Pictish territory on the spiritual foundations laid by Columba. Churches were being founded, communities were being converted and the pagan priesthood was finding itself increasingly marginalised.

It is easy to infer from Bede and Adomnán that the conversion of the Picts should be credited solely to Columba and his successors. There were, however, other monasteries and other saints whose labours received little or no acknowledgement in the Ionacentric annals and hagiography. In Chapter 4 we saw, for example, how the traditions of Abernethy claimed that the first church had been founded by disciples of Saint Brigid of Kildare in the early sixth century. Even if this particular tale is no more than legend, there is no reason to believe that the conversion of the Pictish heartlands was a Columban monopoly. The very early Christian cemetery at Hallow Hill, near St Andrews, suggests that at least one other evangelising initiative was active among the Picts of Fife in the sixth century, perhaps even a decade or two before Columba's visit to Brude's domains further north. Even in the western lands, the abbots of Iona were not the only major players in the fight against paganism. As we shall see below, a number of Pictish communities on the islands and shorelands north of Argyll, and some Gaelic ones too, looked elsewhere for spiritual guidance.

Non-Columban Churches in the West

Columba is such a towering figure in the history of Scottish Christianity, and Iona such an iconic symbol of the so-called 'Celtic Church', that it is easy to see why other saints and other monasteries have been pushed into the shadows. Adomnán cannot be blamed for this: his *Vita Sancti Columbae* achieved its primary aim of glorifying Iona's founder and first abbot. But the growth of Columba's cult elevated Iona above all other churches in northern Britain. This prominence is reflected in texts such as the Irish annals which incorporated older chronicles written on Iona by scribes who carefully filtered newsworthy data to ensure that it reflected well on their own monastery. Religious foundations outside the Columban *familia* or 'family' of churches were rarely mentioned and frequently ignored. Such filtering can be seen in Adomnán's *Vita* which omits, for example, any reference to a saint called Donnan who established a religious community on Eigg.

Like Iona, Eigg is a small Hebridean island whose remoteness was attractive to sixth-century missionaries. Donnan, an Irishman, established a monastery there during the last quarter of the sixth

145

century but little is known of its history. It lay at Kildonan ('Donnan's Church'), on a site now occupied by a sixteenth-century successor. There can be no doubt that its abbots were in contact with their counterparts on Iona throughout the period of its existence. It might seem curious, then, that Adomnán made no reference to a monastery on Eigg when he wrote of a visit made there by Baithéne, Columba's cousin and principal deputy. This might reflect Adomnán's own desire to promote Iona as the main focus of Hebridean Christianity, with competitors duly sidelined. Alternatively, it could simply mean that Donnan had not yet founded his community at the time of Baithéne's visit. An old Irish tale of dubious provenance reports a conversation between Donnan and Columba, but its reliability cannot be verified. If it has any historical value, then Baithéne's visit to Eigg may have been an embassy from Iona to a neighbour whose brethren shared similar objectives. Church dedications to Donnan on the isles of Skye and Uist and in mainland Argyll suggest that his followers were active across a wide area in later times. It is even possible that some of these sites originated as satellite churches while he was still alive, receiving their dedications after his death. Like Iona, Eigg may have lain at the hub of a network or *familia* of religious settle-ments, each of which undertook missionary endeavours among Pictish and Gaelic communities in the Western Isles and on the nearby mainland.

In 617, a band of seaborne marauders arrived on Eigg in search of plunder. Coming to Donnan's monastery they massacred all the brethren including the founder himself. In some Irish texts the culprits are described as violent robbers sent by a rich lady whose wrath Donnan had incurred. This woman has been variously identified by historians as a 'Pictish queen', or as the leader of some kind of proto-Viking warband. In truth, we have no idea who she was or where she lived. She might be a fictional character devised in folklore, a stereotypical heathen villainess. Setting her aside, we can nevertheless accept that the slaughter of Donnan and his companions did occur. The event was noted bleakly in the Irish annals as 'the burning of the martyrs of Eigg' without any reference to Viking pirates or Pictish queens. At first glance, the tragedy seems to illustrate the difficult task facing any group of missionaries who hoped to spread Christianity in remote Hebridean communities. On closer inspection, we may note that Eigg is no more isolated than Iona, both islands being peripheral sites housing vulnerable religious settlements. Why, then was one monastery targeted in the early seventh century while the other remained inviolate for the next two hundred years? The answer might lie in the relationship between their respective abbots and neighbouring potentates. Iona's monks undoubtedly benefited from a high level of protection bestowed by powerful Cenél nGabráin patrons. It is unlikely that Donnan and his brethren strove to undertake their labours without similar local support, but the violence that engulfed them in 617 suggests that their patron's protection was either inadequate or had been withdrawn.

Other religious foundations in Argyll and the Isles included major monasteries on Lismore in the Firth of Lorn and at Kingarth on the island of Bute in the Firth of Clyde. These were founded independently of Iona but functioned as important centres in their own right, their abbots playing influential roles in the affairs of kings. The religious settlement on Lismore lay at Kilmoluag ('Moluag's Church'), occupying a site now occupied by the ruined fourteenth-century cathedral of the bishops of Argyll. Its founder Moluag or Lugaid, an Irishman and contemporary of Columba, was the subject of a *vita* and various hagiographical fragments. Like Columba, Moluag sprang from a high-status family in northern Ireland and had similarly spent the early part of his career at an Irish monastery. In Moluag's case this was Bangor in County Down, founded by Saint Comgall c.552. A typical web of folklore and hagiography surrounds Moluag's arrival on Lismore. One tradition sees him floating across the sea on a rock, while another tells how he and Columba competed for the island in a race which Moluag eventually won. More plausible are the stories of his meeting with the Pictish king Brude, son of Maelchon, and of missionary work among the Picts. The Pictish monastery at Rosemarkie on the northern shore of the Moray Firth, facing Brude's unidentified residence near the mouth of the River Ness, claimed Moluag as its founder, as did other churches in the East. There seems no reason to doubt that what we are seeing here is an evangelising mission by Irish monks operating independently of Iona. The venture's long-term success is unknown, but it is possible that it made more headway than its Columban counterpart and might even have enjoyed a greater share of Pictish royal patronage. Moluag died in 592 and was reputedly buried at Rosemarkie before being taken back to Lismore. Just as Columba sought the patronage of Áedán mac Gabráin, so Moluag must have found a similarly powerful protector and benefactor for his own primary monastery. Given its location, Lismore was almost certainly a spiritual centre for the Cenél Loairn kindred of Lorn and we may cautiously assume that these were Moluag's secular patrons. Their support presumably continued into the seventh century for, as the annals indicate, the monastery continued to thrive after its founder's passing. In 611, the death of Neman, abbot of Lismore, was noted by the annalists. Neman's chronology suggests that he may have been Moluag's immediate successor. A later incumbent, Saint Eochaid, died in 637, but otherwise we know almost nothing about the sequence of Lismore's early abbots.

Further north, another Irish priest called Maelrubai founded a religious settlement at Applecross on the coast of Wester Ross. This was established in 673, two years after Maelrubai's arrival in Argyll. He was around thirty years of age when he left his homeland, having been born c.642 to aristocratic parents. Like Moluag of Lismore, Maelrubai's early career was spent at the Irish monastery of Bangor whose founder, Saint Comgall, was said by later tradition to have been an uncle of Maelrubai's mother. Seven decades of Christian labour separate Moluag's death from Maelrubai's Hebridean mission, leading us to wonder why the latter happened so long after the former. In seeking an explanation we might turn to political events in the vicinity of Applecross at the time of its foundation, especially with regard to the situation on Skye. A prolonged and bitter conflict engulfed the island during the second half of the seventh century as two rival kindreds – Cenél nGabráin of Kintyre and Cenél nGartnait of Skye – fought for supremacy. One phase of hostilities appears to have ended in 668, when the leaders of Cenél nGartnait were forced to seek refuge in Ireland, but another phase seemingly began in 670 when they returned to reclaim their position. Maelrubai's arrival at Applecross three years later looks almost too close in time and space to be a coincidence. When he built his monastery there, on a site facing the east coast of Skye, was he acting at the request of – and with the support and protection of – the chiefs of Cenél nGartnait? Did his ecclesiastical superiors at Bangor see a new opportunity to gain influence in Britain by encouraging Cenél nGartnait to sponsor him? With Moluag's Lismore already established, perhaps under Cenél Loairn patronage, the prospect of setting up another satellite as a counterweight to Iona may have been too tempting for the Bangor hierarchy to resist. If this was indeed the case, then by c.675 the northward ambitions of Iona and her Cenél nGabráin protectors may have faced a political and religious power-bloc comprising Cenél Loairn, Cenél nGartnait and their respective spiritual centres at Lismore and Applecross. With two major footholds in the Hebridean seaways, Bangor perhaps entered the final quarter of the seventh century with its own influential *familia* among the Gaels of Argyll. Adomnan's portrayal of Comgall and Columba as friends might even reflect a personal desire for the two *familiae* to be on amicable terms in the period of his own abbacy.

Whatever his reasons for coming to Britain, Maelrubai evidently journeyed far from Applecross on his evangelising ventures. He is credited with missions not only on Skye and in adjacent mainland districts but also eastward in Moray, northward in Sutherland and north-westward on the Isle of Lewis. How many of these far-flung journeys actually occurred is uncertain, but none of the alleged destinations look implausible for an ambitious abbot. One story, almost certainly spurious, claims that he was slain by Danish marauders while travelling in Sutherland. More reliable are the Irish annals which noted his passing at Applecross in 722, at the age of eighty. His grave, according to local tradition, lies beneath a low mound in the vicinity of the old parish church.

At the southern end of Argyll lay the monastery of Kingarth, traditionally associated with Saint Blaan or Blane, another alleged contemporary of Columba. Located near the southern tip of the Isle of Bute, it was presumably founded by Blane under the patronage of local Gaelic rulers based on the island or on the adjacent mainland in Cowal. In the seventh and later centuries the foremost power in this region was Cenél Comgaill, the kindred descended from Comgall mac Domangairt whose son Conall had played a key role in the founding of Iona. At the time of Blane's death c.590, the people of Bute probably acknowledged one of Comgall's grandsons as king of the shorelands around the Firth of Clyde. A neighbouring kingship in Kintyre was simultaneously held by Comgall's nephew, Aedan mac Gabráin, whose own spiritual needs were served by Columba. Like the monks of Lismore and Applecross, the Kingarth brethren lay outside the Columban orbit and were not under the authority of Iona's abbots.

Little is known of Saint Blane. In a ninth-century Irish text he is called 'Fair Blaan of Cenn Garad'. According to much later Scottish texts of the fifteenth and sixteenth centuries, he was a native of Bute, born on the island to an Irish mother whose brother Saint Cathan lived there as a religious hermit. The story of Blane's childhood incorporates typical hagiographical motifs: he and his mother were cruelly cast out upon the sea in a boat which eventually drifted from Bute to Ireland. There he became a monastic pupil at Bangor, under the benevolent gaze of Saint Comgall, before returning to Bute as a disciple of his uncle Cathan. Much of this story is likely to be fictional, with some parts clearly being 'copy and paste' borrowings from elsewhere, including Classical mythology. None of the Scottish traditions of Blane mention Kingarth but focus instead on Dunblane in Perthshire which had become, by the mid-ninth century, the main centre of his cult. Entries in the Irish annals note the deaths of Kingarth abbots during the previous century and it is tempting to envisage a wholesale transfer of both cult and personnel from Bute to Perthshire thereafter. Such a move would be consistent with the appearance of Viking pirates in the Firth of Clyde after c.800. Prior to these events, Bute's geographical position in the firth might have made Kingarth the premier monastery in southern Argyll. Its *familia* in the seventh and eighth centuries may have included lesser churches at coastal sites around the region, especially at places where a dedication to Blane or Cathan exists today. One likely satellite was Inchmarnock, a small island off the western coast of Bute, where a monastery associated with a saint called Ernan has been the subject of recent archaeological investigation. Kingarth might have played an additional role as an ecclesiastical link between its presumed Cenél Comgaill patrons and the Britons of Alt Clut. The latter, according to much later tradition, had as their own primary saint a figure who bore the nickname 'Mungo'.

Kentigern

Christianity had already gained a foothold among the Clyde Britons when Saint Patrick wrote his letter of complaint to Coroticus, king of Alt Clut, in the second half of the fifth century. Nothing more is known of religious affairs on the Clyde for more than a hundred years, although we can assume that the populace continued to be served by local clergy. At the end of the sixth century, according to much later tradition, a bishopric was established at Glasgow by Kentigern, a Briton of royal parentage. Glasgow's cathedral, St Mungo's, preserves in its dedication his nickname *Munghu*, which means 'dear friend' (or perhaps even 'my dog') in the language of the Britons. His story is told in two *vitae* commissioned by Glasgow's twelfth-century bishops. One was written by Jocelin, a monk of Furness Abbey, who was no stranger to such assignments. The other, commissioned by Bishop Herbert, survives only in fragments and its author's name is unknown. Although both *vitae* are far removed in time from their subject they may incorporate ecclesiastical folklore reaching back to earlier centuries. Together they tell of an early church founded at Glasgow on the site of the present cathedral. From here Kentigern ministered to the Britons as chief royal bishop to the kings of Alt Clut. He himself was not a native of the Clyde but came from Lothian, from the kingdom of Gododdin. His mother Teneu or Thaney was supposedly the daughter of an otherwise unattested king called Leodonus whose centre of power lay on the hilltop fortress of Traprain Law. Both Teneu and her father look suspiciously fictional, the former perhaps being based on Danae, mother of the Greek hero Perseus, while Leodonus seems merely to be an eponym of Lothian.

According to the Glasgow *vitae*, Kentigern was born to Teneu after her seduction by Owain, a son of King Urien of Rheged, who came to her in disguise. Upon learning of the pregnancy, Leodonus grew angry and condemned his daughter to death. She was thrown off a cliff in a cart but miraculously survived. Leodonus then set her adrift in a boat on the Firth of Forth but again she survived, eventually escaping to Fife where she gave birth to her child. This is as far as the fragmentary 'Herbertian Life' goes, the remainder of the story being continued by Jocelin of Furness. From Jocelin we learn that the young Kentigern spent his early years as a fosterling of Saint Serf or Servanus, abbot of the monastery of Culross on the southern coast of Fife. Here the boy trained as a priest before leaving to pursue his destiny. The first event of his independent ecclesiastical career was an encounter with an old man called 'Fregus' ('Fergus') who died in his presence. Kentigern put the body on a cart and went in search of a suitable place for burial. On reaching *Cathures*, also known as *Glasgu* ('Green Hollow'), the young priest found an unused cemetery consecrated many years before by Saint Ninian. After burying Fergus, Kentigern established a church beside the Molendinar Burn on the site of the later cathedral. There he recruited a group of disciples and made contact with local secular elites, not all of whom were friendly. A certain King Morken treated the saint so badly that he was justly rewarded with an untimely death. More productive were Kentigern's dealings with Rhydderch Hael, king of Alt Clut, who appointed him Glasgow's first bishop. After benefiting from Rhydderch's patronage and friendship for many years Kentigern died at Glasgow in old age. His death, according to the Welsh annals, occurred in 612 but should probably be dated more correctly to 614.

How much of the foregoing is historically accurate rather than a blend of folklore and ecclesiastical propaganda is hard to say. The two Glasgow *vitae* were written as hagiography, not as history, and their primary purpose was to glorify the cathedral's founder and first bishop. Any factual elements in the sources consulted by Jocelin of Furness and by the author of the Herbertian 'Life' soon became entangled with legends and miracle stories. Unsurprisingly, both *vitae* contain episodes drawn from a stock of well-used motifs common to the hagiographical genre. These can be disregarded as fictional additions designed to highlight Kentigern's sanctity. They include not only his various miracles but also meetings with the famous saints Columba and David. Face to face encounters between renowned ecclesiastical figures rarely occurred in reality but were a well-used theme in hagiography. By including such meetings in his narrative, the hagiographer was able to forge retrospective links between otherwise unconnected saintly cults. An additional literary tool was the invention of a journey or visit by a saint to a faraway church in order to explain his or her popularity there in the hagiographer's own time. Thus, the 'Life' written by Jocelin of Furness refers to an alleged sojourn by Kentigern in Wales, an area where the saint's cult had a strong presence in medieval times. Peeling away spurious material of this sort, and distinguishing it from genuine early traditions, are the main tasks faced by seekers of real history. Inevitably, any *vita* subjected to this kind of dissection tends to yield few facts but many loose and tangled threads.

Archaeology and hagiography rarely confirm one another but, when they do, the result is often encouraging. In Kentigern's case, the *vitae* associate him with a church at Hoddom in Dumfriesshire, a place far from his primary sphere of activity on the Lower Clyde. Dumfriesshire fell to the Anglo-Saxons before the end of the seventh century and the religious settlement at Hoddom was taken over by an incoming Northumbrian clergy. Archaeological excavations conducted in the 1990s produced evidence of a sixth-century monastery, presumably a community of Britons, which seems to provide a context for Kentigern's visit. Although there is no reason to believe that the area formed an integral part of the kingdom of Alt Clut, a wide hegemony can nevertheless be envisaged for some of the more ambitious Clyde kings. It is possible, then, that parts of Dumfriesshire acknowledged the overlordship of Rhydderch Hael – and the ecclesiastical authority of his bishop – in the years around c.600.

At Glasgow, the results of recent excavations indicate that the cathedral site was used for Christian burial in the sixth century, the time when Kentigern was supposedly active. As yet, there is no evidence of a church dating from this early period, but we may note that it would have been timber-built and unlikely to leave clear traces. It is at least possible that such a church did exist and that its founder was Kentigern. Whether it later became the focus of a bishopric of which he was the first incumbent is an unanswerable question. Equally puzzling is the extent of his influence within and beyond Rhydderch's kingdom, either directly via his own efforts or through those of his disciples and successors. One of his closest followers is said to have been an Irish priest called Conval, the patron saint of Inchinnan near Renfrew. Near the old parish church of Inchinnan stands a shaped stone, known as 'St Conval's Chariot', which is said to have conveyed him from Ireland to Britain. This is actually a cross-base of tenth or eleventh-century date. Less outlandish is the tradition that Conval was buried at Inchinnan. The second part of the place-name is often seen as a reference to the Irish saint Finnian of Moville, but this cannot be confirmed and alternative meanings have been suggested. Conval's alleged link to Kentigern is, in any case, rather doubtful. It probably derives not from sixth-century tradition but from a twelfth-century attempt by the bishops of Glasgow to claim Inchinnan as a satellite under their authority. If the association between Conval and Inchinnan is nevertheless reliable, his tomb may have been located on the site of the old church at All Hallows near the confluence of the rivers Black Cart and White Cart.

Contemporary with Kentigern and Conval, and labouring in the same part of Britain, was the Irishman Mirin or Mirren whose shrine at Paisley in Renfrewshire became a focus for later pilgrimage. The sparse information about Mirin seems to derive from legend and cannot be accepted as historical. One tradition makes him a disciple of Saint Comgall of Bangor but another connects him to the mythical Regulus who is said to have brought relics of Saint Andrew to Scotland. Could Mirin's real historical context lie in an Irish missionary initiative to Renfrewshire? There might even be some genuine connection between him and Conval, especially if the latter's traditional link with Kentigern is a much later invention. With easy access from the western seaways via the Firth of Clyde it is not unfeasible that Conval and Mirin arrived in Renfrewshire at roughly the same time, as emissaries from a monastery in northern Ireland. Perhaps they both came from Saint Comgall's headquarters at Bangor, with a shared remit to minister among the Britons?

One figure whose association with Kentigern is almost certainly spurious is Constantine, patron saint of the old parish church at Govan on the south bank of the Clyde. In the Kentigern hagiography he appears as a Briton of Alt Clut, a royal prince who became a monk under Kentigern's patronage. He is usually identified as the person formerly interred in the impressive stone coffin or sarcophagus now displayed at Govan Old. None of these traditions seem historically reliable. The description of Constantine as a disciple of Kentigern was surely concocted in the twelfth century to portray Govan, the chief royal church of the Clyde Britons, as a subordinate of the newly built Scottish cathedral at Glasgow. Nor is there any evidence to support the idea of a historical connection between Constantine and the Govan Sarcophagus. The former seems to have been a sixth-century saint; the latter was carved no earlier than the late 800s. Modern attempts to equate Constantine with a namesake selected from a shortlist of ninth and tenth-century Pictish and Scottish kings usually proceed from a belief that the Sarcophagus *must* have contained someone who bore this name. Setting the Sarcophagus aside, we see a more plausible candidate for Govan's patron saint in Constantine of Kintyre, an obscure figure commemorated at Kilchousland, 'Constantine's Church', near Campbeltown. Medieval tradition identified him as a sixth-century Briton from Devon or Cornwall, a king who became a monk in Ireland before establishing a church in Kintyre. This tale looks like ecclesiastical fiction and the real figure venerated at Kilchousland may have been Constantine the Great, Rome's first Christian emperor. One modern theory envisages the cult at Kilchousland transferring its personnel and rituals to Govan in the ninth century to escape the menace of Viking raids along the Kintyre coastline. Similar migrations of entire religious communities seem to have occurred around this time, as we have already noted in the case of Kingarth and the cult of Saint Blane. We shall meet the same trend again in Chapter 10. As far as Saint Constantine is concerned, the notion of a ninth-century transfer of cult and clergy to the relative safety of Lower Clydesdale is hardly implausible.

The Conversion of Northumbria

The seventh century witnessed the Christian conversion of the English or Anglo-Saxons, a process partly achieved by priests from Iona. Paganism among the southern English kingdoms was already starting to retreat before 600, Pope Gregory having sent from Rome a mission under the leadership of Saint Augustine. The latter arrived in Kent in 597, the year of Columba's death. At that time, the churches of Continental Europe were pursuing a number of new or revised practices not yet widely adopted in the British Isles. Geographical isolation rendered many of the Insular clergy slow to absorb these reforms and left them clinging to outmoded customs which their Continental peers regarded as improper. Even after the modernising or reformist movement spread from the Continent to southern parts of Britain and Ireland it was stubbornly resisted in northern areas. As we shall see later in this chapter, the differences eventually led to a rift between 'Celtic' traditionalists and their reformed or 'Roman' colleagues.

The Augustinian mission was intended to ensure that the evangelising of the heathen English was undertaken by papal or 'Roman' emissaries rather than by priests of the 'Celtic' tradition. Rome's desire to marginalise and exclude the Celtic clergy stemmed from the latter's retention of certain practices deemed archaic and obsolete. Celtic holy men, for instance, did not trim their hair in the Petrine tonsure or 'Crown of Saint Peter' – the style we commonly associate with medieval monks – but by shaving the scalp in a broad band from ear to ear. This style of tonsure, regarded by Rome as improper, perhaps evolved from ancient druidical practice. Of even greater concern to the reformists was the Celtic method for annually calculating the date of Easter Sunday. Most of the major centres of Western Christendom employed a newer method of calculation which many Celtic monasteries were unwilling to implement. It was this stubborn refusal, the root cause of what became known as the 'Easter Controversy', which made Rome so anxious to prevent a Celtic evangelisation of the English. The problem continued to overshadow ecclesiastical events in Britain and Ireland throughout the seventh century and was not finally resolved until the eighth.

Augustine's mission to Kent was an unbridled success. The Kentish king was baptised and an archbishopric was established at Canterbury, its remit being to offer leadership and guidance to Christian communities in English-controlled lands. Canterbury's influence quickly spread, prompting the creation of subordinate bishoprics in London and other southern cities, but no missionary initiative was directed at the northern English during this early phase. This meant that when the Bernician king Aethelfrith was killed in battle in 617 his family were still pagans, as too were the bulk of his people. The only Christians under his rule were communities of conquered Britons in lands where paganism had already been eradicated by native missionaries. By contrast, Aethelfrith's rival and successor, Edwin of Deira, accepted baptism in the eleventh year of his reign. According to Bede, the baptismal ceremony took place at York on Easter Sunday 627. In the following two centuries both the English and the Britons claimed responsibility for Edwin's conversion, to the profound frustration of modern historians. Bede, a fervent opponent of Celtic religious practices, insisted that Edwin's baptism was performed by Paulinus, an Italian priest sent from Canterbury to establish the first Northumbrian bishopric at York in 625 or 626. The ninth-century *Historia Brittonum* promoted an alternative scenario by crediting the baptism of Edwin to Rhun, son of Urien, a Briton of the royal house of Rheged. Modern attempts to reconcile these opposing accounts envisage two separate baptisms, or a dual ceremony performed jointly by Rhun and Paulinus, but neither theory seems particularly plausible. It is far more likely that only one baptismal ceremony occurred and that only one priest performed it. One recent hypothesis suggests that Rhun sponsored the baptism in a secular role as king of Rheged. This may be the most plausible scenario proposed so far, but it stumbles against a parallel tradition in the *Historia Brittonum* in which Rhun is depicted as an editor of hagiographical texts and, by implication, a cleric. Bede's testimony is usually regarded as superior and we are tempted to accept his story of Edwin's baptism by Paulinus at face value. This does, however, leave us to question why a seemingly incompatible alternative scenario appears in the *Historia Brittonum*.

Leaving aside the question of Edwin's conversion, we need not doubt that Paulinus and the Canterbury clergy became the leaders of Northumbrian Christianity. From his new episcopal see at York, Paulinus began a programme of evangelisation whose main aim was to bring the northern English under Canterbury's wing. As king of Bernicia, in addition to ruling his family's ancestral lands in Deira, the pious Edwin was able to give Paulinus unfettered access to pagan communities in frontier districts bordering the Christian British kingdoms. Whether the rulers of Rheged participated in these developments is unknown, but, if Rhun did indeed play a significant role, some measure of political and ecclesiastical co-operation between Urien's descendants and the Deiran royal family might be imagined. At that time, most churches in areas under North British rule adhered to the old Celtic customs but remained separate from the Irish or Gaelic group represented by Columba's community on Iona and by Saint Patrick's successors at Armagh. The British clergy of Wales, Cornwall and the North constituted three separate ecclesiastical blocs not bound to the abbots and bishops of Gaeldom. It is even possible that the British traditions of Edwin's baptism are simply a garbled folk-memory of a different event. Perhaps they refer to the moment when Rheged's own churches adopted 'Roman' practices acceptable to Paulinus of York and his superiors at Canterbury?

Edwin's victory over Aethelfrith in 617 forced Aethelfrith's children into exile. They escaped northward, beyond the Forth and Clyde, seeking refuge with the Scots and Picts. Eanfrith, the eldest son and crown prince of Bernicia, received a welcome among the Picts where he was treated as an honoured guest. There he was baptised – perhaps by Columban priests attached to the royal court – and there too he married a Pictish princess. His conversion to Christianity was undoubtedly a political gesture instigated by his host, a powerful overking. In earlier times, this Pictish patron would have requested a rite of sacrifice or some other pagan ceremony to set a supernatural seal on the bond of fosterage. In the early seventh century, a Christian ritual with sacred and royal overtones – the baptism of a foster-son by the foster-father's chosen priests – sealed the relationship with a new kind of sanctity.

Eanfrith's brothers and sisters found sanctuary among the Scots. Their father's former adversaries at the battle of Degsastan now became the protectors of his exiled offspring. Under the guidance of Eochaid Buide, king of Cenél nGabráin and overlord of Dál Riata, the Bernician youngsters embraced Christianity and were drawn into the orbit of Iona. Oswald, Aethelfrith's second son and next in seniority after Eanfrith, became especially devoted to the veneration of Columba. Nevertheless, behind this programme of spiritual education lay the same political motives that persuaded Eanfrith to take baptism among the Picts. By presenting the English exiles to the abbot of his royal church on Iona, King Eochaid sanctified their future obligations to his dynasty. These obligations were activated in 634 after Oswald's rout of Cadwallon and triumphal return to Bernicia. A pact of mutual friendship with Cenél nGabráin is likely to have formed part of Oswald's debt to his hosts, but a more significant aspect was a promise that the Bernician people – most of whom still clung resolutely to paganism – would be evangelised not by Canterbury but by Iona.

Back in 633, Cadwallon had destroyed Edwin at the battle of Hatfield. Although himself a Christian, the Welsh monarch's spiritual allegiance lay with the churches of the Britons and he had no love of 'Roman' Canterbury nor of its English devotees among the royal family of Deira. In the wake of the battle, Edwin's widow fled in terror to Kent, the land of her birth, accompanied not only by her younger children but also by Bishop Paulinus of York. Canterbury's hope of spreading its own brand of Christianity among the northern English was thus extinguished, at least for a while. In the following year, Oswald returned from exile to destroy Cadwallon, his victory clearing a pathway for an evangelising mission from Iona.

On the eve of his great victory, according to a story reported by Adomnán, Oswald received a vision in which Columba assured him of success on the battlefield. Behind this tale lay a reminder to Aethelfrith's descendants in Adomnán's own time that their ancestors had been evangelised by Columban monks, just as their dynasty's reinstatement in 634 had been achieved with Cenél nGabráin support. Adomnán plainly wanted the Bernicians to remember their spiritual and material debts to the Gaels. His reminder must have seemed especially timely in the 690s, when Oswald himself was being venerated as a saintly figure within and beyond Northumbria. Canonisation of this Anglo-Saxon king would eventually occur, chiefly because he had suffered the 'red martyrdom' of a violent death at the hands of pagan enemies. As we saw in Chapter 5, he found a suitably barbaric nemesis in Penda of Mercia.

After routing Cadwallon, Oswald became king of all Northumbria, uniting Bernicia and Deira under his rule and receiving homage from Anglo-Saxon realms south of the Humber. Remembering his obligations to the Scots, he sent word to Iona, inviting its abbot to send a Christian mission. A band of Columban monks duly arrived to preach among northern English communities, but its leader failed to gain the people's trust and he was duly recalled. His replacement was Aidan, an Irishman of great humility and piety, who immediately formed a close bond with Oswald. As a gift from the king, Aidan received the island of Lindisfarne on which to build a monastery as a missionary head-quarters. He and his monks were thus able to establish their own 'Iona' off the coast of Bernicia, in a place physically separated from the secular world but conveniently within sight of the hub of royal power at Bamburgh. To ensure the continuity of the mission, Aidan recruited young Northumbrians for monastic training and sent some westward to establish a satellite monastery at Old Melrose on the banks of the Tweed. Under his leadership, and with Oswald's unswerving support, the conversion of Northumbria began in earnest.

After Oswald's death in 642, the kingship passed to his younger brother Oswiu. By then, the Christianising of the northern English was almost complete. At the monastery on Lindisfarne the brethren included Bernician converts trained in the ways of the Columban Church and immersed in the old Celtic customs. Their hair was tonsured in the ear-to-ear style favoured by the Irish and the Britons. Each year, the Northumbrian clergy differed from their peers in other English kingdoms by celebrating Easter on a Sunday chosen by the Celts rather than by Rome. On rare occasions, the two methods of calculation led to the Roman and Celtic celebra-tions coinciding on the same Sunday, but in other years this did not happen and two separate Paschal rituals were observed. This began to cause problems for Oswiu, whose second wife Eanflaed was Edwin's daughter and a devout adherent of the Roman tradition. Oswiu, like Oswald, had been baptised on Iona and valued the continuing presence of Columban clergy in his kingdom. He felt no personal compulsion to change his mode of worship, but nor did he feel at ease when the ecclesiastical calendar obliged him and his queen to celebrate the Resurrection on different Sundays. He was aware, too, that some members of the Northumbrian clergy were keen to fall into line with Canterbury on the Easter issue. The most vociferous of this faction was Wilfrid, abbot of Ripon, a larger than life character whose outward displays of pomp and grandeur contrasted sharply with the simple ascetism of his colleagues. Eventually, after giving the matter much earnest thought, Oswiu summoned an ecclesiastical assembly to debate the controversy in the hope of reaching a solution. The gathering or synod took place in 664 at the monastery of Whitby on the North Sea coast. During the ensuing discussion the pro-Celtic case was argued by Colman, an Irishman who had succeeded to the bishopric of Lindisfarne three years earlier. The spokesman for the Roman side was the eloquent and persuasive Wilfrid. Abbess Hild of Whitby, an Englishwoman of the Deiran royal house, hosted the proceedings while expressing a personal preference for Celtic ways. Colman presented a strong case for keeping Northumbria loyal to the customs of Iona, but Wilfrid's argument carried the debate and secured a momentous victory for Canterbury. The Roman faction triumphed and the northern English churches duly fell into line. Henceforth, all clergy in Oswiu's kingdom were forbidden to follow Celtic practices. This effectively excluded many priests of Irish or Scottish origin from a career in Northumbria and made their positions there untenable. Among the casualties of the reform was Bishop Colman whose devotion to Columba left him no choice but to resign as head of the Lindisfarne community, his place being taken by Tuda, an Irish adherent of the Roman customs. Those few clergymen of English stock who refused to abandon the old traditions kept faith with Colman by accompanying him on the long journey back to Iona.

The synod at Whitby is rightly regarded as one of the most significant ecclesiastical events of the seventh century. Although primarily a defining moment for English Christianity, its repercussions were felt deeply throughout the Celtic North. The decision of the synod drew down the final curtain on Iona's brief period of influence south of the Forth. The Columban Church was confined thereafter to its Gaelic and Pictish heartlands. Wilfrid's success in the debate was not, however, a singular or isolated victory for the reformers and modernisers. On the contrary, it came at a time when the Easter issue was becoming a bone of contention elsewhere across the British Isles. Pro-Roman factions in Ireland had been making progress among their own churches since the early 600s and even on Iona there were murmurs of support for change. At the time of the Whitby synod, most Irish churches had already embraced reform, their adoption of Roman customs leaving the Columban *familia* increasingly isolated. By 679, when Adomnán became abbot of Iona, a small but growing minority among the Columban brethren was eager for reform. He himself, notwithstanding his status as the biographer of Iona's founder, was in fact the most high-profile member of this group.

Adomnán

Adomnán was an Irishman of aristocratic lineage, a scion of the northern Uí Néill. In his time as abbot of Iona, the Columban churches in Ireland and northern Britain continued to flourish despite the ever-increasing pressure for reform. As a supporter of the Roman side, Adomnán tried to persuade the Celtic traditionalists to change, but they steadfastly refused to abandon their old ways. His apparent failure to modernise Iona drew criticism from Bede in the pages of the *Ecclesiastical History*, but elsewhere in the same work the profound esteem in which Adomnán was held among the English clergy shines through. Aside from any failings on reform, Bede regarded Adomnán with the utmost respect and admiration, calling him 'a good and wise man with an excellent knowledge of the Scriptures'. The two probably met in person during Adomnán's two visits to Northumbria in the late 680s, a period when Bede was a teenage monk at Jarrow. The objective of the first visit, and possibly of the second as well, was to secure the release of innocent captives snatched in Ecgfrith's savage raid on Ireland in 684. Such a venture was in keeping with Adomnán's attitude to warfare. He felt particular concern for the plight of non-combatants caught up in the maelstrom of conflict and hoped to devise some means of protection for them. His hope bore fruit in 697 when he proclaimed a new ecclesiastical statute: *Lex Innocentium* (the 'Law of Innocents'), otherwise known as *Cáin*

Adamnáin ('Adomnán's Law'). This served as a code of practice for kings and warlords, placing upon them a sacred duty to minimise civilian casualties. It beseeched the secular powers to grant to all 'innocents' – women, children and clergy – immunity from violence and exemption from military service. To ensure that the new law came into force in as many regions as possible Adomnán summoned kings, bishops and abbots from every realm in which the Columban Church held authority or influence. The kingdoms duly responded, each sending one or more emissaries to the gathering. Adomnán invited all delegates to the monastery at Birr in Offaly, a site close to the traditional boundary between the northern and southern halves of Ireland. Here, the *Lex Innocentium* was ratified and witnessed by the entire assembly of laymen and clergymen. A copy of the list of witnesses or guarantors has survived in a much later manuscript which itself seems to be a copy of a lost ninth-century text. The list is essentially a muster-roll of the royal and religious elites of the Gaelic world. Persuading so many powerful figures to answer the summons, either as attendees in person or as guarantors *in absentia*, was the crowning achievement of Adomnán's career. It demonstrated the respect accorded to him by his peers and testified to the enduring influence of the Columban Church.

Among the signatories of Cáin Adamnáin were the Pictish overking Brude, son of Derile, and his Cenél nGabráin counterpart Eochaid, a grandson of Domnall Brecc. Alongside them stood the chief holy men of their kingdoms. The North Britons were not represented: their clergy were not answerable to Iona, nor were their kings under the spiritual sway of its abbot. Perhaps more surprisingly, or perhaps not so surprising at all, was the apparent non-attendance of Iona's ecclesiastical neighbours in the Hebridean seaways and shorelands. The monastery of Applecross, founded twenty-four years earlier by Saint Maelrubai of Bangor, is absent from the list of witnesses. It was independent of Iona, but then so were many of the Irish monasteries represented at Birr, some of whom answered to mother-churches at Armagh in the north or at Emly in the south. Both the bishop of Armagh and the abbot of

Emly were present, but no delegate came from Applecross, nor from the other major non-Columban churches in north-western Britain: Lismore in the Firth of Lorn and Kildonan on the isle of Eigg. Although 'Lismore' is mentioned in the guarantor list, the reference is to a namesake monastery in south-east Ireland. The absence of the Hebridean Lismore could be explained by its likely affiliation to the royal house of Cenél Loairn, Iona being similarly linked to the rival kindred of Cenél nGabráin. It may, in fact, be no small coincidence that the premier religious centre of Lorn was excluded from a synod summoned by Iona's abbot at a time when their respective secular patrons were engaged in a contest for superiority. This seems consistent with the presence of a Cenél nGabráin king among the guarantors and the absence of a Cenél Loairn counterpart. The omission of Applecross might reflect similar political tensions if, as seems likely, Maelrubai's monastery had close links with Skye. In 697, the year of the synod at Birr, a long-running conflict still simmered between Cenél nGartnait of Skye and a branch of Cenél nGabráin.

No English kingdom was represented at Birr, the synod being essentially a Gaelic gathering. Had the decision at Whitby in 664 accepted Bishop Colman's argument instead of Wilfrid's, the Northumbrian churches would almost certainly have sent a delegation to Ireland thirty-three years later. One renowned Northumbrian cleric did attend, although not as a representative of his homeland. This was Ecgbert, a Bernician, who at that time resided in the Irish monastery of Rathmelsigi where the brethren included many English monks. Ecgbert, like Adomnán, was an active supporter of reform. He looked forward to the day when the Celtic churches would finally adopt Roman practices to bring to an end the divisive Easter controversy. Towards the end of his life he indeed played an important part in healing the rift, as will be seen in Chapter 10. His views on the Paschal issue were shared by Bishop Curetán, the Pictish ecclesiastical delegate at the synod of 697, whose monastery lay at Rosemarkie on the coast of Easter Ross.

CHAPTER 8

The Vikings

Dynasties

The passing of Óengus, son of Fergus, in 761 unravelled his hegemony and liberated Dál Riata from the Pictish yoke. An energetic king called Áed Find ('Áed the White') arose among Cenél nGabráin to claim the overkingship of the Scots. In 768, Áed demonstrated his power by leading an army into the land of the Picts. A battle was fought some-where in Fortriu, the northerly Pictish region around Moray, but its outcome is unknown. The event has significance as the first recorded eastward expedition by Kintyre forces since the time of Domnall Brecc. To contemporary observers it possibly signalled a resurgence of Cenél nGabráin ambitions, but to modern eyes it marks the beginning of a very obscure phase in Scotland's history. Áed died in 778 and was succeeded by his brother Fergus. Two years later, the citadel of the Clyde Britons at Dumbarton was burned. The annalists who noted this event omitted its context, leaving us to guess whether the flames were set deliberately by enemies outside the fortress or acci-dentally by care-less occupants within.

Fergus of Kintyre died in 781. With his departure we enter a period of profound uncertainty. The following decades as far as the mid-ninth century are obscured by a fog of confusion and contra-diction. In trying to make sense of what was happening in these years we face a dearth of reliable information. Even the basic outline of a narrative history is impossible to reconstruct with any confidence. Nowhere is this more true than among the Picts and

Centres of power, sixth to eighth centuries AD

Scots whose respective king-lists become so entangled from this point that we cannot discern which gives a more accurate picture. The situation is less acute south of the Forth–Clyde isthmus where a lengthy royal genealogy continues to provide a loose historical framework for the Britons of Alt Clut as far as c.870. In Northumbria's case we are able to construct a fairly reliable list of kings from various sources.

One confusing aspect of the sources is that they appear to show Pictish kings ruling simultaneously in Dál Riata between the 780s and the 830s. This has led to a belief that the two peoples were ruled as a single overkingship which evolved into a unified realm before c.900. An alternative view envisages royal succession among the Picts and Scots continuing along separate paths before merging in the middle of the ninth century. Our uncertainty is partly due to deliberate manipulation of the source material by Scottish writers of the tenth, eleventh and later centuries. This interference led to Pictish kings being retrospectively 'parachuted' into the king-lists of Dál Riata to give the impression that the lands on either side of Druim Alban were united under one dynasty before 800. If we remove these intrusive Picts from the lists, the picture becomes slightly clearer, although we are still left with many gaps and ambiguities.

It would appear that the successor of Fergus in the kingship of Cenél nGabráin was Donncorci who reigned from 781 to 792. He is an obscure figure who appears in no source outside the Irish annals. Neither his father's name nor his true ancestry are known, but he perhaps represented the continuing dominance of Cenél nGabráin over other kindreds in Argyll. He might have been a son of Fergus, or of Áed Find. Among the Picts, a different Fergus fathered a prince called Constantine ('Causantín') who attained overkingship during the later years of Donncorci's reign in Dál Riata. The name of Constan-tine's father suggests a familial link with Óengus, son of Fergus, and a continuing prominence for the great warlord's family. Constantine's core domains seem to have lain in Perthshire, but we do not know how far his hegemony extended northward. He probably held Atholl under his sway, but whether his authority reached across the Mounth is unknown. His military prowess was shown in a victory over an army of Scots led by Conall, son of Tadg, in 789. Conall is another mysterious figure who, like Donncorci, appears to belong to Cenél nGabráin. Some historians believe that Conall had Pictish ancestry and a legitimate claim to Constantine's throne, but this is not a necessary deduction from the sources. After his defeat by Constantine, nothing more is known of Conall until his reappearance as a contender for the overking-ship of Dál Riata in the early 800s. It is likely that he spent the final decade of the eighth century consolidating his personal power-base in Kintyre. If so, then he and his fellow-Scots soon faced a formidable new foe in the seaways of Argyll.

Norsemen

The first recorded Viking raid on the British Isles came in 793 when a band of Norwegians plundered the Northumbrian monastery of Lindisfarne. By the end of the century more of these 'Northmen' (or 'Norse') were raiding the coasts of Britain and Ireland with increasing frequency. Scotland suffered its first attack in 802 when Iona was ravaged and burned. Four years later, the Columban headquarters was again violated and sixty-eight monks were killed. Religious settlements offered rich pickings to heathen raiders and presented them with soft targets. Decorative gold and silver was ripped from altars and bookbindings, captives were carried off and defenceless monks were cut down. Much as we might condemn these acts of wanton destruction we should remember that the Vikings were not the first to commit such crimes. We have only to recall Dungal of Lorn in 733, or Berht of Bernicia in 684, to meet so-called 'Christians' who casually profaned the sanctity of churches.

Trading links and other forms of communication between Scan-dinavia and northern Britain had undoubtedly been occurring on a minor scale for hundreds of years, but the endemic piracy of the Viking Age was a radical new development. After c.800, frequent and devastating attacks were being directed against exposed shore-lands and islands. Some raiding expeditions were significant ventures involving large numbers of men and ships. Why a considerable number of Scandinavian males were attracted to a life of piracy across the North Sea is an interesting question which continues to exercise the minds of historians and archaeologists. Evidence from the Nordic countries suggests that a combination of social, economic and technological factors lay at the root of the Viking Age. One key factor was a scarcity of agricultural land due to population increases during the eighth century; another was the development of fast keeled longships capable of transporting warbands on swift raiding expeditions. Contrary to some modern theories, there is no evidence that the earliest raiders were interested in acquiring farmland on which to settle their families, nor does it seem that the brutality of their attacks was exaggerated by their own bards or by horrified Christian chroniclers. Phases of large-scale colonisation of the British Isles did indeed occur but only after many years of sustained violence which inflicted enormous terror on the natives. We should not be in any doubt that the typical Scandin-avian visitor in the first half of the ninth century fitted the conventional image of an aggressive marauder seeking loot rather than land. The activities of such men were characterised by hit and run tactics rather than by acquisition of territory. Only after c.850, when per-manent settlements began to appear, did the situation start to change. The first Viking colonies were established in Orkney, Shetland and the Outer Hebrides, and on the Irish coastlands. Some were founded primarily as pirate bases, but others may have served as trading posts where natives and Norsemen could interact peaceably.

Much of what we know about the Viking Age in Scotland comes from contemporary Irish sources, primarily the annals, supplemented by some later English and Scottish texts. All inevitably highlighted the districts in which their compilers maintained a particular interest. We thus encounter references to the western seaways, the Argyll coastlands, Clydesdale and Lothian, and the Pictish heartlands of Perthshire, Aberdeenshire and Moray. But a dearth of information relating to regions further north deprives us of a balanced view of what was happening in Ross and Sutherland and Caithness, and in Orkney and Shetland. These areas had long been regarded as peripheral to the interests of annalists and chroniclers so we should not be unduly sur-prised to find them being sidelined in the ninth, tenth and eleventh centuries. There was, of course, no north-eastern equivalent of Iona to bequeath a record of events in the firths of Dornoch and Pentland. Or, if such a centre of knowledge ever existed, its chronicle has not survived. Ironically, our main sources of information for the history of this region in Viking times are of Scandinavian origin, namely a group of texts known as the Norse sagas. These were written c.1150–1350 and therefore belong to a much later period than the one they claim to describe. Most, if not all, originated in Iceland and were compiled from heroic tales that were themselves originally preserved in oral rather than in written form. Although the information presented by the sagas is rich in detail, only a small percentage of it can be regarded as reliable 'history'. The rest is storytelling, even when the narrative mentions a real event or an attested historical figure.

Picts and Scots

At the beginning of the ninth century, the Scandinavian raids on northern parts of Britain were becoming endemic. The long, broken coastline of Argyll made Dál Riata particularly vulnerable to seaborne assault and its people suffered accordingly. In the face of this growing peril, the overkingship of the Scots wavered as various claimants jostled for power. The disruption and uncertainty of the era are reflected in the sources which present a confusing picture during the transition from the eighth century to the ninth. By 807, when the annals resume their entries on secular events in northern Britain, the sovereignty of Dál Riata was being contested by two men, both of whom bore the name Conall. Their backgrounds are unclear, but both may have sprung from septs or factions among Cenél nGabráin. One was the previously mentioned Conall, son of Tadg, whose forces had been defeated by the Picts in 789; the other, who eventually won the overkingship, was the son of an otherwise unknown Áedán. Their rivalry reached its inevitable conclusion in a battle in Kintyre which took the life of Tadg's son.

Conall, son of Áedán, thereafter ruled as overking of the Scots until 811. According to the sources, his successor was Domnall, a son of the Pictish king Constantine. Domnall's emergence as a paramount ruler in Dál Riata cannot be explained away as a textual error or as an example of manipulation by later writers. It seems that he did indeed rule the Scots during his father's overkingship of the Picts. How this happened can only be surmised, for the sources offer few clues, but one possibility is that Constantine presented his son as a legitimate royal claimant to the Dál Riatan overkingship. Such a claim would have required support and acceptance from the Scots at a time when other candidates were no doubt available. Domnall's claim presumably derived from blood-kinship with one or more royal *cenéla*, perhaps via his maternal ancestry. Was his mother a Gaelic princess? An alternative scenario sees Constantine imposing Domnall on the Scots by force, but this seems unlikely when the sources give no hint of warfare between East and West. Domnall thus emerges as a legitimate contender for the overkingship of Dál Riata rather than as the son of a Pictish conqueror. Constantine died in 820 and the Picts under his rule received his brother Óengus as their new king. With Domnall still reigning as overking in the West, there was probably much co-operation between uncle and nephew. This seems to have permeated down through the aristocracy in their respective kingdoms where it was reflected in social and cultural changes. Of these, the most profound was an increasing Gaelicisation of Pictish society, a process that had probably begun in the previous century. Ironically, it appears that the Pictish dominion imposed on the Scots by Constantine and his family accelerated the eastward spread of Gaelic speech. The process was undoubtedly quickened by the Scandinavian menace in the western seaways and by the real economic difficulties this created. With the sources giving few clues, we are left to envisage a steady migration of Gaelic-speaking elites from Argyll to Perthshire, Moray and other districts east of Druim Alban. It is likely that the Pictish language, a tongue of Brittonic origin, had already adopted some Gaelic characteristics long before 800. During Constantine's reign, there may have been a measure of mutual intelligibility between Picts and Scots, especially among folk of high status on both sides. Perhaps the old Pictish speech gradually slid further down the social hierarchy as it became less attractive to people of ambition? Intermarriage between aristocratic Scots and Picts would have increased the bilingual element in both communities, but it was Gaelic rather than Pictish that eventually became the dominant tongue. We might additionally observe that the ethnic and linguistic distinctions which look so clear-cut today were almost certainly much more blurred in the eighth and ninth centuries.

In the era of co-operation facilitated by one Pictish family's grip on a 'dual overkingship' the main political benefits were military. A Picto-Scottish alliance was surely established in 811, when Domnall gained the overkingship of Dál Riata during his father's reign in the East, and was presumably renewed by Constantine's brother Óengus in 820. Both Domnall and Óengus would have pooled their resources in joint campaigns to protect their respective realms from external foes. The annals mention Viking raids on Irish and Hebridean monasteries during the early ninth century, but non-religious sites were also targeted, even if the attacks upon them went unrecorded. A series of battles can be imagined and, in some of these, Picts and Scots no doubt fought side by side. When, however, Óengus and Domnall died in 834 and 835 respectively, another period of dynastic instability ensued. A new set of ambitious rivals competed for power on either side of Druim Alban. Among the Picts the paramount kingship was claimed by Drust, another son of Constantine, but his authority was not universally recognised and a counter-claim was made by a certain Talorcan. By 837, whatever remained of this overkingship had passed to Drust's cousin Eóganán, a son of Óengus, but his reign was destined to be brief. Sovereignty over the Scots had meanwhile been claimed by Áed, son of Boanta. Áed's origins are unclear but he aligned himself with Eóganán and may have ruled Dál Riata as Eóganán's subordinate. In 839, both kings were struck down by Vikings at an unnamed battle in Moray, the heartland of the old Pictish kingdom of Fortriu. Other casualties of this fateful encounter included Eóganán's brother and probable heir, together with countless numbers of allied troops. In one savage stroke, the Picts and Scots were deprived of their overkings and the warrior-elites of both realms were decimated. In the ensuing turmoil, a mysterious figure called Cináed mac Ailpín claimed the overkingship of Dál Riata. Sovereignty over some part of the Pictish nation was seized by Ferat, son of Barot. The relationship between these two newcomers is unclear, as are their respective origins. Cináed arose among the Scots and was probably a Gaelic-speaker, but he may have been a Pict by birth and ancestry. Of Ferat we know almost nothing beyond an indication in the Pictish king-lists that his reign lasted three years. The dynastic picture thereafter becomes extremely confused, with many contradictions between different king-lists and chronicles. It seems likely that Ferat was slain or deposed, his place being taken by Brude, son of Fochel, whose claim was contested by Ferat's three sons. The latter gained the upper hand and ruled in swift succession, or perhaps simultaneously as rulers of separate Pictish overkingships. They were eventually toppled by Cináed mac Ailpín, presumably after one or more decisive battles.

The territories now under Cináed's rule spanned both sides of Druim Alban. His Pictish domains may have been confined to Perthshire, encompassing lands south of the Mounth, with Moray remaining outside his control. Later tradition associated him with Kintyre and this was probably his main territory in the West. He is usually seen as a pivotal figure in early Scottish history, a king credited with welding the Picts and Scots into a single nation, although this exalted status might owe more to propaganda devised by his descendants than to ninth-century political reality. In the annals, he is described only as *rex Pictorum* ('king of the Picts'), without reference to rank or authority in Dál Riata. Medieval

Scottish tradition linked his ancestry to Cenél nGabráin by making him a descendant of Áed Find, but this might be spurious. In truth, we have no idea where he originated. We may cautiously assume that his preferred language was Gaelic, even if his name and that of his father look Pictish. Beyond this, we cannot say much about his lineage and origins. Stories about Alpín speak of warfare in Galloway, but these are not thought to be reliable. Everything we know about Cináed really begins with his emergence as *rex Pictorum* in the 840s. The sources leave us in no doubt that he established his main seats of power in Perthshire. Chief among his residences was a palace at Forteviot in Strathearn where renowned predecessors such as Constantine, son of Fergus, had formerly held court. A suitable setting for royal rituals and public assemblies was subsequently established at Scone, another low-lying site, where an artificial mound was raised. This feature, the Moot Hill, can still be seen today. It served as an appropriate setting for the Stone of Destiny, a sacred symbol of kingship allegedly transferred by Cináed from a royal centre in Argyll.

As the ninth century progressed, Cináed and his successors presided over the continuing Gaelicisation of Pictish society, a process which led ultimately to the total disappearance of the Picts as a distinct group. Contrary to a belief promoted in later times, this did not involve a programme of 'ethnic cleansing' to expunge the Pictish peasantry from the landscape, nor does it appear to have involved a wholesale migration of Gaelic-speaking farmers from Argyll. In all likelihood, the linguistic change was propelled as much by semi-Gaelicised Pictish nobles as by western immigrants. Groups of high-status Scots nevertheless made the journey across Druim Alban, perceiving the fertile East as a more productive environment for their ambitions than the dangerous shorelands of the West. As noted above, Gaelic language and culture had almost certainly gained a foothold among the Picts during the reigns of Constantine, Domnall and Óengus, between 789 and 835. It is possible, even probable, that these three kings used Gaelic as their own preferred medium in high-level discourse. By the middle of the ninth century, with Picts and Scots acknowledging the rule of a single Gaelic-speaking sovereign in the person of Cináed, the Pictish language may already have been in terminal decline.

By c.850, Cináed's kingdom extended from Kintyre to Fife and from Atholl to the Firth of Forth. Pictish territories further north in Moray seem not to have fallen under his sway. This region lay under the control of a Gaelic-speaking elite whose leaders had migrated from Argyll in the preceding decades. These new rulers of Fortriu sprang from a branch of Cenél Loairn, choosing the seventh-century warlord Ferchar Fota as their real or imagined forefather. Their eastward migration may have been a process rather than a single event, with the first incomers from Lorn perhaps entering Moray via the Great Glen in the late 700s. By the beginning of the ninth century, they seem to have imposed their authority on the Moravian Picts. Why they left their ancestral lands is unknown, but the arrival of Norse raiders on the Lorn shorelands in the 790s would have been an obvious incentive. Their Pictish neighbours further north, in Caithness, might likewise have fallen under the sway of yet another group of Gaelic incomers at roughly the same time. Beyond Caithness lay the Viking colonies of Orkney and Shetland, an area where temporary pirate-bases were now increasingly giving way to settled communities of Scandinavian farmers and fisherfolk. The late 800s would eventually see large-scale Norse settlement in the Northern Isles and in other outlying regions, all of which had previously been ignored by native chroniclers as peripheral and irrelevant.

The Mac Ailpín Dynasty and its Neighbours

The first half of the ninth century brought frequent Norse raids to all parts of the British Isles. By the middle of the century, pirate bands from Denmark were also taking a share of the plunder. In 851, a large Danish fleet appeared in the Irish Sea, perhaps sailing in via the English Channel after raiding on the Continent. The newcomers attacked Norse settlements in Ireland before rampaging in various parts of mainland Britain. Hostilities between Danes and Norsemen continued until 853 when Olaf, an Irish-based Viking of Norwegian stock, emerged as the dominant figure among a number of Scandinavian groups. He eventually established himself at Dublin from where he spent the next twenty years raiding and campaigning on both sides of the Irish Sea. His early activities coincided with the latter part of Cináed's reign and, although there is no record of warfare between the two, Cináed reputedly fought against Danish Vikings. These may have been marauders engaged in plundering raids across Perthshire.

Not all of Cináed's dealings with Viking warlords involved bloodshed. References to political marriages between members of his family and high-born Scandinavians are mostly late and spurious, but the idea of at least one marital union cannot be rejected outright. Such an arrangement, perhaps sealed with oaths of friendship between previously hostile dynasties, could have relieved Cináed's anxieties on his western maritime frontier. He does indeed seem to have pursued his ambitions elsewhere. One text credits him with launching six major raids on English Northumbria, a land already weakened by Danish incursions. He is said to have plundered the Bernician fortress at Dunbar and burned the monastery at Melrose. Loot and prestige, rather than permanent acquisition of territory, would have been his main objectives in these campaigns. Similar motives no doubt prompted the Clyde Britons to plunder the church of Dunblane on Cináed's southern border. This event may have been connected in some way to a dynastic marriage between one of Cináed's daughters and Rhun ab Arthgal, a son of the king of Dumbarton. The betrothal may have sealed a truce between the two kingdoms, ending a period of raid and counter-raid across the River Forth.

A tumour, rather than the sword of an enemy, ended Cináed's life. He died in 858 in his palace at Forteviot beside the River Earn. His brother Domnall succeeded him as overking, maintaining the cohesion of the eastern and western segments of the mac Ailpín realm. One source says of Domnall that 'in war he was a vigorous soldier', although it does not say whom he fought to gain this martial reputation. It is possible that his anonymous foes included rivals within his kingdom, a suggestion which seems broadly consistent with a chronicle reference to 'the Gaels, with their king' assembling at Forteviot during Domnall's reign. This ceremonial gathering seems to have been convened to affirm 'the rights and laws of the kingdom of Áed, son of Eochaid'. The Áed in question was the eighth-century king Áed Find, who, as we have already seen, fought against the Picts in 768. Why he should be mentioned in the context of a later assembly at Forteviot is unclear, but one possibility is that an under-king of Dál Riata, perhaps a member of Cenél nGabráin claiming descent from Áed, came eastward c.860 to swear an oath of fealty to Domnall. Other interpretations of the chronicle record are possible, but there seems little doubt that issues of overkingship and clientship lie behind its ambiguous wording.

In 862, after a brief reign, Domnall died at Rathinveramon, 'the earth-walled fort at the mouth of the River Almond'. The place of his death lay within the crumbling ramparts of the old Roman fort of Bertha, perhaps in a royal church established there for the mac Ailpín family. One tradition asserts that he was assassinated, another that he succumbed to illness. He was succeeded by his nephew Constantine mac Cináeda whose fifteen-year reign was marked by frequent outbreaks of warfare. In later tradition, Constantine was praised as 'the cow-herd of the byre of the cows of the Picts', a poetic way of describing him as protector of the Pictish portion of his kingdom – the lands east of Druim Alban and south of the Mounth. His chief enemies were Scandinavian, most notably Olaf of Dublin and various Danish warlords. At the time of his accession the most northerly parts of Pictish territory already lay under Norse rule. Thus, the archipelagos of Orkney and Shetland, together with some mainland districts, now acknowledged Scandinavian masters. Caithness was apparently still under Pictish or Picto-Scottish rule, but would fall to the Norsemen before c.950. In Moray, the descendants of ninth-century Cenél Loairn immigrants ruled a Gaelicised population of largely Pictish origin and sternly resisted further Norse encroachment. Most of these districts north of the Grampians seem to have lain outside

Constantine's field of vision, his most immediate concern being the continuing menace of Viking attacks on his own domains. During this period, Olaf of Dublin rampaged at will across Ireland and northern Britain, taking captives from many regions and sending them back to the great slave-market in his city. In 870, he and his companion Ivar – perhaps his brother – besieged and sacked Alt Clut, the iconic royal fortress of the Clyde Britons. This was no hit and run raid but a carefully planned assault involving a huge fleet of two hundred longships. There can be little doubt that its objective was the political neutering of the North Britons, perhaps with the collateral aim of establishing a Viking stronghold at Dumbarton. In the longer term, neither of these outcomes was achieved, but the devastating impact of the assault sent shock waves around the western seaways. The beleaguered occupants of the Rock endured a four-month siege before capitulating when their water source ran dry. These unfortunates were then herded onto the waiting longships to be crammed alongside other miserable captives – Picts, Scots and Northumbrians – snatched in previous raids. Among the prisoners was Arthgal, king of Alt Clut, who was taken back to Dublin as a high-status hostage. Constantine mac Cináeda persuaded Olaf and Ivar to assassinate Arthgal two years later, perhaps to clear the way for his son Rhun – husband of Constantine's sister – to attain the Clyde kingship as a puppet. This collusion between Dublin and the mac Ailpíns proved to be temporary. Around the time of Arthgal's murder, Olaf was slain in battle against Constantine while on a plundering expedition. The Norse warlord's demise did not, however, bring any long-lasting respite from Scandinavian raids. In 875, a host of Danes defeated Constantine at Dollar in Stirlingshire before rampaging across his kingdom. Storming northward through Strathtay, they eventually reached Atholl where they lingered for a whole year, no doubt inflicting further misery on the populace. Either they or another band of marauders brought a violent end to Constantine's life in 876 at the 'Black Cave' of *Inverdufatha*, near present-day Inverdovat on the north-east coast of Fife.

The most powerful Viking force at the time of Constantine's

death was the 'Great Army'. This was built around the large Danish force that had first appeared in the British Isles in 851, supplemented by other Scandinavian adventurers, including many of Norwegian blood. In 865, this fearsome power arrived in East Anglia where it camped for a year before moving up to Northumbria. It defeated and slew two Northumbrian kings, set up another in their place, then departed south in search of more loot. By 876, the year when Constantine mac Cináeda died at the hands of a separate Danish force, a portion of the 'Great Army' returned to Northumbria and expelled the English dynasty. A Viking called Halfdan established himself at York as ruler of what is often described as the 'Anglo-Danish' kingdom of Northumbria. His realm stretched from the Humber to the Tyne where it bordered a smaller realm representing a rump of English rule, roughly corresponding to seventh-century Bernicia. The leaders of this territory established their seat of power at the old royal fortress of Bamburgh.

At the time of Constantine's death, the impact of the Vikings had permanently altered the political map of Britain. Three distinct power-blocs were now emerging: the kingdom of the West Saxons in southern England, the mac Ailpín realm in the North and the 'Danelaw' areas of eastern England where Scandinavian warlords held control. Other, less-powerful groups began to position themselves aound these three. In Wales, a patchwork of little kingdoms lay in a crucible of West Saxon, Anglo-Danish and Norse-Irish interests. In the western seaways, bands of Gaelic-speaking warriors from Ireland, the Gall-Gáidhil or 'foreign Gaels', roved and raided like old-style Vikings. Some forged their own small lordships in a broad band of territory between the firths of Clyde and Solway, eventually giving their name to Galloway, while others settled on the coast of north-west England. In the lower valley of the River Clyde, a new kingdom of the Britons arose from the wreckage left by Olaf and Ivar in 870. Its rulers were related to, or identical with, the former dynasty of Alt Clut. The great rock of Dumbarton was reoccupied, but the Viking assault had destroyed its aura of impregnability and it no longer served as the main royal stronghold. A menacing presence lurked in the Firth of Clyde in the dragon-prowed shape of Norse and Gall-Gáidhil longships. This ever-present threat persuaded the Britons to move their centres of power upstream to the confluence of the rivers Clyde and Kelvin at Partick. On the opposite bank, at Govan, the royal family adopted an already ancient church as their primary place of worship and burial. A nearby artificial mound, later known as the Doomster Hill, became their chief ceremonial site. To reflect this move inland to the less-exposed valley the reborn realm was given the name *Strat Clut* ('Strathclyde').

Northward across the River Forth, in Perthshire, another of Cináed mac Ailpín's sons succeeded to the throne in 876. This was Áed, Constantine's younger brother, but within two years of his accession he was dead, falling foul of a new phase of internal strife. According to the Irish annalists he was 'slain by his associates', these being either rogue elements within his army or opportunists among an inner circle of henchmen. The leader of the rebels is named in some sources as Giric, a man of obscure origin who apparently had royal blood. Giric and his co-conspirators made their challenge in a battle at Strathallan, perhaps near Dunblane, where Áed was defeated and mortally wounded. The victory cleared Giric's path to the throne, but whether he ventured along it is something of a mystery. Some sources call him king, while others imply that he stepped aside to make way for Áed's nephew Eochaid, a grandson of Cináed mac Ailpín. Eochaid's parents were Rhun, king of Strathclyde, and a daughter of Cináed whom the sources do not name. Through his maternal ancestry Eochaid was eligible to succeed Áed in the mac Ailpín kingship, but he is unlikely to have been the only claimant. He presumably owed his position to Giric and may have been the latter's protégé, ruling as a figurehead while Giric lurked behind the throne as the real wielder of power. One tradition calls Eochaid the *alumnus* ('foster-son') of Giric, while another ignores him altogether and instead names Giric as Áed's immediate successor. Whatever the truth behind these relationships, both Giric and Eochaid were toppled in 889 by Domnall, son of Constantine and grandson of Cináed. Eochaid may have sought sanctuary with his father's kin on the Clyde, but Giric met a violent death at the old Pictish hillfort of Dundurn in Strathearn. Domnall, Constantine's son, thereafter ruled to the end of the century, his reign coinciding with an important change in the terminology used by contemporary annalists and chroniclers. Unlike his predecessors he was not given the Latin title *rex Pictorum* ('king of the Picts'). Instead, he appears in the sources as the first of his dynasty to bear the Gaelic title *ri Albain* ('king of Alba'). Why this new name was applied to the kingdom is hard to tell, but the Gaelic term *Alba* is an ancient Irish name for the island of Britain as a whole. At the end of the ninth century it evidently conveyed a much narrower meaning. Was it, perhaps, the contemporary Gaelic name for 'Pictland'? Or was it simply an apt label for a part of Britain where Gaelic speech now predominated? Whatever its origin, *Alba* was chosen by the mac Ailpíns as a suitable name for their realm and was presumably acceptable to Picts and Scots alike.

Domnall reigned for eleven years. During this time, the Pictish part of his kingdom was again ravaged by Vikings but he scored a major victory over one group of raiders at a place called *Innisibsolian*. The place-name defies identification, but its first element implies an island, perhaps off the eastern coast of Alba where Domnall was apparently campaigning at the time of his death. He was slain at Dunnottar, a Pictish coastal fortress, most likely by Scandinavian foes. His death occurred in 900, at the dawn of the final century of the first millennium, and coincided with the end of a distinct Pictish history. From the beginning of the tenth century, the sources no longer recognise the Picts as a separate people. Domnall and his successors ruled *fir Albain* ('the men of Alba'), a Gaelic-speaking population to whom contemporary and later writers referred collectively as 'Scots' regardless of their ancestry.

CHAPTER 9
Alba

Constantine mac Áeda

The tenth century heralded a period of political transition in the British Isles. Behind lay an era of small kingdoms and temporary overlordships, a period swept aside by the sudden impact of the Vikings. Ahead lay an era of greater political stability in which smaller realms either vanished altogether or became provinces within large, regional overkingships. By 900, some of the larger entities were beginning to adopt the essential building blocks of statehood: strong monarchies; stable systems of royal succession; the first hints of bureaucracy. Models for these enlarged 'proto-states' were already available in Continental Europe, especially in France and Germany, where the institution of kingship now looked increasingly stable and sophisticated.

An example of the new breed of king was Constantine, son of Áed and grandson of Cináed mac Ailpín, who succeeded his cousin Domnall as king of Alba in 900. Like his forebears, Constantine mac Áeda ruled from a power-base in the southern Pictish heartlands of Perthshire as overking of a much wider realm. The people under his authority were already starting to think of themselves as 'Scots', regardless of whether they lived in Fife or Kintyre. Those born during his forty-year reign grew to adulthood in a land where Gaelic, not Pictish, was now the language of social advancement. Although his kingdom had not yet become the great medieval kingdom of Scotland, it was taking its first tentative steps towards that goal.

Scotland in the Viking Age

When Constantine became king, he found himself facing enemies on several fronts. In the fourth year of his reign, he fought and defeated a Scandinavian army at *Strath Erenn*, probably Strathearn in Perthshire, slaying a warlord called Ivar. The defeated Vikings had previously plundered the church at Dunkeld where precious relics of Saint Columba were housed. They may have been the same marauders who had killed Constantine's predecessor Domnall, at Dunnottar, in which case they had been a menace in Alba for several years. Alternatively, they might have arrived from Ireland, seeking new opportunities in Britain after the expulsion of the Dublin Norse in 902. This is perhaps less likely, for the majority of Dublin refugees settled much further south, on the western shorelands of what are now Cheshire and Lancashire, or along coastal areas of the Lake District, or in Galloway. Constantine's victory in 904 came at a time when Viking power in the British Isles was enduring a brief series of setbacks. Alongside the Irish capture of the long-established Norse stronghold of Dublin, the Anglo-Danish kingdom of Northumbria had reverted to a dynasty of local English kings. However, these setbacks turned out to be short-lived and, within a dozen years of Dublin's fall, Scandinavian warlords were again flexing their ambitions on both sides of the Irish Sea.

Corbridge and Brunanburh

In 914, two Viking fleets fought a naval battle off the Manx coast. The victor was Ragnall, a kinsman of the Ivar slain by Constantine mac Áeda in Strath Erenn ten years earlier. Ragnall's appearance, or reappearance, coincided with the start of a new phase of Scandinavian influence in Ireland. From a base at Waterford, the heathen forces launched raids on the Irish hinterland, their activities creating ideal conditions for an invasion by Ragnall and his brother Sihtric. In 917, after heavy fighting against the Irish, Sihtric recaptured Dublin to turn it once more into a major Viking port. Ragnall remained in Ireland for a while before crossing to northern

Britain where, after a sojourn among Norse colonies on the west coast, he crossed the Pennines to seize the kingship of Northumbria. Ealdred, the incumbent English king at York, fled north to seek sanctuary with Constantine of Alba. Seeing an opportunity to pursue his own ambitions, Constantine marched south to challenge Ragnall, meeting him in battle at the old Roman town of Corbridge beside the River Tyne. Although the fighting ended in stalemate with neither side claiming victory, it left Ragnall still in place as king of Northumbria. With his brother Sihtric ruling at Dublin, a dangerous transmarine alliance of Scandinavian powers now straddled the Irish Sea. The neighbouring kingdoms viewed the situation with understandable anxiety, fearing what such a formidable power-bloc might achieve in the years ahead.

At that time, the main obstacle to further Viking expansion in northern Britain was the mac Ailpín realm of Alba. In southern Britain an even more powerful counterweight was the kingdom of Wessex, the land of the West Saxons. In the early tenth century the West Saxon king was Edward the Elder, son and heir of Alfred the Great. Edward's authority was also acknowledged in the still-English western half of Mercia, the eastern half having long lain within the Danelaw. English Mercia was no longer ruled by its own kings but by an ealdorman owing allegiance to Wessex. During the early years of Edward's reign this office was held by his brother-in-law Aethelred who ruled Mercia as a West Saxon fief. When Aethelred died in 911, Edward's sister Aethelflaed assumed overall control. Being Alfred's daughter, Aethelflaed was no stranger to war and political dealings. She soon showed her mettle by leading her Mercian troops into battle, proving herself a tough and ruthless war-leader. According to one source, she forged a tripartite alliance with Constantine mac Áeda and his Strathclyde counterpart Dyfnwal ab Owain as a counterweight to the Scandinavian threat on her northern frontier in Cheshire. South of the Mersey she harried the Danelaw settlements in the eastern midlands, scoring several major successes and carving a formidable reputation among friends and foes alike. She died in her palace at Tamworth in 919, a year after the battle of Corbridge, but her brother Edward maintained the impetus of her campaigns by building fortresses at key locations across the midlands and by negotiating with the northern powers. In 920, at Bakewell in Derbyshire, Edward successfully brokered a non-aggression pact with the rulers of Alba, Strathclyde and English Northumbria. At this meeting he secured agreements from Constantine, Dyfnwal and the lords of Bamburgh that they would refrain from attacking Ragnall of York as long as Ragnall himself launched no raids south of the Humber. Although depicted by West Saxon propaganda as an act of submission by the northern powers, the outcome at Bakewell was not so much a recognition of Edward's supremacy as a temporary truce in the ruinous cycle of raid and counter-raid. Edward was certainly overlord of substantial parts of southern Britain, but it is unlikely that his hegemony extended north of the Mersey–Humber line. Within a year of the meeting Ragnall was dead, his position at York being taken by his brother Sihtric who came over from Dublin to seize the kingship of Anglo-Danish Northumbria. Three years later, in 924, Edward of Wessex died while campaigning against the Welsh and was succeeded by his son Athelstan, a king whom the Celts and Scandinavians would soon regard as their deadliest adversary.

Athelstan's northern policy began in 926 when he secured the allegiance of York by marrying his sister to Sihtric. When Sihtric died the following year, Athelstan seized York and annexed the kingdom, fighting off a challenge from Sihtric's brother Gothfrith of Dublin. On 12 July 927, Athelstan hosted an assembly of rulers on the banks of the River Eamont near Penrith. There he received pledges of fealty from Earl Ealdred of Bamburgh, Constantine of Alba, Owain ap Dyfnwal of Strathclyde and one or two Welsh kings. The precise location is hard to pinpoint, but the Roman fort at Brougham, the old Northumbrian monastery at Dacre, or a prehistoric henge near Eamont Bridge are possible candidates. Unlike Edward's gathering at Bakewell seven years earlier, the Eamont meeting involved formal recognition of West Saxon overlordship beyond the borders of Wessex and Mercia. It suggests that Athelstan's seizure of Anglo-Danish York in the face of a strong challenge from Dublin had confirmed his status as the most powerful warlord in Britain.

The oaths and pledges sworn in 927 began to unravel in the 930s. Athelstan's relationship with Constantine collapsed in 934 and the English king launched a full-scale invasion of Alba. The cause of the conflict is unknown, but Constantine may have refused to continue paying homage, his defiance thereby inviting a punitive response. In military terms, the invasion was a massive raid to plunder and despoil Constantine's resources and in this regard it was a major success. Leading a large force of West Saxons and Mercians, supplemented by the armies of his Welsh vassals, Aethelstan marched as far as Dunnottar on the Aberdeenshire coast, while his fleet raided even further north in Caithness. At this time, according to one Icelandic saga, the rulers of Caithness were not Scandinavians but Gaels, presumably Scots from Argyll or a Pictish elite who had adopted Gaelic. Athelstan eventually returned home laden with loot, having secured a new oath of allegiance from Constantine. The latter nevertheless remained defiant and conspired with both Olaf Gothfrithsson, king of Dublin, and Owain ap Dyfnwal, king of Strathclyde. In 937, a combined force of Vikings, Scots and Clyde Britons sought a decisive showdown with Athelstan. The ensuing encounter, known to subsequent generations as the 'Great Battle', was a clash of epic proportions. It was commemorated by bards and storytellers on both sides, the most dramatic account being a contemporary English poem incorporated in the *Anglo-Saxon Chronicle*. According to this text, the fighting took place at *Brunanburh*, a location unidentifiable today. Various sites have been suggested as possible candidates, usually on the basis of vague geographical information provided by sources of varying reliability. No consensus has yet been reached, but a setting in northern England or southern Scotland seems plausible and it is to this general area that most historians direct their search for the battlefield. One candidate is Burnswark in Dumfriesshire, a prominent flat-topped hill overlooking a Roman fort and guarding a major communication route. Another is the Lancashire moorland around Burnley, a place whose name means 'meadow of the River Brun'. A third possibility is Bromborough, a village on the Wirral peninsula, but this seems too far south as a destination for the Scots and Strathclyde Britons. Wherever the battle took place, its outcome was a major victory for Athelstan and a clear affirmation of his supremacy. His coins proclaimed him *rex et rector totius Brittaniae* ('king and governor of all Britain'). This boast would have been difficult to challenge after Brunanburh.

The West Saxon poet whose verses praised Aethelstan's triumph gloated on the rout of the allied armies. One group of lines described the humbling of Constantine mac Áeda, a grizzled veteran of many wars who was probably the senior party in the alliance:

> So also the old one
> fled away to his northern country,
> Constantine, hoary battle-man.
> He need not boast of the meeting of swords.
> He was severed from kin, deprived of friends
> on that field, slain at war
> and left his son on the death-ground,
> destroyed by his wounds, young at war.
> He need have no proud words, the white-haired warrior,
> the wily one.

Despite its contemporary fame, the battle caused no major upheaval in the balance of power. Aethelstan emerged with his overlordship intact but with few collateral benefits. Constantine, Olaf and Owain survived the carnage and returned to their own lands. None of the trio was deposed by disgruntled rivals at home, nor is there any hint that they conceded territory to Athelstan. All three seem to have outlived him. He passed away in 939, dying a peaceful but untimely death at the age of forty-three. His younger brother Edmund, a hardy prince who had fought at Brunanburh, succeeded to the West Saxon throne but was unprepared for a sudden attack on Mercia. The onslaught came from Northumbria where the Anglo-Scandinavians of York had shaken off the yoke of vassalage imposed by Athelstan in 927. In a further snub to Edmund, the assault was led by his brother's old adversary Olaf of Dublin, whom the York elite had invited to take up the newly restored kingship.

Olaf marched south of the Humber into Mercian territory, plundering not only Edmund's western fiefs but also the Danelaw areas of the east. Two years later, the York force turned north to ravage the lands of the English lords of Bamburgh. During this campaign Olaf met his death, apparently after the intercession of the eighth-century Bernician saint Baldred, only to be succeeded by an equally ambitious namesake in the shape of his cousin Olaf Sihtricsson, a man more commonly known by the curious epithet *Cuaran* ('Sandal'). More will be said of Olaf Cuaran in the following pages.

Mael Coluim

Constantine mac Áeda resigned the kingship of Alba in 943, having reigned for almost half a century. He spent his twilight years in monastic retirement at St Andrews until his death, at around eighty years of age, in 952. The crown passed to his predecessor's son Malcolm whose name, although shown here in its familiar Anglicised form, represents Gaelic *Mael Coluim* ('Servant of Columba'). Malcolm may have been Constantine's designated heir since 937, when the old king's son Cellach perished at Brunanburh. Alternatively, he may have seized the throne as soon as Constantine abdicated, perhaps pushing Cellach's younger brothers aside. The second of these scenarios seems to be contradicted by a twelfth-century tradition in which the recently retired Constantine encouraged Malcolm to attack Northumbria, thereby hinting at friendship between the two. The raid in question occurred in 949 or 950, penetrating as far south as the River Tees. It resulted in the capture of large numbers of cattle and human beings which were taken back to Alba as loot. A similar quest for plunder may have prompted Malcolm to launch a raid beyond his northern border against Cenél Loairn territory in Moray. At some point during his reign he negotiated a political accord with Edmund, king of the West Saxons, who was rapidly carving a warlike reputation to rival that of his elder brother Athelstan.

In 943, the year of Malcolm's accession, Edmund defeated Olaf

Cuaran in the eastern midlands of England. Olaf was compelled to swear an oath of fealty and returned to York but did not remain there long. The Anglo-Danish nobility withdrew their support from him, transferring their allegiance instead to his cousin Ragnall Gothfrithsson. Both Olaf and Ragnall eventually fled in 944 when Edmund arrived at York with a large army to install an East Anglian nobleman as the new English king of Northumbria. Olaf returned to his family's main power-base at Dublin, having apparently disposed of Ragnall along the way. There he watched and waited while Edmund rose to a position of dominance. It was probably around this time that Malcolm entered into an agreement or alliance with the young West Saxon king, seeing in Edmund the same strength and ambition that had made Athelstan the most powerful English ruler in living memory. At only twenty-three years of age, Edmund was already scaling the heights of supremacy reached by his illustrious elder sibling.

One aspect of the treaty between Edmund and Malcolm was the latter's support or acquiescence in an English invasion of Strathclyde. This attack on the North Britons came in 945, presumably to punish them for incurring Edmund's displeasure. Their king at that time was another Dyfnwal, a son of the Owain who had fought against Athelstan and Edmund at Brunanburh. In an act of cruelty hinting at vengeance, two of Dyfnwal's sons were ritually blinded by English soldiers. They may have been in Edmund's hands before the campaign, perhaps as high-status hostages whose treatment depended on their father's subservience. The fact that they were so brutalised by their captors implies that Dyfnwal broke a pledge of fealty to the English king, thereby inviting a punitive invasion and the mutilation of his children. Strathclyde itself was ravaged by Edmund's troops, its plundered territory being placed thereafter under Malcolm's supervision. The sources speak of Edmund 'leasing' the Clyde kingdom to his Scottish ally, but we have no clear understanding of what this means in a tenth-century context. Formal overlordship of the Britons is likely to have been imposed, or retained, by Edmund himself rather than relinquished to Malcolm so perhaps the terms of the 'lease' merely required the king of Alba to keep a watchful eye on Dyfnwal. This seems consistent with contemporary English opinion, enshrined in the *Anglo-Saxon Chronicle*, which says of Edmund that he leased Strathclyde to Malcolm 'on condition that he be his *midwyrhta* ('together-worker') on land and sea'. From this we might infer that Malcolm was expected to protect Edmund's interests by keeping a tight rein on Dyfnwal's military policy, especially with regard to his dealings with opportunist Vikings in the Firth of Clyde.

Edmund was murdered in 946, in Wessex, while intervening in a petty brawl. The West Saxons elected his younger brother Eadred as king, Edmund's sons being small children at the time of his slaying. Eadred received pledges of loyalty from English lords in Mercia and elsewhere, from Edmund's Welsh clients and from the stalwart ally Malcolm of Alba. A token display of loyalty was shown to Eadred by the Anglo-Scandinavian elite of Northumbria during a meeting at Tanshelf near the Mercian border. By 948, this half-hearted allegiance was exposed when the York nobility, led by the influential archbishop Wulfstan, offered the vacant Northumbrian kingship to a man called Erik. This mysterious figure is sometimes identified as the Viking adventurer Erik Bloodaxe, a Norwegian of royal blood, despite the vagueness of the sources and the likelihood that more than one Erik was active at this time. Regardless of which Erik was appointed as the new king at York, his elevation provoked an angry response from Eadred, who threatened severe consequences if the Northumbrians continued to reject his authority. Fearing another phase of ravaging by West Saxon troops, Archbishop Wulfstan's faction deposed Erik and renewed their oaths of fealty to Eadred. However, the vacant throne soon attracted the attention of Olaf Cuaran who, having recently been chased out of Dublin, now saw an opportunity to resurrect his career. Wulfstan and his aristocratic henchmen accepted the return of their former king and gave him their support until 952 when they reinstated Erik. In the same year, according to the Irish annals, a Viking army defeated a combined force of Scots, Britons and Englishmen. Neither the site of the battle nor the identity of the Vikings was noted by the annalists, but we can speculate that Olaf

Cuaran was probably involved. Perhaps he was the unnamed Scandinavian victor, leading an army of fellow-marauders in a raid on Northumbria's western borderlands? His rival Erik clung to power at York for a further two years before again being expelled by the nobility. Archbishop Wulfstan was already out of the picture, having been removed from office by Eadred, and this time there was no show of defiance against West Saxon overlordship. No new king was appointed, the Northumbrians instead submitting to Eadred by recognising him as their sovereign. Their land henceforth became an earldom under the direct authority of the West Saxon kings, who from this point can be regarded as the first royal dynasty of a more or less unified England.

In the eventful year 952, Constantine mac Áeda died in the monastery at St Andrews. The half-century since his accession to the kingship of Alba had witnessed profound changes in the political landscape of northern Britain. Shifting allegiances had seen Scots hewing Vikings in one battle but standing alongside them in the next, or joining with the Clyde Britons against an English king before abandoning them to the aggressive intentions of his successor. Both Constantine and his cousin Malcolm had sworn oaths of fealty to West Saxon overlords, acknowledging the superiority of English over Scandinavian military power. Within two years of Constantine's death, the once-mighty realm of Anglo-Danish Northumbria, now reduced to an English earldom, was no longer capable of independent action against her Celtic neighbours. A policy of strategic intervention in Northumbria's troubles had enabled first Constantine and then Malcolm to maintain a central role in English and Scandinavian politics. This had brought the additional short-term benefit of keeping dangerous West Saxon warlords mired in the unstable dynastic fortunes of York rather than encamped in the heartlands of Alba.

Royal Rivals

Constantine mac Áeda had been able to concentrate on events

along his southern border because few serious threats were made against him from the far North, from lands across the Mounth. The Viking colonies in Orkney had seemingly given little trouble during his reign, perhaps because their leaders were now exposed to the political ambitions of Norway's kings. Scandinavian lords had evidently ousted the Pictish or Gaelic elite of Caithness, but their immediate neighbours southward were still the Cenél Loairn rulers of Moray. There is no record of conflict between Constantine and the Moravians, the latter presumably concentrating their energies on the Viking menace in Orkney and Caithness. By contrast, Constantine's successor Malcolm seems to have encountered more than one instance of trouble beyond the Grampians. We have already noted his expedition to Moray and it was while on another northward venture that his life was ended. In 954, the year when the kingdom of York came to an end, he was killed near Dunnottar. His slayers were not foreign marauders but local inhabitants of the district. The nature of their grievance against him is a mystery, but it is possible to imagine them as supporters of the man who replaced him on the throne of Alba: his kinsman Ildulb, a son of Constantine mac Áeda. Ildulb's name is a Gaelic spelling of Germanic *Hildulf* and was arguably bestowed on this mac Ailpín prince in memory of some earlier bearer of English, Scandinavian or Continental origin. Little is known of Ildulb's eight-year reign except for one significant event: the transfer of Edinburgh to the kingdom of Alba. The details are sketchy, but the wording of the source suggests that this iconic stronghold, formerly the chief citadel of Gododdin, was evacuated by the English and handed over to the Scots. There is no hint of a siege or any other hostile action. On the contrary, it would seem that the ancient fortress – in Northumbrian hands since the seventh century – was granted to Ildulb by peaceful agreement. Its occupants at the time may have been answerable to a West Saxon overking through a Northumbrian lord – perhaps the ruler of Bamburgh – but we cannot be certain that this was the case at a site on the furthest limit of English authority.

Ildulb eventually met a violent demise, perishing in 962 at

Viking hands near Cullen on the coast of Moray. Following his death, a violent power-struggle broke out between rival branches of the mac Ailpín dynasty, the main protagonists being sons of the two most recent kings: Malcolm's son Dub and Ildulb's son Cuilén. Dub emerged victorious after a battle at the unidentified Ridge of Crup in which the abbot of Dunkeld and the provincial ruler or *mormaer* ('great steward') of Atholl, both of whom presumably fought alongside the defeated Cuilén, were named among the casualties. Dub reigned for five years until kin-strife flared again, at which point he was ejected from the throne in favour of Cuilén, who in turn ruled for a further five years. After Cuilén took the kingship, Dub sought exile in Moray, seeking sanctuary with its Cenél Loairn rulers, before being slain there in 967. His death at Forres was attributed to 'men of Alba' in one source but to 'the treacherous nation of Moray' in another, the former account suggesting that the land of the Moravians was at that time regarded as being as much a part of Alba as the Perthshire domains south of the Grampians. It seems likely that both regions were now under mac Ailpín sovereignty. A story attached to one record of Dub's death speaks of his unburied corpse lying hidden under a bridge at Kinloss, two miles north-east of Forres, an incident curiously reminiscent of a sculptured cameo on the nearby monolith known as Sueno's Stone. Cuilén, meanwhile, continued to reign as king of Alba. He perished in 971 at the hands of the Strathclyde Britons, having incurred their wrath by violating one of their princesses. The girl's father, a son of the aforementioned King Dyfnwal, sought vengeance by slaying Cuilén in battle. This took place somewhere in Lothian and may have marked Strathclyde's rejection of Cuilén's overlordship as much as punishment for a shameful deed. It provides clear proof of the Clyde kingdom's resilience at a time when other once-powerful realms such as Mercia and Northumbria were struggling to retain their identities. The devastating siege of Dumbarton in 870 had severely damaged the Britons, but, as the events of the tenth century confirmed, they eventually recovered their power. Their destruction of Cuilén testifies to their remarkable longevity as a potent force in northern politics. Despite intense pressure from Vikings, Scots and West Saxons, the kings of Strathclyde even managed to expand their hegemony by encroaching on lands formerly held by English Northumbria. By c.970, a wide swath of territory in what is now south-western Scotland had reverted to the Britons. Many parts of this region were restored to native rule for the first time in three centuries.

Cuilén's death was followed by the accession of Dub's brother Cináed to the throne of Alba. He and Dyfnwal of Strathclyde were among a group of Celtic and Scandinavian kings who met with King Edgar of Wessex at a ceremony near Chester in 973. The attendees boarded a boat which they rowed along the River Dee, Edgar taking the helm and his fellow-kings hauling the oars. Later English chroniclers portrayed the event as an act of submission to Edgar, but it was more plausibly a display of co-operation between rival kings. The short voyage along the river no doubt represented the symbolic or ritual aspect of a mutual peace accord. In addition to Dyfnwal, the Strathclyde delegation at Chester included his son Malcolm, a brother of the prince who had slain Cuilén of Alba two years earlier. Malcolm may have been the acknowledged king of the Britons in 973, his father perhaps serving as advisor and mentor. No source describes the political relationship between Strathclyde and Alba at this time, but it was not necessarily warmer than it had been during Cuilén's reign, despite Cináed being the brother of Cuilén's rival.

Cináed bore the auspicious name of the mac Ailpín progenitor and was a man of similarly extensive ambitions. He had apparently disposed of Cuilén's brother Olaf (Gaelic *Amlaib*) on his way to the throne and adopted a similarly aggressive stance throughout his reign. At some point, perhaps before the royal peacemaking ceremony at Chester, he launched plundering campaigns southward. His targets were the Clyde Britons and the Northumbrians, the former faring rather better than the latter. When he attacked Strathclyde, his army was repulsed with heavy loss in a battle at Moin Uacoruar (or Vacornar), a *moin* or 'moss' whose location is unknown. It was presumably to discourage counter-raids by the Britons that he erected defences at the ancient

Fords of Frew on the River Forth, eight miles west of Stirling. His assault on Northumbria proved more successful, bringing his forces as far south as Stainmore and seizing as a high-status hostage an English prince of either the Northumbrian or West Saxon royal houses. Among Cináed's motives in marching down to the River Tees may have been a claim to lordship over English-held estates in Lothian, in which case the prince in his custody was perhaps the son of a 'king' or earl of Bamburgh. If these events occurred prior to the meeting at Chester, they might even have given Cináed considerable leverage in discussions over the status of Lothian. It is unlikely to be a coincidence that later Northumbrian tradition regarded the eventual cession of Lothian to Alba as an outcome of face to face negotiations between Edgar and Cináed.

It may have been in Cináed's time that Orkney formally became a Scandinavian earldom. The Icelandic sagas place this event somewhat earlier, in the reign of King Harald Fairhair (or Finehair) who ruled western Norway from c.872 to c.935. It is possible, however, that the thirteenth-century authors of the sagas did not know the true date, or that their sources gave inaccurate information. The first verifiable Orcadian earl was Sigurd who died in 1014. He might even have been the first formally recognised holder of the title, receiving it not from Harald Fairhair but from a later king of Norway or Denmark. If so, then the earldom may have originated in the last quarter of the tenth century, perhaps at a time when the Danish king Harald Bluetooth was pursuing expansionist policies at home and abroad. If Bluetooth engaged in warfare or diplomacy with Cináed of Alba, there is no record of any such contact. Perhaps their respective territorial ambitions never clashed?

After a reign of eighteen years, Cináed met a violent death in 995, perishing in mysterious circumstances at the instigation of a noblewoman called Finella. His assassination occurred at Fettercairn, ten miles north of Brechin, in the district of Angus where Finella's father Cunchar held authority as a mormaer. The sources speak of Finella's treachery and deceit in arranging the king's murder, but she evidently had a genuine grievance, her only son having been killed by Cináed. Although later tradition wove a fictional tale around these events, we have no reason to entirely disbelieve them, nor should we deny Finella's historical existence. A folk-memory of her name lingers today in the valley of Strath Finella, four miles north-east of Fettercairn, in what were once presumably her family's ancestral lands. Little more can be said about her. The original form of her name in the earlier chronicles is *Finuele*, a form reminiscent of Gaelic *Finguala* (now Fionnuala), but her father's name might represent Brittonic or Pictish-British *Cincar*. It is possible, then, that the stewardship of Angus was held in this period by Gaelic-speakers of Pictish origin, or by a family of immigrants from Dál Riata. The latter might seem more likely if we admit the possibility that the territorial name 'Angus' preserves a memory of Cenél nÓengusa, the rulers of Islay. Did some part of this kindred abandon their Hebridean home in search of new opportunities in the East?

Finella's involvement in Cináed's death may have arisen from more than a desire for revenge. Her political sympathies perhaps lay with his rivals in the house of mac Ailpín, namely the grandsons of Ildulb. One of these, a son of Cuilén called Constantine, made a successful bid for the throne and clung to power for a couple of years. He died in 997, another victim of the feud between royal factions, falling in battle at the confluence of the rivers Almond and Tay. The place of his death was *Rathinveramon*, the old Roman fort of Bertha, where a royal residence doubtless existed at the end of the tenth century. His conqueror and successor was Cináed mac Duib, a son of the Dub toppled by Cuilén in 967, whom we may here call 'Cináed III' for the sake of convenience. During Cináed's reign a major assault against the Strathclyde Britons was launched by the West Saxon king Aethelred 'the Unready'. This occurred at the turn of the millennium, in the year 1000, and resulted in a severe ravaging of Clydesdale by English soldiers. The attack could have been much worse had a fierce storm not intervened to keep Aethelred's naval forces away from the Firth of Clyde. It would appear that the Britons got off lightly, for the English ships changed course by heading instead for the Isle of Man where their crews disembarked to plunder Scandinavian coastal settlements.

Aethelred's nickname, given above in its usual modern form, was actually *Unraed*, meaning 'Poor Counsel' in the sense of 'badly advised'. It was a pejorative epithet alluding to his policy of paying Viking warlords large sums of money to stop ravaging his kingdom. In spite of these 'Danegeld' payments, his most fearsome adversary in the closing years of the tenth century was Sveinn Forkbeard, king of Denmark, who repeatedly raided the coasts of England. Sveinn's depredations in the South seem to have drawn Aethelred's attention away from northern events after the attack on Strathclyde, the distraction no doubt bringing relief to Britons and Scots alike.

Dynastic in-fighting within the mac Ailpín dynasty simmered for a few years before a further eruption of conflict led to yet another royal slaying. On this occasion, the warring parties sprang from the same branch of the family. The protagonists were Cináed III and his cousin Malcolm mac Cináeda, a son of the earlier king Cináed mac Mail Coluim – the proliferation of Cináeds and Malcolms in these years can seem somewhat confusing. The rivals clashed in 1005 at Monzievaird ('Moor of the Bards'), near Crieff in Perthshire. Malcolm emerged victorious and took the kingship. His long reign of almost thirty years was punctuated by military campaigns beyond his south-eastern border, his main foes being the English earls of Northumbria, but he is also credited with wars against Vikings and Britons, both of whom he encountered on his frontiers in the West. One of his first ventures occurred in 1006 when he raided deep into Northumbrian territory. He laid siege to Durham, the seat of an important bishopric, but his army was defeated by an English counter-attack. The event and its outcome were summarised by the Irish annalists:

> A battle between the men of Alba and the Saxons. And the rout was upon the Scots, and they left behind them a slaughter of their good men.

The bane of the Scottish army on this occasion was Uhtred, a young English nobleman whose father-in-law was the bishop of Durham. Uhtred's own father was Waltheof, earl of Bamburgh, in whose domains the Durham bishopric lay. Gathering an army, Uhtred fell upon the besiegers, lifting their blockade and forcing them to flee. The army of Alba suffered heavy casualties, Malcolm himself barely escaping with his life. After the slaughter a grim fate awaited those of his warriors who lay dead upon the battlefield. A near-contemporary source, entitled *De Obsessione Dunelmi* ('On The Siege Of Durham'), gives the gruesome details. It tells how Uhtred:

> ... caused to be carried to Durham the best-looking heads of the slain, ornamented with braided locks as was the fashion of the time, and after they had been washed by four women – to each of whom he gave a cow for their trouble – he caused these heads to be fixed upon stakes and placed around the walls.

Uhtred eventually succeeded his father as earl of Bamburgh. During his tenure of the earldom a major change occurred in the dynastic politics of England. The long line of West Saxon monarchs was broken when Cnut, the half-Polish son of Sveinn Forkbeard, was chosen as king by a faction among the English nobility. A rival faction supported Aethelred Unraed and, later, his son Edmund who claimed the kingship after Aethelred's death in 1016. A brief civil war between Edmund and Cnut raged for several months before the rivals concluded a peace which partitioned the kingdom between them. Edmund died barely six months after his father, his death allowing Cnut to claim sovereignty over all of England. To Malcolm of Alba the change of regime presented an opportunity which he exploited to good effect two years later, in 1018, with an assault on Northumbria. At his side marched Owain Calvus ('the Bald'), king of the Strathclyde Britons, as a trusted ally or loyal vassal. Against them stood the Northumbrians led by an English earl – unidentified in the sources – whom we may cautiously identify as Uhtred of Bamburgh. The opposing forces fought a battle at Carham-on-Tweed from which the northern Celtic powers emerged victorious. In the following year, Uhtred was assassinated while journeying south to pay homage to Cnut, his murder apparently being undertaken on the king's orders. He was succeeded in the earldom of Bamburgh by his brother, Eadwulf Cudel ('Cuttlefish'), who could only watch from the sidelines as Cnut ceded whatever remained of English-held territory in Lothian to Malcolm. The border between England and Alba was formally established along the Tweed as far as the old Bernician heartlands around the river's lower course, thereby reducing Eadwulf's earldom to little more than a northerly outpost of Cnut's realm. It would have been small consolation to the disgruntled Cuttlefish that the kingdom of Owain the Bald, one of the victors at Carham, was soon to disappear completely from the political map. Owain's successors were still ruling on the Clyde in the middle of the eleventh century, but their kingdom, the last outpost of the North Britons, fell under Scottish control before 1070. By then, the kingship of Alba had already passed out of mac Ailpín hands to Donnchad, a grandson of Malcolm mac Cináeda by his daughter Bethoc. This Donnchad is more familiar in his literary guise as the 'King Duncan' killed by Shakespeare's villainous Macbeth who, in turn, was based on a historical ruler of Moray called Macbethad. By 1040, when Macbethad seized the kingship of Alba, the realm was already being referred to as *Scotia*, a Latin name meaning simply 'Scotland'. The era of dynastic change accompanying the new terminology brings us almost to the end of the early medieval period. In the next chapter, our focus switches back to religious affairs in the eighth, ninth and tenth centuries by examining the fortunes of the Church in a time of profound political upheaval.

CHAPTER 10
Kings and Bishops

Church and State

The political changes that led to the foundation of medieval Scotland at the end of the first millennium began several centuries earlier. Gaelicisation of the Picts, for example, was not so much a ninth-century event as a process of interaction and assimilation which accelerated under the mac Ailpín kings. In a similar way, the shaping of today's Anglo-Scottish border was not a one-off occurrence, represented by the formal cession of Lothian in 1018, but rather a later phase in a lengthy sequence of political relationships dating back to the sixth century. One important aspect of these relationships was the evolution of small kingdoms into larger hegemonies and, ultimately, into what we might call 'proto-states'. By c.1000, both Alba in the North and Wessex-dominated England in the South were large kingdoms displaying some of the key attributes of statehood. Both were already starting to exhibit the kind of organisational sophistication seen in contemporary France and Germany, most notably in the delegation of royal authority to provincial stewards such as earls and mormaers. Neither tenth-century England nor contemporary Alba were true states in the modern bureaucratic sense, but nor were they simple political units of the type classified by anthropologists as 'chiefdoms'. Both kingdoms had indeed evolved to become 'complex chiefdoms' moving confidently towards statehood. In this, their rulers benefited from close ties with the ecclesiastical elite – the abbots and bishops of major churches and monasteries – whose expertise in matters of administration and communication made them indispensable advisers to ambitious kings. We see an example of this increasingly symbiotic relationship between 'Church and state', between high priest and monarch, in a chronicle entry for 906. In that year, a great gathering of the elite of Alba took place at Scone, presided over by Constantine mac Áeda with Cellach the bishop of St Andrews at his side. This important event is examined more closely near the end of the present chapter. Here, we may note the key role played in its proceedings by a senior cleric, no less than the chief bishop of the kingdom. As we saw in the cases of Columba and Adomnán, and as we shall see again as the chapter unfolds, direct intervention by ecclesiastical figures in the policies of kings was by no means a ninth-century innovation. We last encountered the figure of the pro-active, politically astute priest in Chapter 7. Here, we pick up the trail at the dawn of the eighth century, in the land of the Picts.

Priests and Kings

The renowned Adomnán, abbot of Iona and promulgator of the Law of Innocents, died in 704 at the venerable age of seventy-seven. In spite of all his great achievements, the conversion of his monks to the customs of Rome eluded him to the last. His passing was followed a year later by that of his friend and pupil, the scholarly King Aldfrith of Northumbria, whose young son Osred succeeded to the throne. In Osred's time the most influential religious figure in the northern English realm was Ceolfrith, abbot of the dual monastery at Wearmouth-Jarrow where Bede was then a senior monk. Ceolfrith had close connections with the Gaelic churches: he had conversed with Adomnán during the latter's visits to Northumbria; he was a friend of Ecgbert, the Bernician cleric who dwelt among the Irish; and his own brother Cynefrith had served as a monk in Ireland. Ceolfrith was known throughout many lands as a man of great piety and as a staunch advocate of conformity with 'Roman' ecclesiastical practices. When the Pictish king

Nechtan, son of Derile, decided to bring the churches of his realm into line, he sought Ceolfrith's advice and assistance.

At that time, the Picts still largely relied on Columban clergy for spiritual leadership. Some Pictish clerics undoubtedly favoured conformity with the Roman Easter, but no major changes could be implemented without the assent of Iona. The impetus for religious reform in Pictland was thus initiated by Nechtan himself in his role as secular patron of all churches within his kingdom. Indeed, he emerges from the sources as a literate and well-informed monarch with a keen interest in religious matters. His initiative began with a letter to Ceolfrith in which he expressed a desire for information and guidance. The Northumbrian abbot was happy to help and the two men began to correspond. Bede included a copy of Ceolfrith's first reply to Nechtan in his *Ecclesiastical History*. The detailed correspondence on spiritual matters ran alongside a *foedus pacis*, a peace pact drawn up between Picts and Northumbrians to end the simmering tensions still lingering in the wake of Brude's victory at Dunnichen. Religious correspondence and secular diplomacy thus formed twin strands of a single peace-making strategy designed to forge political and religious harmony between the two kingdoms. The ensuing negotiations yielded a positive outcome: the peace treaty which Bede described as still being in force when he completed his *magnum opus* in 731. As well as rejoicing at the cessation of frontier skirmishes, Bede was heartened by the successful religious negotiations in which he himself had undoubtedly played a part. It is likely, for instance, that he served as Ceolfrith's chief letter-writer as well as providing detailed scriptural references employed by the abbot to bolster his arguments.

On the secular front, the *foedus pacis* held firm for many years. Hostilities along the Anglo-Pictish border did not break out again until the middle of the century. Meanwhile, among the churches of his kingdom, King Nechtan began a rigorous programme of reform. He soon met stubborn resistance from traditionalists who either rejected the changes or implemented them too slowly for his liking. There might have been additional resentment at such direct royal interference in ecclesiastical affairs. In 716, having become frustrated by the intransigence of anti-reformist clerics, Nechtan ordered them to leave his domains. Like Colman's refugees from the synod of Whitby five decades earlier, these ecclesiastical rebels – perhaps a mixed group of Picts and Gaels – took the road back to Iona. Their defiance of the king was destined to be short-lived: in 717, Iona finally adopted the Roman Easter and the Petrine tonsure. This momentous change was ushered in by the Englishman Ecgbert after his appointment as Iona's bishop in 716.

In 724, Nechtan relinquished his crown to enter monastic life. This happened at a time when dynastic strife was simmering among the Pictish royal kindreds and may have been his response to the growing uncertainty. It is equally possible that the decision was not his own but was forced upon him by rivals. The same could perhaps be said of Selbach, king of Cenél Loairn and claimant on the sovereignty of Dál Riata, who had likewise entered a monastery in 723. Since both kings returned to the secular stage as warlords within a few years, their respective sojourns in holy orders were perhaps either half-hearted or involuntary. In 733, Selbach's son Dungal raided a number of northern Irish monasteries, violating the sanctity of the church on Tory Island by dragging the Pictish prince Brude out of it. At first glance, this looks like a blatant flouting of Adomnán's Law of Innocents, which sought to protect monks and other non-combatants from the perils of war. However, the Law would only have applied to Dungal and his Cenél Loairn kinsmen if they had lain under the spiritual authority of Iona. Their plundering of Irish monasteries suggests that they did not feel bound by the Law and implies rather that their principal church and centre of worship lay outside the Columban *familia*. As we saw in Chapter 7, this church was almost certainly Lismore, the island monastery in the Firth of Lorn opposite the royal stronghold of Dunollie. Its abbot appears not to have been a guarantor of the *Lex Innocentium* in 697.

In the early eighth century, Lismore was not the only non-Columban centre still thriving in the western seaways. Applecross, Eigg and Kingarth all retained their independence of Iona and had sent no delegates to the Synod of Birr. Missionaries from Ireland were, in fact, still arriving on the shores of northern Britain. Some came to preach in peripheral districts where pockets of paganism were most likely to remain. Others sought places of sanctuary away from the cares of the secular world. In the early 700s, three members of a high-ranking Irish family are said to have sailed to Britain in the hope of finding solitude and spiritual fulfilment. These were Kentigerna, the daughter of a king, with her brother Congan and her son Faelan. After establishing a place of peace and contemplation in Strathfillan, in southern Perthshire, the trio went their separate ways. Kentigerna eventually settled on Inchcailloch ('Isle of the Old Woman'), in Loch Lomond, where she died in 734. The similarity of her name to that of Saint Kentigern has not passed unnoticed, with some historians wondering if the two individuals might be one and the same.

Kentigerna's death preceded by one year the passing of the Venerable Bede, who died in the monastery at Jarrow where he had spent almost his entire life. The renowned chronicler of Northumbrian Christianity departed at the age of sixty-two, having borne witness to some of the most important events in the spiritual history of his nation. As a contemporary of leading churchmen such as Ceolfrith, Ecgbert and the great Adomnán himself, Bede had seen some of these events at first hand. He was almost certainly present at Jarrow when Adomnán visited Northumbria, and he probably assisted Ceolfrith during the reform of the Pictish churches. Although he played no active role in the reform of Iona, the fact that this had taken place under the guidance of an English bishop gave him great satisfaction. His network of personal contacts was impressive. It included figures whose childhood memories reached back to the beginnings of Christianity in Bernicia and Deira, to the time of Aidan and Paulinus. At the time of his death, southern Scotland still had an English bishopric at Whithorn in Galloway. This would eventually fall out of Northumbrian control but, in the early eighth century, it testified to the English kingdom's continuing political and ecclesiastical dominance between Clyde and Solway.

Before the Storm

By the middle of the eighth century, most of the native churches of Ireland and northern Britain had embraced reform, thereby rejoining the mainstream of European Christianity. In 768, the clergy of Gwynedd likewise adopted the Roman Easter. It is possible that those of South Wales had already made the change, perhaps copying the example of their Cornish countrymen who seemingly reformed before 700. The churches of the Strathclyde Britons may have followed those of North Wales in the 760s, unless their own acceptance of reform also came earlier. In Pictland, the impact of King Nechtan's ecclesiastical policies remained graven on the landscape long after his death in 732. Many archaeologists and art historians attribute to his reign the first appearance of upright stone slabs inscribed with ornate crosses on the front face and Pictish motifs on the reverse. The oldest examples were produced in the early eighth century and are therefore contemporary with Nechtan's reformist agenda. Their appearance coincided with the building of stone churches founded by Pictish royal patronage and dedicated to Saint Peter of Rome. Nechtan himself endowed the first of these churches and, according to Bede, invited Northumbrian masons to build it. Its precise location is unknown, but both Meigle and Aberlemno are plausible candidates: patronage by high-status individuals and a rich sculptural tradition are evident at both sites. A third candidate is Restenneth, now the site of a medieval priory close to the battlefield of Dunnichen. A lost place-name *Egglespether* ('St Peter's Church') was recorded in later land-holding documents relating to the area, but a similar name was also known in the vicinity of Aberlemno. The most northerly site proposed for Nechtan's earliest stone-built church is Rosemarkie in Easter Ross.

Another Pictish foundation attributed to the eighth-century was *Cenrigmonaid*, now St Andrews, a site perhaps owing its origin to Nechtan's successor Óengus, son of Fergus. Here was built the great royal church of St Andrew, dedicated to the Apostle whose bones were supposedly interred there. One version of the St Andrews foundation-legend tells of a monk named Regulus or Rule who, after experiencing a prophetic vision, brought the apostolic relics from Constantinople to Britain. At a place called *Kylrimont*, more correctly *Cenrigmonaid* ('Head of the Royal Hill'), he allegedly met a certain 'King Hungus' who granted a portion of land for a church in which the sacred remains could be enshrined. Although the tale is largely fictional, the identification of Hungus as Óengus, son of Fergus, is consistent with other evidence. The Irish annals, for instance, include an entry noting the death of Tuathalan, abbot of Cenrigmonaid, in 747. This is the earliest reference to an ecclesiastical settlement at St Andrews and suggests that Tuathalan was the first abbot of a recently founded monastery. Óengus was the paramount Pictish king in the 740s and perhaps appointed Tuathalan to the abbacy. The corresponding archaeological data likewise seems consistent with this chronology, the oldest sculpture at St Andrews being attibuted to the second half of the eighth century. Foremost among a rich collection of Christian sculpture is a sandstone box-shrine or sarcophagus designed to contain the bones of an important individual. This superb example of Pictish craftsmanship, carved between 750 and 800, was set up in the church as a focus of veneration. The identity of the person whose corporeal remains were interred within it is unknown. Did it once hold the bones of the Apostle Andrew, or those of the mighty Óengus himself? Whatever the true purpose of the sarcophagus, the richness of its carving suggests royal patronage and a close connection between king and clergy. If the chief architect of 'church and state' relationships in Pictish territory was Nechtan, son of Derile, then the main beneficiary was a confident, independent religious elite in the time of his successors. The new foundation at St Andrews was home to Pictish monks who were no longer answerable to Iona.

An alternative interpretation of the St Andrews foundation-legend sees the royal patron 'Hungus' or Óengus not as Nechtan's successor but as a namesake who died in 834. This was the Óengus who succeeded his brother Constantine as a Pictish overking in 820. Both siblings may have been involved in the founding or redeveloping of major churches in territory south of the Mounth.

Given the presence of an abbot at Cenrigmonaid in the 740s, it seems unlikely that the later Óengus was responsible for its foundation, but he perhaps endowed it with gifts. Constantine, on the other hand, almost certainly founded the Pictish royal church at Dunkeld. This important religious settlement was established beside the River Tay, below the ancient Fort of the Caledonians, on a site now occupied by the medieval cathedral. Here, the modern visitor can observe two sculptured stones, both of which were probably carved in the ninth century. Within a few decades of its foundation, Dunkeld was earmarked as the premier church of the mac Ailpín kings.

South of Pictish territory and across the Firth of Forth lay Lothian, an area still under English rule in the eighth century. Here, the Northumbrian bishops of Lindisfarne held spiritual authority over a population descended largely from Britons but now thoroughly Anglicised. Among the satellite churches of the Lindisfarne diocese was a monastery at Tyninghame on the coast of East Lothian, eight miles north of the Bernician fortress at Dunbar. Tyninghame was founded by Saint Balthere or Baldred, an obscure figure whose Germanic name is suggestive of English origin. During his abbacy he frequently sought solitude on the Bass Rock, a precipitous feature rising out of the sea near the modern resort of North Berwick. He died in 756 and was buried at Tyninghame where, in later times, his tomb became the focus of a major cult. In the eleventh century, around the time of the cession of Lothian to the Scots, his body was disinterred by the Northumbrian priest Alfred, son of Westou, as part of an initiative to gather the remains of long-dead saints for reburial at Durham. This presumably happened around the time of the battle of Carham when the Anglo-Scottish border was finally fixed along the Tweed. At some point thereafter, Scottish ecclesiastical tradition tried to recast Balthere as a pupil of Saint Kentigern of Glasgow, hence the appearance of two 'Baldreds' in the documentary record. One of these has a a sixth-century context, the other belongs to the eighth. They are essentially one and the same, although the earlier is plainly an invention.

The Storm Breaks

The final decade of the eighth century brought the first Viking raids on the British Isles. As worshippers of pagan gods, the Scandinavian warriors gave no immunity to Christian religious settlements and regarded them as soft targets. Isolated monasteries in the Hebrides were particularly vulnerable to seaborne marauders and offered rich pickings. They often possessed items of great value, such as finely decorated chalices and reliquaries, many adorned with gold and silver. Weaponless monks and nuns, armed only with prayer, gave little or no resistance and were easily slaughtered or enslaved. The earliest record of a Gaelic religious settlement being attacked by Vikings appears in the Irish annals under the year 795, when the island of Rathlin between Ulster and Kintyre was pillaged. Seven years later, Iona endured a devastating assault, the first of many, but the surviving monks resumed their vocation and the primary centre of Gaelic Christendom endured. Nevertheless, the era of Iona's power and influence was drawing to an end. The tiny isle's exposed location made it an unsuitable home for monks in an age when heathen pirates controlled the surrounding seaways.

Viking attacks intensified as the ninth century dawned. In the raid on Iona in 802 the monastery was burned and it is hard to imagine the great library and scriptorium remaining unscathed. Many precious and irreplaceable books undoubtedly perished, together with other unique objects deemed worthless by the heathen plunderers. The human cost, in terms of murder and enslavement, must have been considerable. At that time, the abbot of the monastery was Cellach, a far-sighted man who perceived that his community now lay in deadly peril. In 804, faced with the inevitability of further raids, he obtained land in Ireland for the building of a new monastery. The chosen site lay forty miles north of Dublin at Ceannanus Mór, a place better known today as Kells, where a church allegedly founded by Columba had existed since the sixth century. Construction of what was to become the new Columban headquarters began, but it was a major project and the work required considerable time to complete. In 806, Iona again endured a brutal assault in which sixty-eight monks were mercilessly slaughtered. By the following year, the work at Kells was completed and some of the brethren came down from the Hebrides to take up residence. Their old home was not, however, abandoned: contemporary notices in the Irish annals suggest that it continued as a residence for part of the community. Modern historians are divided on the question of how many monks remained, but the annalists imply that the leaders of the community, perhaps even Abbot Cellach himself, did not immediately transfer to Kells. After Cellach's death in 814, his successor Diarmait seems also to have stayed behind, despite the persistent threat of Viking aggression. One violent raid on Iona in 825 claimed the life of Blathmac, an Irish monk and former soldier, whose murder was described in a contemporary poem. This was written within a decade or two of Blathmac's death and portrays him as a courageous seeker of the bloody 'red martyrdom' bestowed by heathen swords. The story of his last hours tells of his foresight of an impending raid and of his resolve to complete his spiritual duties. Having sent many of his companions to safety, he prepared to celebrate mass in the church, even as the fearsome longships approached. When the Scandinavian warriors eventually arrived, demanding to know the whereabouts of the richly adorned tomb and shrine of Columba, they were confronted by a defiant Blathmac. Enraged by his refusal to divulge the tomb's secret location, they slew him savagely, thereby granting his desire to perish as a 'red' martyr. This brutal episode highlights Iona's unsuitability as a home for the founder's relics, even when the tomb-shrine or reliquary was hidden in the ground. Columba's mortal remains were of little interest to a Viking warband, but their preservation was at risk while their repository lay on an isolated Hebridean isle. After further raids in the 840s, a decision was made to remove the precious bones to safety. Centuries of royal burial meant that Iona was also the ancient spiritual home of Cenél nGabráin. Indeed, it may have been regarded by Cináed mac Ailpín himself as the ancestral church of his dynasty, even after he established his main power-base east of Druim Alban.

Later tradition shows Cináed playing a key role in the decision to move Columba's tomb. He is said to have requested that the bones and other relics be divided between the community's new headquarters in Ireland and his own domains in Perthshire. In 849, when Abbot Indrechtach brought some of the relics to Kells, the rest went eastward to be housed in the mac Ailpín royal church at Dunkeld. A religious house had already been established there by Constantine, son of Fergus, earlier in the ninth century. One tradition attributed its foundation to Cináed, but this is not generally regarded as reliable. It is more likely that Cináed selected Dunkeld for special patronage by his family because it already had a connection with Pictish royalty. He evidently refurbished, expanded or otherwise redeveloped the existing church. In 865, the abbot of Dunkeld was also *prim-escop Fortrenn* ('chief bishop of Fortriu'), a title referring to lands north of the Mounth towards the Moray Firth. This looks like a claim by the ecclesiastical elite of the mac Ailpín kingdom on a Pictish region that may not have been answerable to their secular patrons at that time. By the end of the century, when the southern Pictish overkingship was held by Cináed's grandsons, the dynasty's major seat of spiritual authority had already been transferred to St Andrews.

Blathmac's violent death epitomises the vulnerability of holy men and women in the Viking period, but not every 'red martyrdom' came on the point of a Scandinavian sword. Another member of the Columban brethren, no less a figure than Abbot Indrechtach, was slain while on a pilgrimage to Rome in 854. His assailants were not pagan Vikings but Englishmen, a band of robbers whose religious affiliation was presumably Christian. They slew him during his overland passage through the southern regions of Britain. It seems highly unlikely that they were unaware of his identity or profession. Nevertheless, we are left in no doubt that the principal danger to ecclesiastical personnel and property came from Viking pirates rather than from English brigands. This must have been especially true in the period before the Scandinavian colonies began to embrace Christianity. Iona thus remained vulnerable throughout the entire ninth century, although its value as a source of booty may have waned if precious artefacts were moved to Kells or Dunkeld. Later tradition claimed that the island's ancient burial ground continued to serve as a resting-place for abbots and kings. Both Cináed and his brother Domnall were supposedly interred there, as too were their sons and grandsons. How far these traditions reflect ninth-century fact rather than twelfth-century fiction is unclear, but they are increasingly doubted by historians. Giric, the presumed mentor of Eochaid, son of Rhun, was one of the rulers allegedly buried on Iona after his death in 889. In spite of the mystery surrounding his origins, he emerges as a figure of some importance in contemporary religious developments, at least according to one tradition which asserts that 'he was the first to give liberty to the Scottish Church, which was in servitude up to that time, after the custom and fashion of the Picts'. This curious statement seems to imply that Giric freed the clergy from a burden formerly imposed upon them by Pictish secular authority. It could be a veiled reference to a repeal of the reforms introduced by Nechtan, son of Derile, by royal decree in the early eighth century. Perhaps, as some historians suggest, Nechtan introduced a tax obligation which diverted substantial church revenues to his treasury? If this was indeed the 'servitude' ended by Giric, its removal may have brought the Pictish churches into line with those on the western side of Druim Alban, in the Argyll homelands of the Scots.

The Church in Alba

By the end of the ninth century, some Scandinavian communities around the isles and shorelands of northern Britain were starting to adopt Christianity. Intermarriage with Scots and Picts, or with Britons and Anglo-Saxons, paved the way for a rejection of pagan gods by sons and daughters of mixed parentage. Even the fearsome armies of Viking Dublin now included Norse-Irish warriors of hybrid ancestry and Christian belief. There was, however, no mass conversion of warriors and colonists, nor did the warlords of

Orkney and the Hebridean isles invite missionaries from Kells or Dunkeld or St Andrews to preach the Word among their people. The decline of paganism among the Scandinavian settlers was therefore a random process driven by individual choice and kinship. It was neither imposed nor actively encouraged by their political leaders, but nor does it seem to have been forcefully discouraged.

The principal churches of the mac Ailpín dynasty lay at Dunkeld and St Andrews. Both places enjoyed the patronage of kings and each served as the primary ceremonial centre for a saintly cult. At Dunkeld, a shrine containing Columba's bones was venerated with honour by Cináed and his successors, while at St Andrews the alleged relics of the eponymous Apostle sanctified a major royal monastery. Other places rose to prominence in regional contexts, but Dunkeld and St Andrews retained their special importance as the main royal churches for the early kings of Alba. In the tenth century, St Andrews became a centre of the Culdees or *Céli Dé* ('clients of God'), a movement of religious reformers which had its roots in Ireland. The Céli Dé sought a return to traditional monastic values of asceticism and discipline. They held strong views on the roles of monks, abbots and bishops within the ecclesiastical and secular communities. Their ideas began to appear in southern Irish monasteries in the eighth century and from there permeated the Columban *familia*, reaching Iona before 800 and Dunkeld by c.850. It is even possible that Dunkeld was founded on Céli Dé principles.

The tenth century saw the development of an additional role for Columba as a spiritual standard-bearer in time of war. This role was not without precedent: three hundred years earlier, the Northumbrian king Oswald had received the saint's blessing in a dream on the eve of his decisive battle against Cadwallon. In the last century of the first millennium, Columba's role in warfare evolved into something more tangible. Not only did the soldiers of Alba invoke his name in prayers for victory, they also carried his staff or crozier when they marched into battle. This holy totem was borne in the front rank and became known as *Cathbuaid* ('Battle Triumph'). In peacetime it was probably kept at Dunkeld with other relics, but, unfortunately, it has not survived. Other items associated with Columba seem to have conferred less protection from hostile foes. In 920, a Scandinavian force attacked and devastated Kells, the Irish headquarters of the *familia*, where some of the founder's remains were enshrined. During the onslaught, many monks were wantonly slain as they prayed in the church. Dunkeld, too, suffered similar outrages during the same century, as in 903 when it was caught up in a Norse raid.

Attacks on the churches and monasteries of northern Britain continued to the end of the millennium, despite the adoption of Christianity by some Scandinavian colonies. In the Hebrides there were many folk of mixed blood – descendants of early Norse colonists who had intermarried with local natives – who turned their backs on paganism. Others stayed fiercely loyal to the old beliefs and continued to maintain a callous disregard for Christian sites. At Tyninghame in 941, the church founded by Saint Balthere was plundered and burned by Olaf Gothfrithsson of Dublin. More puzzling, and perhaps more shocking to contemporaries, were acts of violence directed at holy places by Christian allies of the heathens. An example of this type of sacrilege was the plundering of Kells in 969 by a Viking force accompanied by Irishmen from Leinster who, we may presume, were men of Christian birth. Equally disturbing, at least to modern eyes, is a reference to a battle in 965 where Abbot Donnchad of Dunkeld was listed among the casualties. The event in question occurred at the unidentified 'Ridge of Crup' where the rival mac Ailpín princes Dub and Cuilén contested the kingship of Alba. Whether or not Abbot Donnchad took part in the fighting is unknown, but the fact that he perished on the battlefield suggests that he was no passive bystander. Indeed, we may note that military service by clergymen was not unheard of in this period, in spite of Adomnán's prohibitive Law.

Aside from the risk of robbery and destruction, the churches of Alba continued to fulfil their spiritual role. The reforms traditionally ascribed to King Giric in the late ninth century were presumably still in place at the dawn of the tenth. Further changes were implemented by Constantine mac Áeda, grandson of Cináed mac Ailpín, in the early years of his reign. In 906, at Scone in Perthshire, Constantine summoned the great assembly mentioned at the start of this chapter. Here, the secular and religious elites of Alba gathered to witness a royal pronouncement on ecclesiastical matters. At Constantine's side stood Cellach, bishop of St Andrews, taking the role of high priest of the kingdom. Together, these two decreed that 'the laws and disciplines of the faith and the rights in churches and gospels should be kept in conformity with the Scots'. The venue for the ceremony was Moot Hill, a man-made mound whose focus was the revered Stone of Destiny. It seems likely that the event marked a change in the relationship between the mac Ailpín dynasty and the senior clergy of Alba. Perhaps Constantine used the occasion to grant greater autonomy to the bishops? Something significant certainly occurred, even if the precise context cannot now be recovered.

During Constantine's reign a young nobleman called Catroe embarked on a remarkable religious career that began in Perthshire and ended in France. Catroe was born around 900, at the start of Constantine's kingship, among a wealthy Gaelic-speaking family. His mother might have been a Briton connected to the royal house of Strathclyde. Whatever her origin, she and Catroe's father were devoted to the memory of Columba and probably worshipped at the saint's shrine in Dunkeld. They gave their son into the keeping of Saint Bean, an obscure figure holding ecclesiastical rank either at Dunkeld or at another Perthshire monastery. Under Bean's guidance Catroe trained as a monk and, after studying in Ireland, returned to Alba to instruct his mentor's other pupils. At around forty years of age, c.941, Catroe grew restless and felt a strong urge to embark on a pilgrimage. His journey took him first to a church dedicated to Saint Brigit, perhaps at the old Pictish monastery at Abernethy, where he met King Constantine. From there he travelled south under royal protection to Strathclyde, where he stayed as a guest of King Dyfnwal, described as his kinsman. The Clyde Britons escorted Catroe on the next stage of his pilgrimage, bringing him to their border with Anglo-Scandinavian Northumbria at a place called *Loida* which may have been on the River Lowther near

Penrith. From there he journeyed east to York before turning south and eventually reaching the royal palace of Wessex at Winchester. The West Saxon king Edmund instructed no less a personage than the archbishop of Canterbury to arrange Catroe's safe passage across the English Channel. On the European mainland, various high-ranking members of the Frankish secular and religious elites offered patronage to the Scottish pilgrim, whose piety and austerity won him many admirers. He was eventually chosen as abbot of the great cathedral at Metz, close to the centres of eastern Frankish imperial power. It was while travelling back there from a visit to the court of the Empress Adelaide in 971 that he died. In later times, his tomb at Metz became a place of veneration and he was accorded the honour of sainthood.

Catroe was in the early stages of his Continental career when Constantine mac Áeda exchanged the rich trappings of royalty for the robes of a cleric. Racked by age and infirmity, and after a forty-year reign, the king of Alba abdicated to spend his remaining days as abbot of St Andrews. The religious community there included many Céli Dé and it was these reformist brethren whom the old warrior-king now found himself leading. He was not the only tenth-century ruler to relinquish earthly authority in the twilight of life. In 965, the Irish prince Áed, a son of King Maelmithid of Brega, journeyed as a pilgrim to St Andrews and died there. Ten years later, a rather longer voyage of penitence was made by Dyfnwal, the king of Strathclyde who had given hospitality to Catroe. Like his kinsman and erstwhile guest, Dyfnwal embarked on a pilgrimage, but he died *en route* to Rome. He had already transferred the Clyde kingship to his son Malcolm, with whom he had hauled the oars of King Edgar's boat on the River Dee in 973.

Dyfnwal's fellow-pilgrims among the powerful men of the time generally chose destinations closer to home, such as St Andrews or Iona. In the late tenth century, the old Hebridean home of the Columban monks still held an allure for penitents opting out from the world of secular politics. One of its more unusual pilgrims was Olaf Cuaran, the archetypal Viking warlord whose activities were noted in Chapter 9. He arrived on Iona as an old man after relinquishing the throne of Dublin in 980. In the place where his heathen countrymen had inflicted so much distress he lived out his final years as a pious Christian convert, perhaps even being interred in the ancient burial ground. By then, of course, the role of the old monastery was dwindling. It was still occupied by monks and still ruled by an abbot, but the headship of the Columban *familia* had already passed to men based at Irish churches such as Kells and Armagh. In 986, an unidentified abbot of Iona was slain by Vikings while celebrating Christmas on the island with his brethren. He was not, however, the head of the wider *familia*, for the symbolic title *comarba Coluim Cille* ('successor of Columba') was at that time held by a contemporary whose own violent death at heathen hands occurred in Dublin.

Acts of destruction at holy sites remained a hallmark of Viking raids until Norway, Denmark and the overseas Scandinavian colonies adopted the Christian faith. The slow process of conversion began in the ninth century and continued to the end of the tenth, not attaining its final goal until Iceland adopted Christianity around the year 1000. Among the settlements in northern Britain, those on Orkney were converted after the baptism of Earl Sigurd in 995 on the orders of the Norwegian king Olaf Tryggvasson. Olaf subsequently encouraged the people of Shetland and the Faeroe Islands to abandon paganism, thereby bringing the outer Scandinavian colonies into the Christian fold. By then, most of the Viking lordships in the western seaways were already moving along the same path, under the guidance of Irish and Scottish missionaries. The age of the heathen marauder was almost over.

CHAPTER 11
Overview: the Birth of Medieval Scotland

Anglo-Norman Kings

As the upheavals of the Viking Age subsided, a new wave of Scandinavian adventurers – the Normans – crossed from their territory in northern France to impose their rule on England. They were led by Duke William, a descendant of a Viking called Rollo or Rolf to whom the Frankish king had granted the lower valley of the River Seine in 911. Under Rollo's successors Normandy ('land of the Northmen') became an independent duchy with substantial military resources. By the middle of the eleventh century its ruling family already had close dealings with West Saxon kings and, in 1066, Duke William crossed the Channel to claim the English throne. William defeated his rival, Harold Godwinson, to become William the Conqueror, the first Norman monarch of England.

In the wake of the Norman victory, the Scottish king Malcolm III raided northern England, apparently in support of rebellious English factions opposed to King William. The latter's retribution came in 1072, with an attack on Scotland, but Malcolm sued for peace and swore allegiance to the Conqueror in a ceremony at Abernethy. This act of homage began to look hollow in the ensuing years, when Malcolm launched further raids on Northumbria. In 1091, he swore a new oath of allegiance, this time to the Conqueror's son William Rufus, but later reacted forcefully when he felt that its terms were not being honoured. He died two years later, near Alnwick in Northumbria, perishing alongside one of his sons in a battle against Anglo-Norman forces. Homage to William Rufus was subsequently offered by another son, Edgar, who secured the Scottish throne in 1097 after a period of dynastic strife. Similar pledges of loyalty were given by Edgar's younger brothers, Alexander and David, who followed him in the kingship in 1107 and 1124 respectively. The Anglo-Norman monarch to whom these two gave homage was Henry I, youngest son of the Conqueror. Out of these cross-border relationships developed the strong Norman influence on Scotland and, in the longer term, the factors that would ultimately spark conflict in the time of Wallace and Bruce.

Peoples

The end of the early medieval period witnessed a final farewell to two of Scotland's indigenous peoples: the Picts and the Britons. Neither group disappeared in a physical sense – indeed, they remained *in situ* in their respective ancestral lands – but both slipped out of the historical record and no longer played any role in political events. They became part of the Scottish kingdom that emerged during the eleventh and twelfth centuries and, by c.1150, both had effectively ceased to exist. Their descendants saw themselves as integral parts of the *fir Albain* ('the men of Alba') and were indistinguishable from other 'Scots'. In the case of the Picts, as we have seen, this evolutionary process happened much earlier. The Gaelicisation of the Pictish heartlands may have started as far back as the eighth century but accelerated rapidly in the ninth and was probably complete by 1000. At that time, the Picts were still remembered as a people who had fought alongside the Scots during the turmoil of the Viking period. In the eleventh and twelfth centuries, however, their role in the foundation of Scotland was rewritten in line with current political needs. They were portrayed as an awkward obstacle to the unified Gaelic-speaking kingdom of the mac Ailpín dynasty. In this revised vision of the beginnings of Scottish nationhood, the Picts played a subordinate role to the Scots, who were presented as invaders and conquerors from the West. To contemporary English chroniclers engaged in anti-Scottish propaganda the Picts served a different purpose as savage barbarians still identifiable among the ranks of Scottish armies. English writers reporting the Anglo-Scottish wars of the twelfth century believed that the warriors of Galloway, whom they castigated as brutal and primitive, were Picts. This stereotype fitted snugly onto the Galwegians who, as descendents of the Gall-Gáidhil or 'Irish Vikings' of earlier times, no doubt had a roughness that made it easy for enemies to demonise them. In truth, they had no real connection with the Pictish homelands, which lay much further north than the Solway. But the idea of a Pictish population in Galloway long endured to outlive the twelfth-century propaganda that spawned it. Remarkably, it was still appearing as a serious notion in academic discourse in the late twentieth century. Its modern supporters imagined a significant Pictish population in south-western Scotland, pointing to anomalous scraps of 'evidence' such as the isolated example of a symbol stone on Trusty's Hill near Gatehouse-of-Fleet. The presence of this sculpture in such a southerly location is indeed noteworthy, but it is more probably a one-off rather than an indication of Pictish settlement. Most historians now reject the notion of 'Galloway Picts' and prefer to regard Trusty's Hill as a place where a Pictish craftsman – or a local Briton imitating the Pictish sculptural style – carved a couple of symbols for some purpose that we cannot hope to identify.

Even in their ancient home in the Highlands the real, historical Picts began to be seen as enigmatic and mysterious. They attracted the kind of folklore normally associated with supernatural beings and, in one medieval folk-tale, were actually described as 'small, wee folk' like the inhabitants of Faerie. By the end of the Middle Ages, the Picts had almost faded into a mythical twilight, their important role in the formation of Scotland dwindling in the popular consciousness alongside their ever-shrinking physical stature. They were destined to become figures of folklore and jest, a furtive race of pygmies whose descendants dwelt secretly in brochs, souterrains and other ancient structures of forgotten purpose. This image can be traced back to twelfth-century Norwegian tradition but survived until comparatively recent times, being discarded only in the past hundred years or so. Its persistence partly explains why the Picts still exude such an enticing scent of mystery. Their rehabilitation to the mainstream of Celtic society was not fully achieved until the final decades of the twentieth century. Even today, despite the continuing scholarly efforts of historians and archaeologists, the enigmatic aura has not entirely gone away. On the other hand, academic study of the Picts is now accepted as a serious pursuit and is no longer dismissed, as it once was, as a whimsical venture undertaken by a rather eccentric breed of scholar.

If the Pictish identity had already disappeared by 1000, then that of the North Britons was facing similar extinction. Within three generations of the Battle of Carham, the kingdom on the Clyde was finally absorbed into the kingdom of Alba. The architect of the Britons' downfall was the Scottish king Malcolm III who subjugated Strathclyde in an unrecorded military campaign sometime around the middle decades of the eleventh century. It is likely that the final *coup de grâce* was inflicted between 1060 and 1070, at the time of the Norman conquest of Anglo-Saxon England. By 1100, the Clyde estuary and its hinterland had become a royal province ruled as a princedom by Malcolm's youngest son, the future King David of Scotland. During the following century, the Britons lost the most important feature of their identity: their ancient language. Gaelic officially replaced Brittonic as the speech of economic life and social advancement, its ascendancy reducing the indigenous tongue to a relic spoken by a dwindling number of old folk among the peasantry. Some aspects of British society, including fragments of ancient law, survived the transition to find a place in the new order, but the rest were swept away. In later years, the same medieval historians who rewrote the history of the Picts were probably aware that a substantial proportion of Lowland 'Scots' were descended from Britons. Nevertheless, in all practical aspects of everyday life, the Britons ceased to be a distinct element within Scotland's population after the early twelfth century. Traces of their language still linger today in the place-names of the Lowlands, where some names exhibit a distinctly Welsh character. Renfrew, for example, is a town and shire on the southern shore of the Clyde bearing a Brittonic name that in modern Welsh would be *Rhyn Frwd* ('Point of Current'). Likewise, the place-name Peebles derives from a Brittonic word similar to Welsh *pebyll* ('tent'), to which 's' was later added to give an Anglicised plural form. Ironically, the most famous place associated with the old kingdom of Strathclyde now has a name of Gaelic rather than of indigenous origin: Dumbarton, *Dun Breattain* ('Fortress of the Britons').

A more lasting linguistic legacy was left by the English, a people who colonised parts of Lothian and south-west Scotland during the long period of Northumbrian supremacy. Territory gained north of Solway and Tweed by Bernician warrior-kings such as Aethelfrith, Oswald, Oswiu and Eadberht was relinquished during the Viking Age to be absorbed into the realm of Alba. Lowland place-names such as Pennersax, derived from Brittonic *Pen yr Sax* ('Saxon's Head') and Glensaxon, Gaelic *Gleann Sasunn* ('Glen of the Saxons') show where Englishmen made new settlements or took over British farms and hamlets. In some areas, the English language resisted the southward encroachment of Gaelic to survive in everyday speech, eventually being incorporated into the dialect known today as 'Scots'. This was used by Scotland's national bard, Robert Burns, who thus composed his poems in what was essentially a form of medieval English originating ultimately in the Bernician conquests of the sixth, seventh and eighth centuries. After the battle of Carham in 1018, English-speakers north of the Tweed and Solway became subjects of the Scottish king. To what extent this affected their own perception of their identity is uncertain, although later evidence suggests that such issues mattered less to Border folk than Scottish and English monarchs might have preferred. Within a hundred years of the battle of Carham, the new frontier was already being regarded with ambivalence and indifference by folk dwelling on either side of it. By the 1300s, the Anglo-Scottish border country was a volatile region where families of brigands, the fore-runners of the fearsome Border Reivers, held sway over 'debatable' lands contested by English and Scottish monarchs. Nowhere was disregard of the Tweed–Solway frontier more evident than at the battle of Pinkie in 1547, when soldiers recruited from the Border clans fought on both sides. According to reports circulating after the battle, the main concern among contingents of Scottish and English borderers was to avoid getting entangled in combat with one another.

One group of invaders who left an enduring mark on the landscape of medieval Scotland were the Romans. Modern archaeology has uncovered the remains of their stone buildings, such as the military bath-house at Bearsden, as well as an impressive collection of inscribed memorials from various forts. These discoveries and their subsequent public presentation contrast with the disinterest shown towards Scotland's Roman settlements by folk in early medieval times. The six centuries between 400 and 1000 saw some reuse of erstwhile Roman sites for specific ceremonial purposes, but the continuity of habitation seen in England is not evident north of Hadrian's Wall. Along the Wall itself, several forts were still being used as dwelling places for many decades after the collapse of Roman Britain. On the Antonine Wall, by contrast, the forts were already derelict two centuries before the abandonment of the Hadrianic line and were thereafter left to decay. The military and civil settlements along the Forth–Clyde isthmus had little relevance to the native elites who arose in the second half of the millennium. This does not mean that surviving traces of the short-lived Roman occupation of Scotland were completely disregarded. The massive scale of some structures meant that they still dominated their environments hundreds of years after they fell into disuse. Thus, the Antonine Wall continued to serve as a prominent geographical feature long after its second-century abandonment, its turf ramparts slowly disintegrating but still extant. In the eighth century, Bede gave a brief description of how it looked in his own time, telling his readers that 'the clearest traces of the work constructed there, in the form of a very wide and high wall, can be seen to this day'. His words show how a contemporary observer, gazing at the ancient barrier from a southerly viewpoint, perceived Rome's most impressive legacy to the Scottish landscape. How the Wall appeared to contemporary Pictish eyes observing from the northern side is unknown, but the fact that the Picts had their own name for the eastern end – *Peanfahel* ('Head of the Wall'), now Kinneil – implies that the old frontier still played an important role as a marker in the landscape. Scotland's most enigmatic Roman monument lay slightly north of the Antonine Wall and was probably associated with it. This was a circular stone building, roofed by a dome, which formerly stood on the northern side of the River Carron. Sketches made in the eighteenth century suggest that it may have been erected by Roman troops to celebrate the completion of the Wall, but, sadly, it was demolished in 1743 to make way for an industrial dam. No trace of it survives today. In medieval times its origins were forgotten by local people who instead associated it with the legendary King Arthur by giving it the name 'Arthur's O'on' ('Oven'). Its other name was Stenhouse ('Stone House') which is still preserved in the place-name Stenhousemuir. The monument itself was a significant landmark in medieval and modern times and may already have become embedded in local folklore before its assimilation into Arthurian legend.

The first few centuries of the second millennium saw the amalgamation of Scotland's constituent peoples into one nation. The Celtic groups – Picts, Britons and Gaels – and their Germanic neighbours – the Vikings of the Isles and the English of Lothian – were all brought together as 'Scots' under the rule of a single sovereign. This process was once seen as the final victory of a Gaelic-speaking, immigrant group whose ancestors colonised Argyll sometime around 500 from a base in Ireland. We saw in Chapter 3 that such views hold little ground among the current generation of historians and are now regarded as obsolete. More credible, and more consistent with the archaeological evidence, is an alternative view seeing the Scots as an indigenous people of northern Britain who adopted Gaelic speech because of an affinity with the Irish. Here, in this concluding chapter, a brief and simple observation may be made, namely that the Scots were the true survivors of the first millennium AD. As one of the native peoples of northern Britain they were present at the beginning of the millennium, when the first Roman soldiers arrived. To the Romans they were *Scotti*, and this is the name they bore throughout the succeeding centuries. They were still there at the dawn of the second millennium when the power of the Vikings was waning, when the Clyde Britons were entering their own twilight, when the English of Lothian were answerable to the kings of Alba and when the Picts had already vanished. Biologically, of course, neither the Picts nor the Britons, nor the Norse colonists, nor the Northumbrians were expunged from the land. All these groups simply lost the political and cultural identities that had formerly defined them as separate peoples. They eventually became Scots. Conversely, the original Scots themselves lost little or nothing of their character in the upheavals of the period. They emerged in the eleventh century with their identity not only preserved but redefined and strengthened, their language in a dominant position and their name attached to the most powerful kingdom ever seen in northern Britain. They had watched the Romans arrive and depart; they had witnessed the rise and fall of English Northumbria; they had endured the Viking onslaught. By 1000, they were the undisputed masters of the North, a status they fought hard to preserve through the Middle Ages and beyond.

Perceptions

Today, the story of Scotland's origins in the early centuries AD is readily accessible in both the written word and, more tangibly, in an impressive archaeological corpus. In terms of a textual legacy, the first millennium still offers numerous unsolved puzzles but is by no means a blank page in Scottish history. It is not, for instance, an especially mysterious era about which few facts are known. This is not to deny or ignore the many gaps in the documentary record but merely to acknowledge that similar literary lacunae are found in other regions of medieval Europe. The society of early medieval Scotland, between the Roman and Norman periods, was essentially a pre-literate one in which writing was the exclusive preserve of an ecclesiastical elite who were also the keepers of records. Inevitably, the output of written works was far smaller in those times than in our modern era of mass literacy, but this does not mean that the picture is always hazy or indistinct. Even the destruction of monastic libraries at the hands of Viking raiders did not totally obliterate the documentary record. Sufficient data has certainly survived to enable today's historian to study early Scotland as a viable academic topic. It cannot be denied, however, that substantial parts of the picture are likely to remain forever incomplete. Misconceptions springing from gaps in our knowledge continue to thrive. In the absence of reliable texts, and under the influence of romanticised perceptions of Celtic society, all kinds of tenuous theories are able to flourish. Thus, the first three centuries AD are sometimes seen as a heroic struggle waged by primitive but noble Celts against ruthless Roman efficiency, a view distilled from the propaganda of Tacitus but almost certainly inaccurate. The real story of Scotland's contact with Rome was rather less straight-forward. It was more likely to have been a tangled web of trade agreements, short-lived alliances, broken pledges and failed diplomacy. Likewise, the later centuries of the millennium are popularly perceived as a murky 'Dark Age' in which the Scots fought the Picts in a series of more or less obscure conflicts until Cináed mac Ailpín unified them as one people. Alongside this imagined scenario of ethnic conflict runs a parallel religious story of nature-loving Celtic monks creating beautiful manuscripts and concocting herbal medicines in an ascetic utopia disturbed by occasional Viking raids. In so far as such perceptions offer a snapshot of the period 500 to 1000 they are not totally devoid of accuracy, even if they are somewhat misleading. Many bitter wars were certainly waged in this period, by Picts and Scots and Vikings and others, but the textual sources are far more informative than popular perception might sometimes believe. Much of what is not known can be surmised or inferred by critical examination of the various texts. A great deal is known, too, about the part played by 'Celtic' Christianity, especially as seen through the eyes of important figures such as Bede and Adomnán who witnessed the key spiritual and political developments of the period. Thus, when modern mystical notions about 'Celtic' priests are cast aside, the picture presented by the sources shows a sophisticated ecclesiastical elite operating alongside its secular counterpart. Both comprised ambitious, powerful men and women whose close co-operation shaped the great events of early Scottish history. Kings and abbots, queens and bishops, warriors, monks and nuns were all bound together in symbiotic relationships which furthered the respective interests of each.

Where the documentary record fails to shed enough light, the gaps can sometimes be filled by archaeologists. The function of hilltop fortresses, for example, is barely alluded to in the sources despite many references to battles, burnings and other events occurring at such places. Archaeological excavation has now answered some of the questions posed by historians, chiefly by unearthing evidence of how forts and other defensible sites were used and what kind of people dwelt there. New discoveries continue to be made at various types of settlement – palaces, farmsteads, churches and cemeteries – all over Scotland. Knowledge of the country's early history is therefore increasing, because each new archaeological discovery adds a little more clarity to the picture. Thus, although no more manuscripts are likely to be found, the surviving annals and chronicles are continually being supplemented by new physical data. The best and most impressive archaeological findings can be viewed at museums and other heritage centres, or are visible *in situ* where they were erected by the people of long ago. Numerous examples of Pictish sculpture, for instance, are accessible either in indoor collections or in landscape settings chosen by their original creators. The social and geographical contexts of monuments and artefacts are often explained by accompanying signboards or leaflets. Where no such information is displayed on-site, the visitor can usually access it via literature produced by local tourism agencies or by perusing detailed coverage in books and journal articles. Recent years have seen an increasing number of publications whose objective is to present Scotland's ancient and early medieval archaeology to audiences outside academic circles. This has run in tandem with improvements in how objects and sites are displayed and conserved for the benefit of visitors. At the heart of these programmes of publication and conservation is Historic Scotland, the official body responsible for the safekeeping of the nation's archaeological heritage. The majority of this heritage is protected by law, a statutory safeguard that extends even to numerous sites whose inaccessibility renders them 'off the beaten track' in so far as public appreciation is concerned. Some places inevitably fall outside Historic Scotland's remit, usually because their geography lacks precision or because their historical context is too obscure. Thus, while the famous battlefields of Bannockburn (1314) and Culloden (1746) each possess designated visitor centres and are regarded as important parts of the national heritage, similar commemoration and protection would not be expected at places where lesser-known battles were fought. Military encounters that were undoubtedly significant in early medieval times, such as the defeat of Domnall Brecc at Strathcarron in 643 or the great battle of Carham in 1018, have no marker in the modern landscape. The level of protection and conservation also varies according to different types of sites and monuments and, in some cases, can become an emotive topic. Many Pictish stones, for example, still stand in their original settings and inevitably attract substantial public interest at local, national and international level. Unfortunately, these unique sculptures are vulnerable to environmental factors, such as acidity, and would certainly fall into decay if left untended. One solution involves encasing the stones in glass cases which allow them to be seen and admired while protecting them from the ravages of Nature. Such intervention has not always been welcomed. A prime example is Sueno's Stone, mentioned in Chapter 9 of this book, which although now well-protected is no longer easy to photograph because of the reflective aspect of its casing. Another option is to move monuments inside buildings, either by adding them to collections such as those at Meigle, St Vigeans and Govan or by creating new places of safety for individual items. A further alternative is replacement by a weatherproof replica, a method employed, for example, at Fowlis

Wester and Dunnichen where the original Pictish monuments have been removed indoors. For many visitors, however, the texture of resin or fibreglass is a poor substitute for the unique vibrancy of stone. Notwithstanding the various objections, it is generally agreed that some form of protection for the most important items is necessary. Statutory protection under law is sufficient, hopefully, to prevent the kind of wanton vandalism seen in the eighteenth century when Arthur's O'on was destroyed by a local industrialist. But any monument left outside without protection remains vulnerable to environmental damage. The weather poses a severe and continuing threat to patterns and figures carved so painstakingly a thousand years ago. We need only to glance at the fine drawings of John Romilly Allen (1847–1907) to remind ourselves that two-dimensional images might be all that we have left if the original stonework erodes away. Risks are inevitably minimised when a monument is placed inside a building. In Perthshire, for instance, both the Crieff Cross-Slab and the Dupplin Cross are now displayed indoors, the former in a tourist information centre, the latter in the ancient church of St Serf. It is reassuring to know that these two sculptural masterpieces, and others of similar quality, are protected from the elements. Wise custodianship today ensures that future generations will be able to admire at first hand, and in three dimensions, the breathtaking craftsmanship of the past.

Genealogies

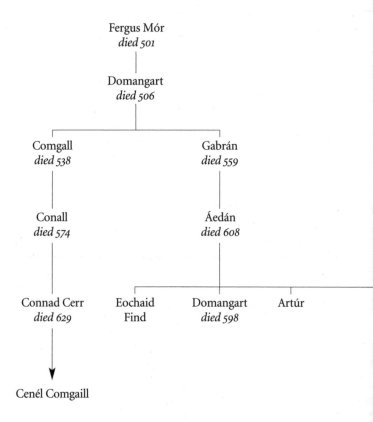

Cenél nGabráin

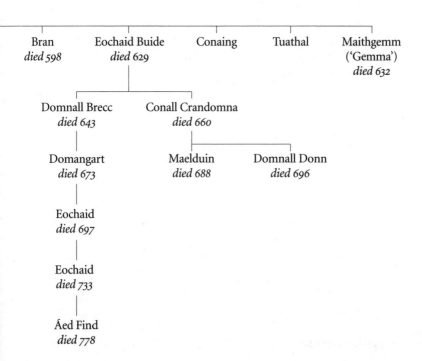

Bran
died 598

Eochaid Buide
died 629

Conaing

Tuathal

Maithgemm
('Gemma')
died 632

Domnall Brecc
died 643

Conall Crandomna
died 660

Domangart
died 673

Maelduin
died 688

Domnall Donn
died 696

Eochaid
died 697

Eochaid
died 733

Áed Find
died 778

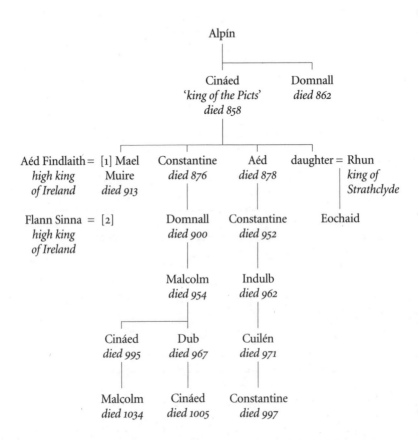

The mac Ailpín dynasty of Alba

Timeline

AD

43	Roman invasion of Britain
82	Agricola attacks Caledonia
83	Agricola's second Caledonian campaign
84	Battle of Mons Graupius
122	Emperor Hadrian orders a wall to be built between Tyne and Solway
143	Antoninus Pius orders the construction of a second wall
208	Septimius Severus begins his war against the Caledonii and Maeatae
367	Barbarians unite to attack Roman Britain
410	Emperor Honorius tells the Britons to govern themselves
460	Approximate date of Saint Patrick's letter to Coroticus
563	Saint Columba arrives in Britain
584	Death of the Pictish king Brude son of Maelchon
597	Death of Columba
603	Defeat of Áedán mac Gabráin at Degsastan
617	Death of Aethelfrith of Bernicia
634	Oswald defeats Cadwallon
642	Death of Oswald
643	Battle of Strathcarron
655	Oswiu of Northumbria defeats Penda of Mercia
664	Synod of Whitby
670	Death of Oswiu and accession of Ecgfrith
673	Foundation of Applecross by Maelrubai
684	Northumbrian raid on Ireland
685	Battle of Dunnichen
694	Death of Brude son of Bili
697	Promulgation of the Law of Innocents
704	Death of Adomnán
717	Expulsion of Columban clergy by Nechtan son of Derile

735	Death of Bede
734	Óengus son of Fergus launches Pictish assault on Cenél Loairn
744	Battle of Mugdock
756	Alt Clut besieged by Picts and Northumbrians
761	Death of Óengus
768	Áed Find of Cenél nGabráin defeats Picts in Fortriu
793	Viking raid on Lindisfarne
802	First Viking raid on Iona
820	Death of the Pictish overking Constantine son of Fergus
825	Martyrdom of Blathmac on Iona
839	Scots and Picts defeated by Vikings
848	Cináed mac Ailpín defeats his rivals to become *rex Pictorum*
858	Death of Cináed
870	Vikings besiege Alt Clut
889	Death of Giric
900	Constantine mac Áeda becomes king of Alba
906	Constantine and Bishop Cellach at Scone
917	Vikings recapture Dublin from the Irish
918	Battle of Corbridge
934	Athelstan of Wessex invades Alba
937	Battle of Brunanburh
939	Death of Athelstan
945	Edmund of Wessex attacks Strathclyde
952	Death of Constantine mac Áeda
971	Death of Saint Catroe
973	Northern kings meet Edgar of Wessex at Chester
995	Baptism of Earl Sigurd of Orkney
1005	Battle of Monzievaird
1006	Malcolm of Alba besieges Durham
1018	Battle of Carham

Further Reading

PRIMARY SOURCES

Adomnán, *Vita Sancti Columbae*. R. Sharpe (ed.) (1995) *Adomnán of Iona: Life of Saint Columba* (London)

Ailred, *Vita Niniani* (Life of Ninian). A.P. Forbes (ed.) (1874) *The Historians of Scotland: V – Lives of St Ninian and St Kentigern* (Edinburgh). Reprinted 1989 in *Two Celtic Saints: the lives of Ninian and Kentigern* (Felinfach)

Aneirin, *Y Gododdin*. Jarman, A.O.H. (ed.) (1988) *Aneirin: Y Gododdin* (Llandysul)

Annales Cambriae (Welsh Annals). J. Morris (ed.) (1980) *Nennius: British history and the Welsh annals* (Chichester)

Anglo-Saxon Chronicle. A. Savage (ed.) (1997) *The Anglo-Saxon Chronicles* (Godalming)

Bede, *Historia ecclesiastica gentis Anglorum*. J. McClure and R. Collins (eds) (1994) *Bede: The ecclesiastical history of the English people* (Oxford)

Berchan's Prophecy. B.T. Hudson (ed.) (1996) *The Prophecy of Berchan: Irish and Scottish high-kings in the Early Middle Ages* (Westport)

Gildas, *De Excidio Britanniae*. M. Winterbottom (ed.) (1978) *Gildas: the ruin of Britain and other works* (Chichester)

Historia Brittonum. J. Morris (ed.) (1980) *Nennius: British history and the Welsh annals* (Chichester)

Jocelin of Furness, *Vita Sancti Kentigerni* (Life of St Kentigern). A.P. Forbes (ed.) (1874) *The Historians of Scotland: V – Lives of St Ninian and St Kentigern* (Edinburgh) Reprinted 1989 in *Two Celtic Saints: the lives of Ninian and Kentigern* (Felinfach)

Patrick, *Epistola* and *Confessio*. A.B.E. Hood (ed.) (1978) *St Patrick: his writings and Muirchu's Life* (Chichester)

Orkneyinga Saga. Palsson, H. and Edwards, P. (eds) (1981) *Orkneyinga Saga: the history of the earls of Orkney* (Harmondsworth)

Taliesin. M. Pennar (ed.) (1988) *Taliesin Poems* (Felinfach)

EARLY SCOTLAND

Aitchison, N. (2003) *The Picts and the Scots at War* (Sutton)

Alcock, L. (1993) *The Neighbours of the Picts: Angles, Britons and Scots at war and at home* (Rosemarkie)

Alcock, L. (2003) *Kings and Warriors, Craftsmen and Priests in Northern Britain, AD 550–850* (Edinburgh)

Anderson, A.O. (1922) *Early Sources of Scottish History, AD 500–1286* Vol. 1 (Edinburgh)

Anderson, M.O. (1973) *Kings and Kingship in Early Scotland* (Edinburgh)

Chadwick, H.M. (1949) *Early Scotland: the Picts, the Scots and the Welsh of southern Scotland* (Cambridge)

Cowan, E.J. and McDonald, R.A. (eds) (2000) *Alba: Celtic Scotland in the medieval era* (East Linton)

Driscoll, S.T. and Nieke, M.R. (eds) (1988) *Power and Politics in Early Medieval Britain and Ireland* (Edinburgh)

Duncan, A.A.M. (1975) *Scotland: the making of the kingdom* (Edinburgh)

Foster, S.M. (2004) *Picts, Gaels and Scots: Early Historic Scotland* 2nd edition (London)

Laing, L. and Laing, J. (1993) *The Picts and the Scots* (Stroud)

McNeill, P. and Nicholson, R. (eds) (1975) *An Historical Atlas of Scotland, c.400–c.1600* (St Andrews)

Meldrum. E. (ed.) (1971) *The Dark Ages in the Highlands* (Inverness)

Moffat, A. (2010) *The Faded Map: the story of the lost kingdoms of Scotland* (Edinburgh)

Nicolaisen, W.F.H. (1976) *Scottish Place-names: their study and significance* (London)

Ritchie, A. and Breeze, D.J. (1991) *Invaders of Scotland* (Edinburgh)

Smyth, A.P. (1984) *Warlords and Holy Men: Scotland, AD 80–1000* (London)

Taylor, S. (ed.) (2000) *Kings, Clerics and Chronicles in Scotland, 500–1297: essays in honour of Marjorie Ogilvie Anderson on the occasion of her ninetieth birthday* (Dublin)

Watson, W.J. (1926) *The History of the Celtic Place-names of Scotland* (Edinburgh)

Woolf, A. (ed.) (2006) *Landscape and Environment in Dark Age Scotland* (St Andrews)

PICTS

Carver, M. (1999) *Surviving in Symbols: a visit to the Pictish nation* (Edinburgh)

Clarkson, T. (2010) *The Picts: a history* Revised edition (Edinburgh)

Cummins, W.A. (1995) *The Age of the Picts* (Sutton)

Evans, N. (2008) 'Royal succession and kingship among the Picts' *Innes Review* 59: 1–48

Forsyth, K. (1997) *Language in Pictland: the case against 'non-Indo-European Pictish'* (Utrecht)

Forsyth, K. (1998) 'Literacy in Pictland' in H. Pryce (ed.) *Literacy in Medieval Celtic Societies* (Cambridge), 39–61

Henderson, I. (1967) *The Picts* (London)

Henry, D. (ed.) (1997) *The Worm, the Germ and the Thorn: Pictish and related studies presented to Isabel Henderson* (Balgavies)

Konstam, A. (2010) *Strongholds of the Picts: the fortifications of Dark Age Scotland* (Oxford)

McHardy, S. (2010) *A New History of the Picts* (Edinburgh)

Nicholl, E. (ed.) (1995) *A Pictish Panorama: the story of the Picts and a Pictish bibliography* (Balgavies)

Ritchie, A. (1989) *Picts* (Edinburgh)

Ritchie, A. (1994) *Perceptions of the Picts: from Eumenius to John Buchan* (Rosemarkie)

Small, A. (ed.) (1987) *The Picts: a new look at old problems* (Dundee)

Wainwright, F.T. (ed.) (1955) *The Problem of the Picts* (Edinburgh)

Woolf, A. (2006) '*Dun Nechtáin*, Fortriu and the geography of the Picts' *Scottish Historical Review* 85: 182–201

PRE-ROMAN SCOTLAND

Armit, I. (ed.) (1990) *Beyond the Brochs: changing perspectives in the Later Iron Age in Atlantic Scotland* (Edinburgh)

Armit, I. (1997) *Celtic Scotland* (London)

Armit, I. (2002) *Towers in the North: the brochs of Scotland* (Stroud)

Feachem, R.W. (1977) *Guide to Prehistoric Scotland* 2nd edition (London)

Harding, D.W. (2004) *The Iron Age in Northern Britain: Celts and Romans, natives and invaders* (Abingdon)

Hartley, B. and Fitts, L. (1988) *The Brigantes* (Gloucester)

Hingley, R. (1998) *Settlement and Sacrifice: the later prehistoric people of Scotland* (Edinburgh)

Moffat, A. (2009) *Before Scotland: the story of Scotland before history* (London)

Oram, R.D. (1997) *Scottish Prehistory* (Edinburgh)

Piggott, S. (ed.) (1962) *The Prehistoric Peoples of Scotland* (London)

Ritchie, A. (1988) *Scotland BC* (Edinburgh)

Rivet, A.L.F. (ed.) (1966) *The Iron Age in Northern Britain* (Edinburgh)

Ross, S. (1991) *Ancient Scotland* (Moffat)

Smith, B.B. and Banks, I. (eds) (2002) *In the Shadow of the Brochs: the Iron Age in Scotland* (Stroud)

ROMAN SCOTLAND

Breeze, D.J. (1982) *The Northern Frontiers of Roman Britain* (London)

Breeze, D.J. (1996) *Roman Scotland* (London)

Breeze, D.J. (2006) *The Antonine Wall* (Edinburgh)

Campbell, D.B. (2010) *Mons Graupius, AD 83: Rome's battle at the edge of the world* (Oxford)

Crawford, O.G.S. (1949)*The Topography of Roman Scotland North of the Antonine Wall* (Cambridge)

Fraser, J.E. (2005) *The Roman Conquest of Scotland: the battle of Mons Graupius, AD 84* (Stroud)

Frere, S. (1978) *Britannia: a history of Roman Britain* 3rd edition (London)

Hanson, W.S. (1987) *Agricola and the Conquest of the North* (London)

Hanson, W.S. and Maxwell, G.S. (1986) *Rome's North West frontier: the Antonine Wall* 2nd edition (Edinburgh)

Hogg, A.H.A. (1951) 'The Votadini' in W.F. Grimes (ed.), *Aspects of Archaeology in Britain and Beyond: essays presented to O.G.S. Crawford* (London), 200–20

Hunter, F. (2007) *Beyond the Edge of the Empire: Caledonians, Picts and Romans* (Rosemarkie)

Keppie, L.J.F. (1986) *Scotland's Roman Remains* (Edinburgh)

Maxwell, G.S. (1989) *The Romans in Scotland* (Edinburgh)

Maxwell, G.S. (1998) *A Gathering of Eagles: scenes from Roman Scotland* (Edinburgh)

Moffat, A. (2010) *The Wall: Rome's greatest frontier* (Edinburgh)

Reed, N. (1976) 'The Scottish campaigns of Septimius Severus' *Proceedings of the Society of Antiquaries of Scotland* 107: 92–102

Rivet, A.L.F. and Smith, C. (1981) *The Place-names of Roman Britain* (London)

Woolliscroft, D.J. and Hoffmann, B. (2006) *Rome's First Frontier: the Flavian occupation of northern Scotland* (Stroud)

FIFTH TO ELEVENTH CENTURIES

Aitchison, N. (2006) *Forteviot: a Pictish and Scottish royal centre* (Stroud)

Barrow, G.W.S. (1981) *Kingship and Unity: Scotland, 1000–1306* (London)

Broun, D. (1998) 'Pictish kings, 761–839: integration with Dál Riata or separate development?' in S.M. Foster (ed.) *The St Andrews Sarcophagus: a Pictish masterpiece and its international connections* (Dublin), 71–83

Clancy, T.O. (2004) 'Philosopher-king: Nechtan mac Der-Ilei' *Scottish Historical Review* 83: 125–49

Clancy, T.O. (2008) 'The Gall-Ghaidheil and Galloway' *Journal of Scottish Name Studies* 2: 19–50

Cruickshank, G. (1991) *The Battle of Dunnichen* (Balgavies)

Driscoll, S.T. (2002) *Alba: the Gaelic kingdom of Scotland, AD 800–1124* (Edinburgh)

Duncan, A.A.M. (1976) 'The battle of Carham, 1018' *Scottish Historical Review* 55: 20–8

Fraser, J.E. (2002) *The Battle of Dunnichen, 685* (Stroud)

Fraser, J.E. (2009) *From Caledonia to Pictland: Scotland to 795* (Edinburgh)

Hudson, B.T. (1994) *Kings of Celtic Scotland* (Westport)

Woolf, A. (2000) 'The 'Moray Question' and the kingship of Alba in the tenth and eleventh centuries' *Scottish Historical Review* 79: 145–64

Woolf, A. (2001) 'The Verturian hegemony: a mirror in the North' in M. Brown and C. Farr (eds) *Mercia: an Anglo-Saxon kingdom in Europe* (Leicester), 106–11

Woolf, A. (2005) 'Onuist son of Uurguist: *tyrannus carnifex* or a David for the Picts?' in D. Hill and M. Worthington (eds) *Aethelbald and Offa: two eighth-century kings of Mercia* BAR British Series 383 (Oxford), 35–42

Woolf, A. (2007) *From Pictland to Alba, 789–1070* (Edinburgh)

CHRISTIANITY

D. Broun and T.O. Clancy (eds) (1999) *Spes Scotorum, Hope of Scots: Saint Columba, Iona and Scotland* (Edinburgh)

Carver, M. (2008) *Portmahomack: monastery of the Picts* (Edinburgh)

Clancy, T.O. (2001) 'The real St Ninian' *Innes Review* 52: 1–28

Crawford, B.E. (ed.) (1998) *Conversion and Christianity in the North Sea World* (St Andrews)

Dumville, D.N. *et al.* (1993) *St Patrick, AD 493–1993* (Woodbridge)

Herbert, M. (1988) *Iona, Kells and Derry: the history and hagiography of the monastic* familia *of Columba* (Oxford)

Hill, P. (1997) *Whithorn and St Ninian: the excavation of a monastic town* (Stroud)

Hughes, K. (1970) *Early Christianity in Pictland* (Jarrow)

Laing, L., Laing, J. and Longley, D. (1998) 'The Early Christian and later medieval site at St Blane's, Kingarth, Bute' *Proceedings of the Society of Antiquaries of Scotland* 128: 551–65

Macquarrie, A. (1997) *The Saints of Scotland: essays in Scottish church history, AD 450–1093* (Edinburgh)

Taylor, S. (1998) 'Place-names and the early church in Scotland' *Records of the Scottish Church History Society* 28: 1–22

Thomas, A.C. (1968) 'The evidence from North Britain' in M.W. Barley and R.P.C. Hanson (eds) *Christianity in Britain, 300–700* (Leicester), 93–122

SCOTS

Anderson, M.O. (1982) 'Dalriada and the creation of the kingdom of the Scots' in D. Whitelock, R. McKitterick and D. Dumville (eds) *Ireland in Early Medieval Europe* (Cambridge), 106–32

Bannerman, J. (1974) *Studies in the History of Dalriada* (Edinburgh)

Campbell, E. (2001) 'Were the Scots Irish?' *Antiquity* 75: 285–92

Campbell, E. (1999) *Saints and Sea-kings: the first kingdom of the Scots* (Edinburgh)

Dumville, D.N. (2002) 'Ireland and north Britain in the earlier Middle Ages: contexts for the *Miniugud Senchusa Fher nAlban*' in C. O'Baoill and N. McGuire (eds) *Rannsachadh na Gaidhlig 2000* (Aberdeen), 185–212

Fraser, J.E. (2005) 'Strangers on the Clyde: Cenél Comgaill, Clyde Rock and the bishops of Kingarth' *Innes Review* 56: 102–20

Lane, A. and Campbell, E. (2000) *Dunadd: an early Dalriadic capital* (Oxford)

Marsden, J. (1997) *Alba of the Ravens: in search of the Celtic kingdom of the Scots* (London)

Marsden, J. (2010) *Kings, Mormaers and Rebels: early Scotland's other royal family* (Edinburgh)

Nieke, M.R. and Duncan, H.B. (1988) 'Dalriata: the establishment and maintenance of an Early Historic kingdom in northern Britain' in S.T. Driscoll and M.R. Nieke (eds) *Power and Politics in Early Medieval Britain and Ireland* (Edinburgh), 6–21

BRITONS

Alcock, L. (1983) '*Gwˆyr y Gogledd*: an archaeological appraisal' *Archaeologia Cambrensis* 132: 1–18

Broun, D. (2004) 'The Welsh identity of the kingdom of Strathclyde, c.900–1200' *Innes Review* 55: 111–80

Chadwick, N.K. (1976) *The British Heroic Age: the Welsh and the Men of the North* (Cardiff)

Clarkson, T. (2010) *The Men of the North: the Britons of southern Scotland* (Edinburgh)

Jackson, K.H. (1955) 'The Britons in southern Scotland' *Antiquity* 29: 77–88

Jackson, K.H. (1969) *The* Gododdin: *the oldest Scottish poem* (Edinburgh)

Koch, J.T. (1997) *The* Gododdin *of Aneirin: text and context from Dark-age North Britain* (Cardiff)

Lowe, C. (1999) *Angels, Fools and Tyrants: Britons and Anglo-Saxons in southern Scotland, AD 450–750* (Edinburgh)

McCarthy, M.R. (2002) 'Rheged: an early historic kingdom near the Solway' *Proceedings of the Society of Antiquaries of Scotland* 132: 357–82

Macquarrie, A. (1993) 'The kings of Strathclyde, c.400–1018' in A. Grant and K.J. Stringer (eds) *Medieval Scotland: crown, lordship and community* (Edinburgh), 1–19

ANGLO-SAXON NORTHUMBRIA

Alcock, L. (1981) 'Quantity or quality: the Anglian graves of Bernicia' in V.I. Evison (ed.) *Angles, Saxons and Jutes* (Oxford), 168–85

Blair, P.H. (1947) 'The origin of Northumbria' *Archaeologia Aeliana* 25: 1–51

Blair, P.H. (1954) 'The Bernicians and their northern frontier' in N.K. Chadwick (ed.) *Studies in Early British History* (Cambridge), 137–72

Brooke, D. (1991) 'The Northumbrian settlements in Galloway and Carrick: an historical assessment' *Proceedings of the Society of Antiquaries of Scotland* 121: 295–327

Dumville, D.N. (1989) 'The origins of Northumbria: some aspects of the British background' in S. Bassett (ed.) *The Origins of Anglo-Saxon Kingdoms* (Leicester), 213–22

Hawkes, J. and Mills, S. (eds) (1999) *Northumbria's Golden Age* (Stroud)

Higham, N.J. (1993) *The Kingdom of Northumbria, AD 350–1100* (Stroud)

Hope-Taylor, B. (1977) *Yeavering: an Anglo-British centre of early Northumbria* (London)

Jackson, K.H. (1959) 'Edinburgh and the Anglo-Saxon occupation of Lothian' in P. Clemoes (ed.) *The Anglo-Saxons: studies in some aspects of their history presented to Bruce Dickins* (London), 35–47

Kirby, D.P. (1991) *The Earliest English Kings* (London)

Lowe, C. (1999) *Angels, Fools and Tyrants: Britons and Anglo-Saxons in southern Scotland, AD 450–750* (Edinburgh)

Rollason, D. (2003) *Northumbria, 500–1100: creation and destruction of a kingdom* (Cambridge)

Stancliffe, C. (1995) 'Oswald, most holy and most victorious king of the Northumbrians' in C. Stancliffe and E. Cambridge (eds) *Oswald: Northumbrian king to European saint* (Stamford), 33–83

Yorke, B. (1990) *Kings and Kingdoms of Early Anglo-Saxon England* (London)

VIKINGS

Backlund, J. (2001) 'War or peace? The relations between the Picts and the Norse in Orkney' *Northern Studies* 36: 33–48

Barrett, J. (2003) 'Culture contact in Viking Age Scotland' in J. Barrett (ed.) *Contact, Continuity and Collapse: the Norse colonization of the North Atlantic* (Turnhout), 73–111

Batey, C.E., Jesch, J. and Morris, C.D. (eds) (1994) *The Viking Age in Caithness, Orkney and the North Atlantic* (Edinburgh)

Brunsden, G.M. (2009) *Thorfinn the Mighty: the ultimate Viking* (Stroud)

Crawford, B.E. (1987) *Scandinavian Scotland* (Leicester)

Downham, C. (2007) *Viking Kings of Britain and Ireland: the dynasty of Ivarr to AD 1014* (Edinburgh)

Etchingham, C. (2001) 'North Wales, Ireland and the Isles: the Insular Viking zone' *Peritia* 15: 145–87

Fellows-Jensen, G. (1991) 'Scandinavians in Dumfriesshire and Galloway: the place-name evidence' in R.D. Oram and G. Stell (eds) *Galloway: land and lordship* (Edinburgh), 77–95

Graham-Campbell, J. and Batey, C.E. (1998) *Vikings in Scotland: an archaeological survey* (Edinburgh)

Hudson, B.T. (2005) *Viking Pirates and Christian Princes: dynasty and empire in the North Atlantic* (New York)

O'Corrain, D. (1998) 'The Vikings in Scotland and Ireland in the ninth century' *Peritia* 12: 296–339

Oram, R.D. (1995) 'Scandinavian settlement in south-west Scotland with a special study of Bysbie' in B.E. Crawford (ed.) *Scandinavian Settlement in Northern Britain* (London), 127–40

Ritchie, A. (1974) 'Picts and Norsemen in northern Scotland' *Scottish Archaeological Forum* 6: 23–36

Ritchie, A. (1993) *Viking Scotland* (London)

Sellar, W.D.H. (1966) 'The origins and ancestry of Somerled' *Scottish Historical Review* 45: 123–42

Smith, B. (2001) 'The Picts and the martyrs or did the Vikings kill the native population of Orkney and Shetland?' *Northern Studies* 36: 7–32

Wainwright, F.T. (1950) 'The battles at Corbridge' *Saga-Book of the Viking Society* 13: 156–73

Woolf, A. (2005) 'The origins and ancestry of Somerled: Gofraid mac Fergusa and "the Annals of the Four Masters"' *Medieval Scandinavia* 15: 199–213

Woolf, A. (ed.) (2009) *Scandinavian Scotland – twenty years after* (St Andrews)

ART AND SCULPTURE

Cummins, W.A. (1999) *The Picts and their Symbols* (Stroud)

Fisher, I. (2001) *Early Medieval Sculpture in the West Highlands and Islands* (Edinburgh)

Foster, S. (ed.) (1998) *The St Andrews Sarcophagus: a Pictish masterpiece and its international connections* (Dublin)

Foster, S. and Cross, M. (eds) (2005) *Able Minds and Practised Hands: Scotland's early medieval sculpture in the 21st century* (Leeds)

Fraser, I. (1999) *Pictish Symbol Stones: an illustrated gazetteer* (Edinburgh)

Henderson, G. and Henderson, I. (2004) *The Art of the Picts: sculpture and metalwork in early medieval Scotland* (London)

Jackson, A. (1984) *The Symbol Stones of Scotland: a social anthropological resolution of the problem of the Picts* (Stromness)

Jackson, A. (1989) *The Pictish Trail: a guide to the old Pictish kingdoms* (Kirkwall)

Jones, D. (1998) *A Wee Guide to the Picts* (Edinburgh)

Ritchie, A. (ed.) (1994) *Govan and its Early Medieval Sculpture* (Stroud)

Spearman, R.M. and Higgitt, J. (eds) (1993) *The Age of Migrating Ideas: early medieval art in northern Britain and Ireland* (Stroud)

Sutherland, E. (1997) *A Guide to the Pictish Stones* (Edinburgh)

Index

Aberlemno 207
Abernethy 84, 216, 219
Adomnán xiii, 61, 138, 140, 145–6, 160, 163–5, 203
Áed, son of Boanta 174
Áed mac Ainmerech 92–3, 142
Áed mac Cináeda 181
Áed Find 166, 178
Áedán mac Gabráin 90–93, 105–8, 142
Aeron 102
Aethelflaed 186
Aethelfrith 104–10, 157
Aethelred the Unready 198–200
Agricola, Roman governor 17–26
agriculture 13–14
Aidan (saint) 161
Ailred of Rievaulx 81
Ainfcellach 129–30
Alba 182, 195
Alchfrith 121–2
Aldfrith 126–7, 203
Alfred, son of Westou 209
Alpín, 8th century Pictish royal claimant 133
Alpín, father of Cináed 175
Alt Clut *see also* Dumbarton
    adoption of Christianity 76–7, 151–6
    besieged by Vikings 179
    extent of kingdom 59
    origins 93–4
    resurgence as Strathclyde 181
    relations with Northumbria 115, 120, 123, 136
    relations with Picts 76, 136, 177
    relations with Scots 88, 92, 119, 129, 151
    royal epithets 101
    royal succession 109
Ammianus Marcellinus 40
Amrae Coluimb Chille 140
Andrew (saint) 155, 207–8
Anglo–Saxon Chronicle 189, 192
Anglo-Saxons, origins of 50, 55–8, 65, 96–7
Angus (district) 93, 197
annals
    Irish xi–xii, 86, 116, 145, 199, 211
    Welsh 103, 152
Antonine Wall 29–33, 224–5
Antrim 60–3, 90
Applecross 148–9, 164–5
arcani 47, 49–50
Ardae Nesbi, battle of 130
Arfderydd 102
Argyll *see* Scots
Arthgal, king of Alt Clut 179
Arthur, legendary king 225
Arthur's O'on 225
Arthuret 102

Athelstan 187–9
Atholl 124, 179, 195
Attacotti 49
Augustine (saint) 156–7
Ayrshire 45, 102, 136

Báetán mac Cairill 90–1
Baithéne 144, 146
Baldred (saint) 190, 209
Ballachulish 69
Balthere (saint) *see* Baldred
Bamburgh 97, 180, 197, 199–201
Bangor (Co. Down) 147–50, 155
Barbarian Conspiracy 49
Bass Rock 209
Bean (saint) 216
Bede
    Ecclesiastical History xi
    on Adomnan 163
    and the Antonine Wall 224
    death of 206
    on the battle of Degsastan
        105–6
    on the battle of Dunnichen 127
    on Bernician origins 97, 103
    on the Britons 97–8
    on Brude, son of Maelchon
        141–2
    on Columba 80, 138, 141
    on Ecgfrith 126
    on Edwin 111, 157–8
    and the name 'Northumbria'
        108
    on Ninian 80
    on Oswiu 121
    on Pictish Christianity 204
    on Pictish matrilineal
        succession 66
    on Scottish origins 59–60
Bennachie 22
Berchan's Prophecy xiv
Berht 126, 128

Bernicia 96–7, 103–4, 108–11, 121–2,
    160–1
Bertha (Roman fort) 23, 74, 178, 198
Bewcastle 72
Birdoswald (Roman fort) 58
Birr 164
Birrens (Roman fort) 34, 72
Blane (saint) 150–1
Blathmac (saint) 211
Border Reivers 223
Boresti 22
Boudica 16
Brigantes 16–18, 35–6, 57–8
Brigantia (goddess) 69, 73
Brigid (saint) 84
Britons
    adoption of Christianity 74–83,
        151–6
    post-Roman kingdoms 56–9,
        93–105
    relations with Bernicia and
        Deira 96–9, 103–10, 115–16,
        120, 136–7, 157–8
    relations with Picts 46, 50, 136,
        177
    relations with Rome 15–19,
        34–40, 44–52
    relations with Scots 59–64,
        117–20, 125, 195–6, 200–1
    relations with Vikings 179
    relations with West Saxons
        186–9, 191–2, 198
    *see also individual kingdoms
        by name*
brochs 8–9, 43
Broichan 143
Brude, son of Bili 124–8
Brude, son of Derile 128, 132
Brude, son of Maelchon 87, 91,
    141–5, 147
Brude, son of Óengus 131, 134–5, 205
Brunanburh, battle of 188–9

Burnswark 32, 188
Bute, Isle of 88, 150–1

Cadwallon 111, 113–14
Cadzow 101
Caesar, Julius 6, 15–16, 68–9
Cáin Adamnáin 163–5
Caislen Credi, battle of 133
Caithness 71, 176, 178, 188, 194
Calchfynydd 96
Caledonians (Caledonii, Caledones) 20–5, 33, 37–41, 43
Calgacus 21
Camelon (Roman fort) 23, 29
Camulos 69, 72
Candida Casa see Whithorn
Cano, son of Gartnait 129
Canterbury 157–8, 162
Caracalla 39–40
Caratacus 16
Carham-on-Tweed, battle of 200
Carlisle 17, 58, 94
Carpow 39–40
Carriden (Roman fort) 36
Carron (river) 119, 225
Cartimandua 17, 37
Carvetii 58
Cassius Dio 38
Cathan (saint) 150–1
Cathbuaid ('Battle Triumph') 214
Catraeth 98–9, 105, 114
Catroe (saint) 216–17
Catstane 82–3, 106
Catterick 98–9
Céli Dé 214, 217
Cellach, abbot of Iona 210–11
Cellach, bishop of St Andrews 203, 216
Celts 3–5, 14, 43
Cenél Cathbach 129
Cenél Comgaill 88, 107, 113, 150–1
Cenél Loairn 88, 119, 125, 129–35, 148, 165, 176, 178, 190, 194, 205
Cenél nGabráin
    origins 87, 107
    relations with Britons 119, 129
    relations with Northumbria 112–13, 159–60
    relations with other cenéla 107, 119, 122–3, 125, 129–31, 165
    relations with Picts 123, 135, 166, 168–9, 172–5, 178
    royal burial 211
Cenél nGartnait 122–3, 129, 149, 165
Cenél nOengusa 88, 198
Cenn Delgthen, battle of 112
Ceolfrith 203–4, 206
Chester 109, 196
Christianity
    and barbarian kings 75
    'Celtic' 227–8
    conversion of the Britons 75–83, 151–6
    conversion of the English 156–63
    conversion of the Picts 83–5, 138–49
    conversion of the Scandinavians 213–14, 218
    Easter controversy 157, 161–3, 165, 203–4
Cináed mac Ailpín 174–7, 211–12, 227
Cináed mac Duib 198
Cináed mac Mail Coluim 196–8
Circinn 93
Clackmannan 38, 70
Claudian, Roman poet 41, 51
Clochmabenstane 70
Clyde (river) 45, 101, 181
Cnut 200–1
Cocidius (Celtic god) 72
Colman, bishop of Lindisfarne 162
Colman Bec (Irish king) 89–90

Columba (saint) xii–xiii, 80, 92, 138, 140–5, 160, 211, 214–15
Comgall, son of Domangart 87
Comgall of Bangor (saint) 147–50, 155
Commodus, Roman emperor 33
Conall, son of Áedán 172
Conall, son of Comgall 89, 141–2
Conall, son of Tadg 169, 172
Conall Crandomna 122–3
Coninia 83
Connad Cerr 113
Constantine, Roman usurper 51
Constantine (saint) 155–6
Constantine, son of Fergus 168–9, 172–3, 209
Constantine mac Áeda 183–90, 193, 203, 215–16
Constantine mac Cináeda 178–9
Constantine the Great, Roman emperor 44, 74, 156
Conval (saint) 154
Corbridge 31, 74, 186
Cornavii 71
Coroticus 76–7
Cowal 88, 150
Craig Phadraig 6, 143
Cramond (Roman fort) 40
crannogs 9
Crieff Cross-Slab 230
Cruithne 65
Crup, Ridge of see Ridge of Crup
Cuilén, king of Alba 195
Cul Dreimne, battle of 141
Culdees see Céli Dé
Culross 152
Cumméne 144
Cunchar, ruler of Angus 197–8
Cunedda 50
Curetán (saint) 165

Dál Fiatach 90–3, 113

Dál Riata see Scots
Dál nAraidi 112
Damnonii 18, 45–7, 56, 59
Danes 176–7, 180
Darlugdach 84
David I, king of Scotland 220, 222
De Obsessione Dunelmi 200
Deira 96–7, 122, 158
Degsastan 105–7
Delgu, battle of 90
Dere Street 30–1, 106
Dollar 179
Domangart 'son of Ness' 86
Domangart, son of Domnall Brecc 123, 125
Domnall, son of Constantine (died 835) 172–3
Domnall, son of Constantine (died 900) 181–2
Domnall mac Ailpín 177–8, 213
Domnall Brecc 112, 117, 119–20
Domnall Donn 128
Donnan (saint) 145–7
Donnchad, abbot of Dunkeld 215
Donnchad ('Duncan'), grandson of Malcolm 201
Donnchad, son of Conall 90
Donnchad Bec 130
Donncorci 168
druids 69, 143, 157
Druim Alban 63
Druim Cett 92–3, 142–3
Druim-Derg-Blathuug, battle of 134
Drust, 8th century Pictish royal claimant 132–4
Drust, son of Constantine 173
Drust, son of Erp 66
Dub, king of Alba 195
Dublin 177, 179, 185, 187
Dumbarton 59, 76, 91, 93, 136, 166, 179, 180, 223

Dumfriesshire 19, 26, 45, 70, 154
Dumyat 38
Dunadd 135, 142
Dunaverty 88, 130, 142
Dunbar 177
Dunblane 150, 177, 181
Duncrub 22
Dundurn 125, 182
Dungal, son of Selbach 130–1,
    134–5, 205
Dunkeld 22, 185, 195, 209, 212–16
Dunnichen, battle of 127
Dunnottar 125, 182, 188, 194
Dunod the Stout 102–3
Dunollie 128–9, 135
Dunragit 94
duns 9, 62
Dupplin Cross 230
Durham 199–200, 209
Dyfnwal ab Owain, king of
    Strathclyde (c.920) 186
Dyfnwal ab Owain, king of
    Strathclyde (died 975) 191–2,
    196, 216
Dyfnwal ap Teudubur, king of Alt
    Clut 136

Eadberht, king of Northumbria
    136–7
Eadred, king of Wessex 192–3
Eadwulf Cudel, earl of Bamburgh
    201
Eamont (river) 187
Eanflaed 121, 161
Eanfrith 111, 159
East Angles 110
Easter controversy see Christianity
Ecgbert, bishop 165, 203, 205
Ecgfrith 123–7
economy 13–14
Edgar, king of Scotland 220
Edgar, king of Wessex 196

Edinburgh 57, 94, 116, 194
Edmund, king of Wessex 189–92,
    217
Edmund, son of Aethelred the
    Unready 200
Edward the Elder 186–7
Edwin 108, 110–11, 157–60
Eigg 145–7, 165
Eildon Hills 7, 26
Elmet 57, 104, 109
English see Anglo-Saxons
Eochaid, king of Cenél nGabráin
    c.726 131
Eochaid, son of Rhun 181
Eochaid Buide 107, 109, 112, 159
Eoganán, son of Óengus 173–4
Epidii 60, 63–4, 71
Epona 71
Erik, king of Northumbria 192–3
Eumenius 40
exactatores 134
exploratores 46–7

Feradach of Cenél Loairn 135
Ferat, son of Barot 174
Ferchar Fota 125, 128, 176
Fergus mac Eirc (Fergus Mór)
    59–60, 86, 88
Fettercairn 197
Fid Eoin, battle of 113
Fife 84, 124, 127, 145, 152, 179
Finella 197–8
Finglen, battle of 130
Finnian (saint) 82, 154
foederati 46, 48, 50
Forres 195
Forteviot 175, 177
Forth (river) 119, 177, 197
Fortriu 41, 133, 166, 174, 212 see also
    Moray
forts
    of the Iron Age 4–7

Roman 23, 52, 224
see also individual sites by name
Frew, Fords of 197

Gabrán 87
Gaelic language *see* languages
Gall-Gáidhil 180, 221
Galloway 19, 45, 77–82, 94, 175, 180, 221
Gartnait, son of Domelch 84
Gask Ridge 23
genealogies 47, 56
Gildas 64–5
Giric 181, 213, 215
Glasgow 151–5
Glind Mairison, battle of 119
Goddeu 101
Gododdin (kingdom) 56–7, 94, 104, 115–6
Gododdin (poem) 98–9
Govan 77, 137, 155–6, 181, 229
Gowrie 87
Grampian Mountains 22
Grannus (Celtic god) 73
Gurci 102–3
Guriat, king of Alt Clut 122
Gwenddoleu 102
Gwynedd 50, 111, 207

Hadrian's Wall 28–9, 32, 44–6, 49–50, 58–9, 114, 224
hagiography xiii, 81, 138, 140, 151–3
Hallow Hill (Pictish cemetery) 84–5, 145
Hamilton 101
Hatfield, battle of 111
Henry I, king of England 220
Hexham 114
Hild (saint) 162
hillforts 4–7
Historia Brittonum 104, 158
Historic Scotland 229

Hoddom 153–4
Honorius, Roman emperor 51–3

Iceland 171, 218
Ida 97, 103
Idle (river) 110
Ildulb, king of Alba 194–5
Inchcailloch 206
Inchinnan 154
Inchmarnock 151
Inchtuthil 23, 27
Indrechtach, abbot of Iona 212
Innisibsolian, battle of 182
Inverdovat 179
Inveresk (Roman fort) 31, 36, 73
Iona
    annals xi–xii
    and Bernicia 159–62
    and the Céli Dé 214
    and Dunkeld 213
    and the Easter controversy 162–3, 203–5
    foundation 138, 141–2
    and the Picts 142–5, 203–4
    royal burials 211–13, 218
    royal pilgrims 218
    Viking raids 169, 210–12
Ireland, Irish 59–63, 76, 89–93, 112, 119, 126, 185, 210
Irish annals *see* annals, Irish
Islay 88
Iudeu 121–2
Ivar, king of Dublin (9th century) 179

Jarrow 127, 203–4
Jocelin of Furness 151–3

Kells 210–11, 215
Kelso 95–6
Kentigern (saint) 151–5, 206
Kentigerna (saint) 206

Kildare 84
Kingarth 150–1
Kinneil 225
Kintyre 60, 86, 156, 172, 174
Kirkmadrine 78–9

La Tène 14
languages
    Brittonic (British) 3, 62–4,
        222–3
    English 58, 62, 223–4
    Gaelic 3, 62–4, 172–3, 175–6, 220,
        222
    Gaulish 3
    Pictish 42–3, 67, 172–3, 175–6,
        220
Latinus 78
Law of Innocents 163–5, 205, 215
Leithreid, battle of 91
Leodonus 152
Liberalis 83, 100–1
Liddel Strength 102
Liddesdale 83, 102
Lindisfarne 104, 137, 161–2, 169, 209
Lismore 147–8, 165, 205
literacy 15, 226–7
loci 34
Lorn 88
Lothian 99–100, 152, 195, 201, 209,
    223
Lugus (Celtic god) 71

Mabon *see* Maponus
Macbethad ('Macbeth') 201
Maeatae 37–40, 91, 105
Maelduin 125
Maelrubai (saint) 148–9
Mag Rath *see* Moira, battle of
Magusanus (Celtic god) 70
Malcolm III (Mael Coluim mac
    Donnchada) 219, 222
Malcolm ap Dyfnwal, king of

Strathclyde 196
Malcolm, son of Cináed
    (Mael Coluim mac Cináeda)
    199-201
Malcolm, son of Domnall (Mael
    Coluim mac Domnaill) 190–4
Man, Isle of 91, 198
Manau 38, 70, 91, 105
Manor Water 83
Maponus 70, 72–3
Marcus Aurelius, Roman emperor
    33
matrilineal succession 66–7, 133
Meigle 207, 229
Melrose 161, 177
Mercia 108–9, 111, 186, 189
Metz 217
Miathi *see* Maeatae
Mirin (saint) 154–5
Mithras 74
Moin Uacoruar, battle of 196
Moira, battle of 119
Moluag (saint) 147–8
Moncrieffe Hill, battle of 133
Mons Graupius 20–22
Monzievaird, battle of 199
Moray 41, 124, 174, 176, 178, 190,
    194–5 *see also* Fortriu
Morbihan Bay 15
Mount Carno, battle of 133–4
Mugdock, battle of 136
Mugint 82
Muiredach of Cenél Loairn 131,
    134–5
Mull of Kintyre 60
Mungo (saint) *see* Kentigern

Naturae (Picts) 81, 83
Nechtan, son of Derile 132–4,
    204–5, 207, 213
Nechtan Morbet 84
Neithon, king of Alt Clut 109

Netherby (Roman fort) 40, 46–7, 102

Newstead (Roman fort) 26–7, 31, 33, 73

Ninian (saint) 79–82, 152

Normans 219–20

Norsemen, Norse 169–70, 176–9 *see also* Vikings

Norse sagas 171, 197

North Britons *see* Britons

Northumbria *see also* Bernicia *and* Deira
    adoption of Christianity 156–62
    relations with Britons 96–8, 103–10, 114–16, 120, 136, 157–8
    relations with Mercia 117, 120–2, 125–6
    relations with Picts 123–8, 177, 204–5
    relations with Scots 105–13, 159–62, 196–7, 199–201, 219
    relations with Vikings 180, 186–7, 191–3

Novantae 18, 45, 56, 83, 94

Nudd Hael 101

Ochil Hills 38

Óengus, son of Fergus (died 761) 132–7, 166, 168, 207–8

Óengus, son of Fergus (died 834) 172–3, 208–9

Olaf, king of Dublin (9th century) 177–9

Olaf Cuaran 190–3, 217–18

Olaf Gothfrithsson 188–90, 215

oppida 6–7

Orkney 91, 125, 178, 197, 218

Osred 203

Oswald 112–17, 159–61, 214

Oswine, king of Deira 117, 121

Oswiu 115, 117, 120–4, 161–2

Outigirn 97

Owain ap Bili, king of Alt Clut 117, 119–20, 122

Owain ap Dyfnwal, king of Strathclyde 187–9

Owain ab Urien 103, 151

Owain the Bald, king of Strathclyde 200–1

Padarn Pesrut 47–8

paganism 15, 68–75, 156–7, 210

Paisley 154

Partick 181

Patrick (saint) 76–7

Paulinus 157–8

Pecthelm 80

pedigrees *see* genealogies

Peebles 223

Penda 113, 117, 120–2

Peredur 102–3

Picti 40–1

Picts
    and Christianity 80–1, 138, 143–5, 146–8
    in folklore 221
    king-list 65–7
    language 42–3, 67, 172–6
    matrilineal succession 66–7, 133
    relations with Britons 46, 50, 64, 76
    relations with Northumbria 122–8, 177, 203–5
    relations with Rome 40–4, 48–52, 64
    relations with Scots 49, 87, 123, 134–5, 172–8, 220–1
    stones (carved) *see* sculpture
    symbol stones *see* symbols (Pictish)

Pinkie, battle of 224

poetry (Welsh) 94–5, 98–100

Prophecy of Berchan xiv

Ptolemy, Greek geographer 24, 45

Ragnall, king of York (died 921)
185–7
Ragnall Gothfrithsson 191
Rathinveramon 178, 198 *see also*
Bertha
Rathlin 210
Redwald 110
Regulus (saint) 155, 208
Renfrew 222–3
Renfrewshire 155
Restenneth 207
Reuda 61
Rheged 94–5, 99–100, 103–5, 115, 158
Rhun ab Arthgal 177, 179
Rhun ab Urien 115, 158
Rhydderch Hael 91–2, 101, 104, 152,
154
Ridge of Crup, battle of 195, 215
Rieinmellth 115, 121
Rome, Romans
antiquities 224–5
forts 23, 26–31, 44, 224
invasion of Britain 15–16
relations with Caledonians
20–5, 34
relations with North Britons
34–6, 44–8
relations with Picts 40–4, 48–51,
64
religion 72–4
roads 30–1
withdrawal from Britain 52–3
Rosfoichne, battle of 131
Rosemarkie 147, 207
roundhouses 8–9
Royth 115
Rule (saint) *see* Regulus

St Andrews 207–9, 212, 214, 216–17
St Andrews Sarcophagus 208
St Vigeans 229
Saxons 50, 55

Schiehallion 22
Scone 175, 203, 216
Scots
origins 59–64, 225–6
relations with Britons 59–64,
91–2, 117, 119–20, 125, 177,
195–6, 199–201
relations with Northumbria
105–7, 109–13, 159–62, 196–7,
199–201, 219
relations with Picts 87, 122–3,
134–5, 168–9, 172–6, 220
relations with Roman Britain
48–9, 226
relations with Vikings 173–80,
182–3, 185–9, 194
relations with West Saxons
186–97
sculpture
of the Britons 77–9, 82–3, 155
of the Picts 84, 207–8, 221,
228–30
Selbach 129–31, 205
Selgovae 18, 46, 56, 83, 95
Serf (saint) 152
Severus, Roman emperor 39
Shetland 178
Sihtric 185–7
Sigurd, earl of Orkney 197, 218
Skye 122, 129, 148–9
society 10–13, 35
Solway Firth 94–5
souterrains 10
sources x–xiv
Stilicho, Roman general 51
Stirling 31, 121
Stone of Destiny 175, 216
stones (carved) *see* sculpture
Strathallan 181
Strathcarron, battle of 117, 119–20
Strathclyde 181, 186–9, 191–2, 195–6,
198, 200–1, 216–17, 222–3

Strathearn 124, 175, 182, 185
Strathfillan 206
Strathmore 124, 127
Strathyre, battle of 123
Sueno's Stone 195, 229
Sveinn Forkbeard 199
symbols (Pictish) 84, 207, 221
Synod of Birr 164–5
Synod of Whitby 162

Tacitus 17–22, 26
Taliesin 94, 99–100, 103
Talorc, son of Congus 134–5
Talorcan, son of Drostan (died 739)
    132
Talorcan, son of Eanfrith 111, 123
Talorcan, son of Fergus 135–6
Tarain 128
Tarbert (in Kintyre) 129–31
tattoos 41
Teloch *see* Delgu, battle of
Teneu (Thaney) 152
Teudubur, king of Alt Clut 136
Theodosius, Roman general
    49–50
Thule (Thyle) 24
tonsure 157, 161
Tory Island 131, 134, 205
Traprain Law 7, 152
Trent (river) 125
Trusty's Hill 221
Tuathalan, abbot of Cenrigmonaid
    208
Tweed (river) 46, 83, 95–6, 100–1,
    201

Tyninghame 209, 215

Uhtred 199–201
Uí Néill 89–93, 112, 119, 127, 141
Uinniau 82
Urien 94–5, 99–100, 103–4, 115

Verturiones 40–1, 43
vici 35–6
Vikings 169–71, 173–4, 176–82,
    185–99, 210–13, 218 *see also*
    Norsemen, Danes
vitae xiii, 138, 140, 151–3
vitrification 6
Votadini 19, 46–8, 50, 56–7, 83 *see*
    also Gododdin (kingdom)

Wales 109, 153, 180, 207
Wearmouth-Jarrow *see* Jarrow
Welsh annals *see* annals, Welsh
West Saxons 180, 186–93, 196,
    198–200, 219
Whitby 162
Whithorn 78–82, 206
Wilfrid (saint) 161–2
William, duke of Normandy 219
William Rufus, king of England 219
Winwaed, battle of 122
Wradech (Feradach), Pictish king
    66
Wulfstan, archbishop of York 192–3

Yarrow Stone 83, 100–1
Yeavering 110–11
York 157–8, 187